Ciutadella

Alaior

Maó

MENORCA

Pollença

Alcúdia

Inca

MALLORCA

Artà

Capdepera

Manacor

Llucmajor

Felanitx

Campos

Santanyí

Colònia
de Sant Jordi

Cabrera CABRERA

Menorca
Pages 94–115

Mallorca
Pages 46–93

D0207613

0 kilometres   20
0 miles   20

MALLORCA
MENORCA & IBIZA

EYEWITNESS TRAVEL

MALLORCA
MENORCA & IBIZA

Main Contributor **Grzegorz Micula**

Produced by Wydawnictwo Wiedza i Życie S.A., Warsaw

Senior Graphic Designer Paweł Pasternak

Editors Robert G. Pasieczny, Anna Moczar-Demko

Graphic Design Paweł Kamiński, Piotr Kiedrowski

Typesetting and Layout Paweł Kamiński, Piotr Kiedrowski, Elżbieta Dudzińska

Cartography Magdalena Polak

Photography Bartłomiej Zaranek

Illustrations Bohdan Wróblewski, Michał Burkiewicz, Monika Żylińska

Contributors Grzegorz Micuła, Katarzyna Sobieraj, Robert G. Pasieczny, Eligiusz Nowakowski

Consultant Carlos Cassas Marrodan

For Dorling Kindersley
Translator Magda Hannay

Editor Matthew Tanner

Senior DTP Designer Jason Little

Production Controller Sarah Dodd

Printed in Malaysia.

First American edition, 2004

15 16 17 18 10 9 8 7 6 5 4 3 2 1

Published in the United States by DK Publishing,
345 Hudson Street, New York, New York 10014

Reprinted with revisions 2006, 2008, 2010, 2012, 2014, 2016

Copyright © 2004, 2016 Dorling Kindersley, London
A Penguin Random House Company

A catalogue record for this book is available from the Library of Congress.

Published in Great Britain by Dorling Kindersley Limited.

ISSN 1542-1554

ISBN 978-1-46544-022-8

Floors are referred to throughout in accordance with British usage; ie the "first floor" is the floor above ground level.

MIX
Paper from
responsible sources
FSC
www.fsc.org   FSC™ C018179

**The information in this
DK Eyewitness Travel Guide is checked regularly.**
Every effort has been made to ensure that this book is as up-to-date as possible at the time of going to press. Some details, however, such as telephone numbers, opening hours, prices, gallery hanging arrangements and travel information are liable to change. The publishers cannot accept responsibility for any consequences arising from the use of this book, nor for any material on third party websites, and cannot guarantee that any website address in this book will be a suitable source of travel information. We value the views and suggestions of our readers very highly. Please write to: Publisher, DK Eyewitness Travel Guides, Dorling Kindersley, 80 Strand, London, WC2R 0RL, Great Britain, or email: travelguides@dk.com.

Front cover main image: Idyllic waters of Cala Fornells

◀ Spain, Balearic Islands, Mallorca, Cala S'Almonia beach

Contents

Baroque sundial in one of Palma's palaces

Introducing the Balearic Islands

Horse-cab ride through the streets of the Old Town, Palma

A sunny morning on the beach near S'Arenal harbour

Sign of a restaurant serving Mallorcan food

A stall selling watermelons at the weekly market in Inca

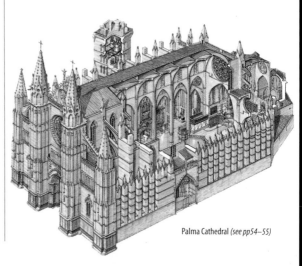
Palma Cathedral *(see pp54–55)*

HOW TO USE THIS GUIDE

This guide will help you to make the most of your visit to the Balearic Islands. The first section, *Introducing the Balearic Islands*, locates the islands geographically and gives an outline of their rich history and culture. Individual sections describe the main historic sights and star attractions on each of the four archipelago islands. Help with accommodation, restaurants, shopping, entertainment and many recreational activities can be found in the *Travellers' Needs* section, while the *Survival Guide* provides useful tips on everything you need to know, from money and language to getting around and seeking medical care.

The Balearic Islands Area by Area

In this guide, each of the islands has been given its own chapter. Within each chapter there is an introduction, a Regional Map, and a detailed listing of all the best sights.

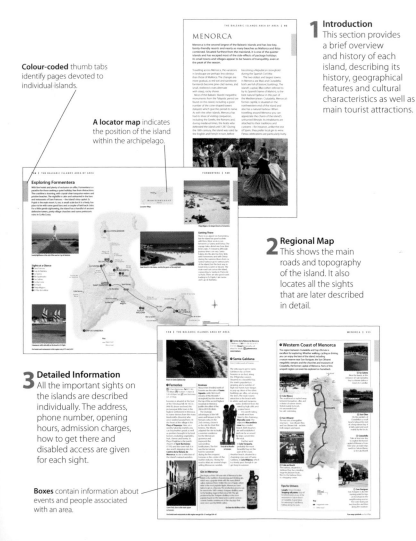

Colour-coded thumb tabs identify pages devoted to individual islands.

A locator map indicates the position of the island within the archipelago.

1 Introduction
This section provides a brief overview and history of each island, describing its history, geographical features and cultural characteristics as well as main tourist attractions.

2 Regional Map
This shows the main roads and topography of the island. It also locates all the sights that are later described in detail.

3 Detailed Information
All the important sights on the islands are described individually. The address, phone number, opening hours, admission charges, how to get there and disabled access are given for each sight.

Boxes contain information about events and people associated with an area.

4 Major Towns
At least two pages are devoted to each major town, with a detailed description of the historic remains and local curiosities that are worth seeing.

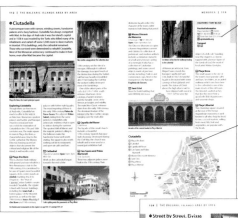

A Visitors' Checklist provides tourist and transport information, including opening hours of tourist attractions, admission charges, and details of local festivals and market days.

A town map shows the location of all the main sights within the town centre and provides tourist information on post offices and car parks.

5 Street-by-Street Map
This gives a bird's-eye view of a particularly interesting sightseeing area described in the section.

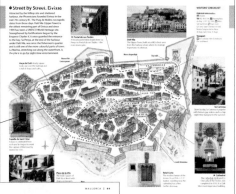

A suggested route for a walk is shown in red.

Stars point out the best sights or exhibits that no visitor should miss.

6 Star Sights
At least one page is dedicated to each major sight. Historic buildings are dissected to reveal their interiors, and parks are illustrated to show the main attractions.

Photographs illustrate the most interesting areas and the most impressive sights within an attraction.

Cut-outs show the sight in its surroundings and some parts of the interior.

INTRODUCING THE BALEARIC ISLANDS

DISCOVERING THE BALEARIC ISLANDS

The itineraries mentioned below have been designed to include most of the major sights of Mallorca, Menorca and Ibiza. Listed first is a summary of the highlights you could aim for on all three islands, followed by three short itineraries covering Palma, Menorca and Ibiza. The final itinerary is a 14-day tour concentrating on Mallorca. Note that there are many frequent flights and ferries between the islands, but you should avoid renting a car as you can't take it on all the ferry routes between islands. Pick, combine and follow your favourite tours, or simply dip in and out and be inspired: if, for example, you only have five days in Mallorca, spend a day in Palma *(see p12)*, followed by Days 5 to 8 of the two-week Mallorca itinerary.

A harbour view of Dalt Vila, Eivissa
Ibiza's oldest remaining part, Dalt Vila, with its intriguing history and beautiful sights, is a UNESCO World Heritage Site and a must-visit for tourists.

0 kilometres 15
0 miles 15

3 days in Ibiza

- Explore **Eivissa town**, its handsome squares and cobbled streets enclosed within formidable-looking fortifications.

- No trip to Ibiza is complete without a visit to one of the island's heaving nightclubs, such as **Pacha**.

- Enjoy **Els Amunts**, the rolling mountains along the island's north coast.

◀ Pretty fresco painted by an Arab artist

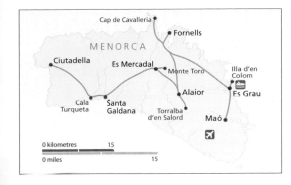

4 days in Menorca

- Sample the small-town delights of both **Maó**, the island capital, and pretty **Ciutadella**, with its compact centre crowded with attractive stone mansions that nudge up towards the harbour.

- Amongst the resorts, aim for **Fornells**, the prettiest resort on the island, with a scattering of cottages sitting tight against a rocky slice of coast.

- Relax on an isolated cove beach, such as the beautiful **Cala Turqueta**.

- Head to the top of **Monte Toro**, Menorca's highest point, which has fabulous views.

Key

— 5 days in Mallorca
— Two weeks in Mallorca
— 4 days in Menorca
— 3 days in Ibiza

A view of Deià, Mallorca
The lovely mountain town of Deiá was home to the well-known English novelist and poet, Robert Graves.

5 days in Mallorca

- Spend time in **Palma**, the wonderful capital city of the Balearics, rich with historical attractions.

- Take the vintage train over the mountains to **Sóller**, once a fruit merchants' town.

- Explore the verdant gardens of the **Jardines d'Alfàbia** and the picturesque resort of **Port de Sóller**.

- Investigate the various nooks and crannies of **Pollença**, a charming little town.

- Visit the **Monestir de Lluc**, home to the much-revered statue of the Virgin Mary.

Two weeks in Mallorca

- Admire the magnificent scenery of Mallorca's northwest in the mountain hamlets of **Deià, Banyalbufar, Estellencs** and **Valldemossa** which has a beautiful monastery.

- Relax and unwind at **Port de Pollença**, the archetypal family resort which has a great vibe, and sits alongside a lovely sandy beach.

- Explore the medieval hilltop town of **Artá** and the prehistoric site of **Ses Païsses**.

- Enjoy the easy charms of **Porto Cristo**, an agreeable port and resort with an attractive centre and a harbourside beach.

- Take the passenger boat to **Cabrera Island National Park**, renowned for its rare plant species and marine life.

For map symbols *see back flap*

2 days in Palma

- **Arriving** Son Sant Joan international airport is about 11km (7 miles) from Palma. Public buses run approximately every 15 minutes into Palma, and taxis are also available.

- **Moving on** Inter-island flights are frequent. A car is recommended for exploring the island.

Day 1

Morning Begin your visit to **Palma** at the **cathedral** (p54), a beautiful sandstone edifice, whose mighty buttressed walls soar high above the seafront. Explore the cathedral which has exquisite Gothic architecture and then pop over to the **Palau d'Almudaina** (p52), once a royal palace and now home to a small but superb collection of Renaissance tapestries. Admire the sculptures in the courtyard of the **Palau March (Fundación Bartolomé March)** (p58) and walk over to the **Museu Diocesà** (p59) – the Diocesan Museum – which has a remarkable collection of medieval religious paintings.

Afternoon Stroll down the narrow lanes of the **Old Town** that are lined by ancient stone houses, and go for a walk along part of the old **city wall** (p59), stretching out behind the seafront. Be sure to visit the old Arab baths, the **Banys Àrabs** (p59) and **Santa Eulàlia** (p58), the handsome church with an imposing

interior. Round off the afternoon with a tour of the **Basilica de Sant Francesc** (p59), which stands illuminated inside by a splendid rose window and is littered with the tombs of the local aristocracy.

Day 2

Morning Start the day by strolling up the elegant **Passeig d'es Born** (p53), once the city's main thoroughfare sheltered from the sun by ancient palm trees. Enjoy the charm of one of Palma's most distinguished old mansions, **Palau Solleric** (p53), and continue onto **Es Baluard Museu** (p58), a prestigious museum of modern art located in a massive Renaissance bastion. Thereafter, proceed to **Plaça Mercat** (p53) to sample the freshest of food at Palma's biggest and best market. Visit the **Plaça Major** (p58), a handsome open square. Don't forget to check out the modern art of the fascinating **Museu Fundación Juan March** (p60).

Evening Take a tour to the **Castell de Bellver** (p61), a medieval castle perched high on a hill overlooking Palma. Be sure to examine the collection of classical sculptures inside and enjoy the views out over the Bay of Palma. Keep aside a couple of hours for the intriguing **Fundació Pilar i Joan Miró** (p62), where the famous artist lived and worked for several decades – at a safe distance from Franco the dictator. Here, you should spend time in the Miró museum, with its prized collection of the artist's work, and even pop into his former studio.

Part of the Renaissance city wall in Palma, dating back to the 1500s

3 days in Ibiza

- **Arriving** Ibiza Airport is approximately 7 km (4 miles) away from Eivissa and is well-connected by a public bus service.

- **Transport** Eivissa town is best explored on foot, but a car is essential for the rest of this itinerary.

Day 1

Eivissa Town Spend at least a day in **Eivissa town** (pp120–23), exploring the ancient buildings and narrow lanes and alleys of the old town, known as **Dalt Villa** (p121). Highlights include the cathedral and the imposing city walls that zigzag around the city centre. Also, look out for the antique exhibits of the excellent **Museu d'Arqueològic** (p122) and drop by the **Museu d'Art Contemporani** (p122), which boasts a collection of modern art. Round off the day with a visit to a nightclub – Eivissa has some of the best in Europe.

Day 2

West Coast Head for Ibiza's lovely west coast, stopping just for the short hike up to the **Mirador des Savinar** (p130) viewpoint and watchtower. Carry on to **Cala d'Hort** (p130), where you can unwind on a shingly cove beach. Lounge about in **Cala**

The Gothic cathedral of La Seu, towering over Palma, Mallorca

Vedella *(p130)* nearby, an appealing mini-resort with a strip of golden sand arching round the back of a slender cove. Continue north along to **Cala Molí** *(p130)*, where a lovely sandy beach is framed by pine dusted hills. Proceed further north, and enjoy the assorted water sports of **Cala Bassa** *(p131)*, a large beach resort teeming with life.

Day 3
North Coast Escape the tourists by heading inland to **Santa Agnes de Corona** *(p127)*, a pretty little village set in the heart of the countryside. Hike out of the village to the chapel of **Santa Agnes** *(p127)*, an unusual grotto church of ancient provenance. Thereafter, proceed east along the main road with farmlands on one side and the peaks of the **Els Amunts** *(p132)* mountain range on the other. Junipers, fan palms, carobs and strawberry trees dot the mountains. Keep an eye out for falcons, greenfinches, goldfinches and hoopoes.

> **To extend your trip…**
> Eivissa town is just a short ferry ride from the fourth inhabited Balearic island, **Formentera** *(p136–43)*, a small, flat island with several splendid beaches, the longest of which is **Platja Migjorn** *(p142)*.

Enjoying the sunshine on Platja Migjorn, Formentera

The shores of Es Grau, a small fishing village with a wide beach

4 days in Menorca

- **Arriving** Menorca's airport is a short journey from the main town, Maó. Shuttle buses and taxis connect the airport to Maó.

- **Transport** A car is required to explore the island.

Day 1
Maó Enjoy the cosy, small-town atmosphere of **Maó** *(p98)* and admire its exquisite harbourside setting – Maó has one of the finest harbours in the Mediterranean. Explore the old town, visiting the bustling **Mercat** (market) on **Plaça Carme** *(p98)* and the intriguing church of **Santa Maria** *(pp98–9)*. With ample time in hand, visit **Museu de Menorca** *(p100)* – the most enjoyable museum on the island with an excellent collection of prehistoric and Roman artifacts. Wander down the harbour around **Xoriguer Distillery** *(p100)* that stands testimony to bygone days when the Menorcans supplied the British sailors with gin.

Day 2
North Coast Heading north from Maó, make a beeline for **Es Grau** *(p102)*, an intimate, pocket-sized resort draped around a sandy bay. Take a boat ride to the craggy, offshore islet of **Illa d'en Colom** *(p102)*, where you can hike up to the lighthouse or laze on the beach. Continue north to **Fornells** *(p108)*, a beguiling village that strings along a rocky, sun-bleached coast. The bay here is ideal for windsurfing –

there is almost always a breeze – or you can push on to the beautiful **Cap de Cavalleria** *(pp108–9)*, a rugged headland with empty beaches and an ancient British watchtower.

Day 3
Inland towns and villages Don't miss the town of **Alaior** *(p104–5)*, whose attractive old centre towers over the top of a steep hill. Cheese is the big deal here – be sure to sample some of the local produce. Take a detour to **Torralba d'en Salord** *(p105)*, an impressive prehistoric ruin. Proceed onto Es Mercadal *(p105)*, a quaint hamlet at the base of **Mone Toro** *(p105)*, the island's highest hill. Drive to the top to visit the monastery. The next target is **Santa Galdana** *(p110)*, a resort that nestles in a steep wooded gully, which is conveniently located near several delightful beaches: **Cala Turqueta** *(p110)* would be the pick.

Day 4
Ciutadella Spend the day in Ciutadella *(p112)*, the pearl of Menorca, where beautiful, honey-coloured stone mansions fan out from the **Plaça d'es Born** *(p112)*, the town's elegant main square. Explore the **cathedral** *(p112)*, a handsome medieval structure, and investigate the assorted antiquities of the **Museu Diocesà** *(p113)*. Wander along the **harbour** *(p114–15)*, where fishing boats dock and restaurants line the quay. Finally, drop by the **Museu Municipal de Ciutadella** *(p114)*, where an excellent collection of prehistoric finds is lodged within the safe confines of the old city wall.

Two weeks in Mallorca

- **Arriving** Mallorca's international airport is a short bus or taxi ride from Palma, capital of the island.

- **Transport** Palma is best explored on foot, but a car is essential for the rest of this itinerary. You should take the vintage train which runs across the island from Palma to Sóller (6–7 times daily; *see p74*).

- **For a shorter trip** If you only have five days in Mallorca, select a day in Palma from the two-day itinerary on p12, take the vintage train (*p74*) from Palmer to Sóller and then follow days 5 to 8 of this itinerary.

Green waters of Estellencs, a charming town on the northwestern coast

Day 1: Palma

Pick from the Palma itineraries on p12.

Day 2: Port d'Andratx; Sant Elm; Parc Natural de Sa Dragonera

Enjoy the charming pine-covered hills to **Sant Elm** (*p65*), an unassuming place, with a relaxed air and a small beach. From here take a boat trip to the offshore island of **Sa Dragonera** (*p65*), for its hiking trails, cove beaches and bird life.

Day 3: Estellencs; Banyalbufar; Port de Valldemossa; Valldemossa

Explore the rugged **northwestern coast of**

Tourists enjoy the beach on Cala Tuent

Mallorca (*p66*), beginning with the charming little village of **Estellencs** (*p66*). Push on to **Banyalbufar** (*p67*), which is – if anything – even prettier with its honey-coloured stone houses ringed by terraced olive groves. Take the minor road as it zigzags over the mountains to the dramatic cove of **Port de Valldemossa** (*p70*), home to a wide, shingly beach. Finish the day with a visit to **Valldemossa** (*p70*), a handsome old town whose famous monastery once sheltered the composer Chopin.

Day 4: Son Marroig; Deià; Cala Deià

Sense the history of Mallorca at **Son Marroig** (*p72*), a fascinating manor house perched high above the ocean. Linger at **Deià** (*p72*), a beautiful mountain village made famous by the English poet and writer Robert Graves, who lived here for several decades. Visit the intriguing museum devoted to him – **La Casa de Robert Graves** (*p73*). Brave the steep, curving road to reach **Cala Deià** (*p72*), a narrow cove battered by the surf and home to two excellent beachside restaurants.

Day 5: Sóller town; Jardines d'Alfabia; Port de Sóller

Savour the charms of **Sóller** (*p73*), the prettiest town on Mallorca, where an exquisite collection of old stone houses flanks a cobweb of narrow cobbled lanes and alleys. Detour south to the **Jardines d'Alfabia** (*p75*), a lush garden of

water fountains and jasmine trellises, waterlily ponds and bulrushes – all set behind an attractive manor house. Be sure to take the vintage train, which clanks down from Sóller to **Port de Sóller** (*p74*), a family-friendly resort that arches around a beautiful horseshoe-shaped bay.

Day 6: Cala Tuent; Sa Calobra; Monestir de Lluc

Escape the tourist throng by driving over the mountains to **Cala Tuent** (*p75*), where soaring peaks frame a wide shingle beach. Admire the even more dramatic coastal scenery at tiny **Sa Calobra** (*p75*), a popular day-trippers' destination, which is famous for the impressive box canyon, where the River of the Twins crashes down to the seashore. Make a beeline for the **Monestir de Lluc** (*p76*), a beautiful monastery set in a shallow valley amidst the mountains and home to a revered statue of the Virgin Mary, known as La Morenta.

Day 7: Pollença; Port de Pollença; Cap de Formentor

Explore **Pollença** (*p78*), a lovely little town of fine old mansions and distinguished stone churches. Be sure to climb its **Via Crucis** (Way of the Cross), a long and wide stone stairway that leads up to a shrine with great views over land and sea. Take a stroll along the long sandy beach at **Port de Pollença** (*p79*), a charming family-friendly resort that is especially popular with the

For practical information on travelling around the Balearic Islands, see pp190–93

British. Venture out to the **Cap de Formentor** (p79), at the tip of a wild and mountainous peninsula.

Day 8: Alcúdia; Port d'Alcúdia; Parc Natural de S'Albufera

Be sure to visit **Alcúdia** (p79), an amenable little place with medieval walls and a clutch of Roman remains; the best time to visit is on market days – Tuesdays and Sundays. Relax on the beach at **Port d'Alcúdia** (p79), an immaculate arc of golden sand crowded with tourists, or take a boat trip around the bay. Introduce yourself to the island's wonderful birdlife at the **Parc Natural de S'Albufera** (p80), a reedy, marshy wetland backing onto Alcúdia bay.

Day 9: Interior towns: Muro; Sineu; Petra

Avoid the more commercialized parts of Mallorca by heading inland to the towns of the central plain. Begin with **Muro** (p80), a sleepy place with a handsome main square and church, the imposing Sant Joan Baptista. Proceeding south, you soon reach **Sineu** (pp80–81), a lively and particularly pretty little town where the kings of Mallorca once held court, and then **Petra** (p81), where the prime target is the birthplace of Junipero Serra, one of the first Europeans to explore modern-day California.

Day 10: Interior towns: Vilafranca de Bonany; Els Calderers; Randa; Llucmajor

Sample the atmosphere of rural Mallorca at **Vilafranca de Bonany** (p85), a quiet village where they sell the freshest of produce – especially peppers. See how the local landed gentry while away the hours at **Els Calderers** (p85), an elegant manor house surrounded by a working farm, and then go up to the top of **Puig de Randa** (pp90–91) to visit the hilltop monastery and its beautiful shrine. Complete the day with a quick ramble around **Llucmajor** (p90), a quiet town with a particularly pleasant main square.

The medieval battlements of the Artà fortress

Day 11: Artà; Capdepera; Cala Rajada

Begin the day with an exploration of **Artà** (p82), a pretty hilltop town with a splendid set of medieval walls. Clamber up to the sanctuary at the top of the town for the magnificent views over land and sea. Stroll over to **Ses Païsses** (p82), one of the island's most atmospheric prehistoric sites. Push on to **Capdepera** (p82), the proud possessor of a medieval castle, and round off the day at **Cala Rajada** (p82), an agreeable resort and fishing port with several lovely sandy beaches.

Day 12: Coves d'Arta; Cala Millor; Safari–Zoo

Don't miss the **Coves d'Artà** (p82), one of the most impressive cave systems on the island with huge stalactites and stalagmites illuminated in a variety of striking colours. Push further down the coast to **Cala Millor** (p84), a large, sprawling resort with a striking sandy beach and facilities for all sorts of water sports. For something rather different, take a tour of the neighbouring **Safari–Zoo** (p84), a somewhat idiosyncratic mix of a zoo and a leisure park.

Day 13: Porto Cristo; Coves del Drac; Felanitx; Parc Natural Mondrago

Enjoy the charms of **Porto Cristo** (p84), an agreeable port and resort with an attractive centre and a harbourside beach. Stroll over to the **Coves del Drac** (p84) – the Dragon's Caves – a subterranean maze of caves, where you can take a boat ride on an underground lake to the sound of a string quartet. Pause at **Felanitx** (p86) for a brief look around this historic town and continue onto the **Parc Natural Mondragó** (p86), a protected slice of coast offering peaceful country walks and a delightful pine-covered beach.

Day 14: Colonia de Sant Jordi; Cabrera island

Relax at **Colònia de Sant Jordi** (p87), the pick of the resorts dotting the south coast, a charming combination of an old seaport and a holiday destination. Laze on one of the resort's several beaches or head off to **Es Trenc** (p87), a long strip of sandy beach that extends as far as the eye can see. Catch the passenger boat to **Cabrera Island National Park** (pp88–9), a bare and rocky archipelago renowned for its wildlife – and its picnic-eating lizards.

Yachts in the coves of Parc Natural Mondragó

Putting the Balearic Islands on the Map

This little group of islands off the east coast of Spain is the Mediterranean's westernmost archipelago. An autonomous province, the Balearic Islands are 82 km (51 miles) from the Iberian Peninsula, a three-hour journey by ferry. The total area of the islands is slightly over 5,000 sq km (1,930 sq miles). Mallorca, the largest island, has an area of 3,640 sq km (1,405 sq miles). The smallest of the four main islands is Formentera.

Northern coast of Mallorca
The northern shores of the Balearic Islands descend steeply via craggy cliffs. There are few beaches here, but clifftop trails are highly recommended.

Bird's-eye View of Eivissa, Ibiza
The Old Town at the centre of Ibiza is particularly interesting when viewed from above. One can see the maze of narrow streets layered within the beautiful old city walls.

Formentera
El Mirador's restaurant terrace provides a stunning island view.

Barcelona

Sólle
Ma-11
Ma-10
Palma
Sa Dragonera Andratx
Ma-1
Pa
Mallc

Valencia

Valencia, Dénia

Ibiza
Valencia
PM810
Sant Antoni de Portmany
C-733
Dénia
C-731
Santa Eulària des Riu
PM803
Eivissa
Ibiza

Valencia, Dénia

La Savina
Sant Francesc *Formentera*
PM820

Key
— Motorway/highway
— Major road
— Minor road
---- Ferry route

0 km   15
0 miles   15

For map symbols *see back flap*

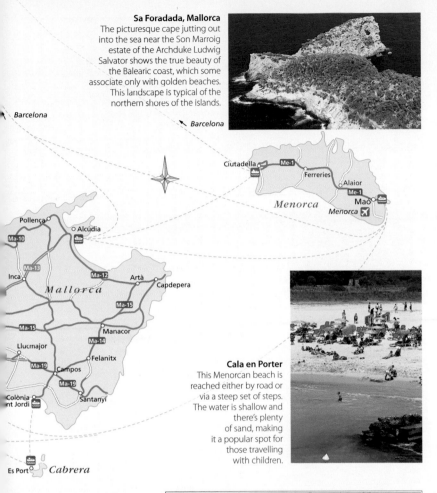

Sa Foradada, Mallorca
The picturesque cape jutting out into the sea near the Son Marroig estate of the Archduke Ludwig Salvator shows the true beauty of the Balearic coast, which some associate only with golden beaches. This landscape is typical of the northern shores of the islands.

Cala en Porter
This Menorcan beach is reached either by road or via a steep set of steps. The water is shallow and there's plenty of sand, making it a popular spot for those travelling with children.

Location of the archipelago
A short hop from Spain, the Balearic Islands are one of the most popular European resorts. Flights from northern Europe take less than three hours. As a result, the islands attract many visitors all year round.

A PORTRAIT OF THE BALEARIC ISLANDS

The Balearic Islands are blessed by a hot Mediterranean sun that is tempered by cool sea breezes. Holidaymakers crowd onto the beaches every summer while the young make the most of the clubs and bars. Away from the resorts, time has moved at a gentler pace and inland the islands are quiet and undeveloped.

An ideal staging post between Europe and Africa, these beautiful islands have had their fair share of invaders, including the Phoenicians and the Romans who made the islands part of their Empire. In recent times, the islands have fallen to a full-scale invasion of tourists, which began in the 1960s.

The islands' nightlife, particularly on Ibiza and Mallorca, is legendary and attracts a young crowd. There is far more on offer than clubs however, and if chic cafés are more your thing, the Balearic Islands can supply these too. Indeed, the islands have proved to be popular with the rich and famous, many of whom have homes on the hillsides, away from the prying lenses of the paparazzi.

Even before the influx of tourists, the islands' climate attracted celebrities. The composer Frédéric Chopin journeyed to Mallorca with his lover George Sand in the winter of 1838–9. Other artists, including the painter and sculptor Joan Miró and the poet Robert Graves, liked it so much that they settled down here.

Menorca is quieter than Mallorca or Ibiza. It has low-key resorts, golden beaches and a rocky landscape that is rich in fascinating prehistoric remains.

Formentera, 4 km (2 miles) south of Ibiza, is the smallest of the Balearic Islands. Tourism is still light though the island's population doubles in the summer as daytrippers come to enjoy what is still a rural haven.

Cala Tarida on the western shores of Ibiza

◀ Charming old fishing neighbourhood of Sa Penya, Ibiza's Eivissa district

Rocky coast near Coves d'Artà in Mallorca

Tourist Paradise

It was in the early part of the 19th century that tourists first began to arrive on the Balearic Islands, and since that time the local economy has taken full advantage of the opportunities these new arrivals offered. Over 11 million visitors arrive every year to enjoy the islands' many attractions.

Mallorca, the largest island, is by far the most culturally rich, but the other islands are not short of attractions. Ibiza is famous as the clubbing capital of Europe; Menorca is an ideal resort for families, while those in search of peace and quiet head for Formentera. You may even spot the occasional celebrity – Annie Lennox, Claudia Schiffer and

Portal of the main entrance to Palma's cathedral

Michael Schumacher all have homes on Mallorca, while Elle MacPherson, Roman Polanski and Noel Gallagher (to name but a few) have opted for life on Ibiza. The Balearic Islands are also very popular with politicians and royalty, including the Spanish royal family with their summer residence in Palma.

The Balearics have many fascinating historic sights ranging from Neolithic remains and castle ruins to stunning cathedrals and fine examples of British colonial architecture. Gourmets can delight in the famous Menorcan cheeses and Mallorcan wines, as well as sample the products of the local distilleries, including gin (inherited from the English) and the potent Ibizan herbal liqueurs. The famous *caldereta de llagosta* (Menorcan lobster stew) is not to be missed.

Natural Treasures

The greatest riches of the archipelago are its landscape and natural beauty. The local authorities, hoping to preserve these assets for future generations, have issued several legal decrees that are aimed at protecting the natural environment. Currently, over 40 per cent of the archipelago is legally protected. There is a total of 82 areas of outstanding natural beauty, while the whole of Menorca is designated as a UNESCO Biosphere Reserve, with 18 designated sites that are currently assigned special protection. Mallorca's stunning Parc Natural de S'Albufera is a unique ornithological reserve and is one of southern Europe's most precious water marshes. Among Mallorca's parks and nature reserves are Cala Mondragó and Dragonera Island.

Cabrera Island National Park, to the south of Mallorca, also enjoys special protection. The number of boats permitted to land here is strictly limited. This has halted the mass influx of tourists, who come here to experience its unique natural beauty and swim in its crystal-clear waters. Here, the island's landscape is protected, as well as its surrounding waters.

National parks can be explored on foot or by bicycle, using special trails and signposts. There are also organized tours. The natural wonders of the islands can also be seen outside the parks. Some charming places are to be found, particularly in the valleys of the Serra de Tramuntana mountain range in Mallorca and in the secluded coves of the northwestern part of the island, as well as along most of the coastline of Menorca. The Pitiusan (Pine Trees) archipelago, comprising Ibiza, Formentera and

Fishermen sorting the catch in Eivissa's harbour

numerous neighbouring uninhabited rocky islands, forms a combined ecosystem visible from the air. A region of outstanding ecological value in Ibiza is the system of salt marshes, Ses Salines, which includes areas inhabited by thousands of birds. Since the Carthaginians discovered the islands these salt marshes have been used to supply salt extracted from seawater.

In Ses Illetes in Formentera, declared a World Heritage Site by UNESCO, the seabeds are carpeted with fields of *Posidonia oceanica*, a sea-grass species, which gives the water its crystal-clear appearance and makes it ideal for scuba diving.

People and Events

Although the impact of tourism has been far reaching, island customs and traditions have survived intact. This is particularly apparent in the rural areas. To see this side of island life, visit a local farmers' market in one of the small inland towns, or sit down with the locals in a village bar.

Solemn procession held during Corpus Christi

Entrance to El Palacio Hotel in Palma

The Arts

The islands have long been a draw for artists. Frédéric Chopin came to Valldemossa on Mallorca, though the weather was far from ideal (one of his Mallorcan compositions was the *Raindrops Prelude*). The picturesque Mallorcan village of Deià was for many years the home of the English writer Robert Graves, whose guests included Pablo Picasso and the actors Alec Guinness and Peter Ustinov. The most famous artist associated with Mallorca, however, is Joan Miró, whose works can be seen in the Fundació Pilar i Joan Miró, on the outskirts of Palma.

Another important element of island life is the numerous national, local and religious holidays and fiestas. Normally these are days devoted to the patron saints of local parishes, but they can also be held at the end of harvest time or to celebrate an anniversary of an important public event.

A long calendar of fiestas begins in January with the Festa de Sant Antoni in Mallorca. Perhaps the most colourful is the Festa de Sant Joan in Ciutadella, Menorca (23–24 June), with horseback processions along the narrow streets, firework displays and a jousting tournament. *(See pp30–33 for more on fiestas and holidays.)*

Sports

The archipelago is famous for its water sports, particularly the many races held on the waters of the Badia de Palma. The most important of these are held under the patronage and with the participation of King Felipe VI. They are attended by leading members of the yachting world. The big events, including the King's Cup and Queen Sofia's Cup, are celebrated as public holidays.

Sun-worshippers on the beach in Son Xoriguer, Menorca

Felipe VI, the King of Spain

Bullfights *(corridas)*, popular in mainland Spain, enjoy more limited popularity in the Balearics. A bullfight can be seen in one of the arenas in Mallorca, but the standard of shows is not high.

The true local passion is *fútbol* (football). Real Mallorca, based in Palma, is one of the leading Spanish sides and won the 1998 Spanish Cup. It is worth attending a match, not just as a sporting event but to enjoy the good-natured enthusiasm of the crowd.

Other sports strongly associated with the islands include yachting, windsurfing, horse riding and golf. Excellent golfing conditions exist in the islands, even in winter.

Present-Day Balearics

Once removed from the mainstream of international life, the Balearic Islands have now found themselves drawn in, thanks to tourism. Before World War I,

they were visited by the English King Edward VII and the German Emperor Wilhelm II. This high-society tourism reached its peak in the 1930s, when the poet Adam Diehl built the luxurious Hotel Formentor on Pollença Bay. In the 1960s, Ibiza was "discovered" by hippies. Soon after, charter flights began operating to Mallorca. Mass tourism developed rapidly after the death of General Franco in 1975.

In 1983, the islands became an autonomous region of Spain. The authorities made Catalan and its local dialects (*Mallorquín* on Mallorca, *Menorquín* on Menorca and *Eivissenc* on Ibiza) the joint official language with Spanish and introduced strict control of the local economy.

Following a string of environmental protest marches in 1998 and 1999, an "eco-tax" was introduced in 2002. The tax, levied on visitors to the islands, was intended to tackle some of the environmental havoc that had been wreaked by unregulated tourism over the last 30 years. In its first year the tax's benefits included funding the demolishing of a number of unsightly hotels. The "eco-tax" was always controversial, however, and the government finally decided to scrap it in 2003.

Bullfight in the Mallorcan arena

Architecture of the Balearic Islands

The Balearic Islands boast a rich and diverse architectural heritage. The sights worth seeing range from prehistoric chamber tombs to magnificent aristocratic mansions and palaces. Palma has the most to see, notably the fine Gothic cathedral which was renovated by Antoni Gaudí, while Menorca has many remains from the Talayotic period. Ibiza's houses, influenced by the Arabs, have inspired some of the greatest architects of the 20th century including Le Corbusier and Walter Gropius.

Main entrance to a residence in Els Calderers in Mallorca

Country Houses

The typical village landscape is marked by low, often whitewashed houses. Built of the local stone, many have aged to a yellow-brown colour, blending with their surroundings. Thick walls and few openings ensure that the interior stays cool even on the hottest days. A farmstead often also includes some modest outbuildings; the whole surrounded by a garden and fields.

Whitewashed stone walls

Small window in a recess

Narrow entrance door

More modest homes are often adjoined by farm buildings, with a small granary on top. Village houses are almost always single-storey dwellings.

Country Estates

At the centre of each country estate was a fine *hacienda* (or *possessió*). Their owners vied with each other by building ever more extravagant dwellings attesting to their wealth and importance. The interiors were furnished with magnificent furniture and paintings. The accommodation included formal apartments, private rooms and domestic quarters. Some are now let as holiday homes.

Great country houses, such as La Granja on Mallorca's southwest coast, belonged to wealthy landowning families and were run according to a feudal system.

Villas

This form of architecture appeared on Mallorca in the 19th century. Villas, serving as summer residences, were built in line with the fashion of the day. Their numbers rose with the increasing popularity of the island.

Modern villas are often owned by the rich and famous. They stand in beautiful, secluded spots on many of the islands.

Old villas, with their delightful architecture, can be seen in many large town centres and in seaside resorts on Mallorca.

Churches

Whitewashed churches are typical of Ibiza, although they can also be seen on Menorca and Formentera. Often they stand at the centre of the village or on a hillside at its outskirts. The entrance to the dark interior is usually preceded by a triple arcade.

Triple arcades

Typical small belfry

Three crosses on the façade – the symbol of Golgotha

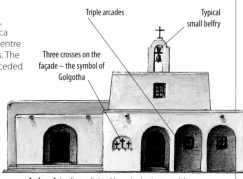

The belfry on a village church is usually a simple affair. It consists of a distinctive arcade rising above the façade, crowned with an iron cross and housing a bell.

A church is often adjoined by a single-storey parish building or a vestry. It may be surrounded by a low stone wall and feature an enclosed forecourt.

Watchtowers

The stone towers that can be seen along the coastline were built to protect the islands from attacks by pirates, mainly from North Africa, who raided the ports and inland towns. The towers stand in secluded, inaccessible spots, so that they could be easily defended. Most of the towers are deserted, and closed to visitors. A few are used as viewpoints.

Towers on Mallorca are slender. For extra protection, their entrances were high above the ground. Their walls feature narrow loopholes.

Towers on other islands are lower. Built of stone, they resemble the fortresses built in the Canary Islands.

Windmills of the Balearic Islands

Stone-built windmills are another typical feature of the Balearic landscape. Early mills were used to grind grain; later they were used to pump water. Most stone-built mills are no longer in use and are slowly falling into disrepair. Some have lost their sails, and they now resemble watchtowers. Others have been converted into restaurants, with the machinery and millstones serving as tourist attractions.

Windmills were built mostly on the plains among green fields, and were used to grind corn or to drive the pumps of deep-water wells. Because they are cheaper to run than petrol-driven pumps, some farmers still use wind power to pump water even today.

Typical windmills were built near towns with food markets, and were used for grinding grain. Often the miller would actually live in the tower.

Landscape and Wildlife of the Balearic Islands

Thanks to the huge variety of habitats, from mountains and cliffs to sandy beaches and wide plains, the Balearics have a wide diversity of wildlife including some rare birds and reptiles. Mallorca's characteristic terrain is *garrigue*, an open scrubland, interspersed with small pockets of forest. At higher altitudes the scrub is replaced by *maquis* – a mix of mainly rosemary, broom and laurel. Menorca, in particular, is noted for its wild flowers and shrubs while large swathes of Ibiza are covered by forests of pine.

The craggy cliffs, sharp-edged and forbidding, appear inaccessible. Consisting of limestone, they are sparsely covered with vegetation.

Forests are rare on the islands. The largest woodland areas can be found in Mallorca. These are mainly pine forests, featuring Aleppo pine mixed with holm oak.

Olive groves are seen mainly in Mallorca, inland as well as near the coastline. Tree trunks and boughs are sometimes twisted into curious shapes.

The northern shores of the islands are mostly steep and craggy. Inland, the vegetation is dense and lush. There are few beaches and those that are accessible are rocky or pebbly. The northern shores have been less affected by tourism, and provide stunning views as well as excellent natural areas to explore.

Balearic Landscape

Of all the Balearic Islands, Mallorca's landscape is the most diverse. As well as its many secluded coves, it has magnificent green plains and the Serra de Tramuntana mountain range.

Cove beaches are one of the features that make the islands so attractive. Some are now resorts. Others can be difficult to reach, but their soft sands, gentle waves and clear water attract a steady flow of visitors.

High mountains are found only in the northern part of Mallorca. Puig Major – the highest peak in the Serra de Tramuntana – rises to a height of 1,445 m (4,740 ft).

Flora

There are some 1,500 species of flowering plant on the islands, of which 50 or so are native. Some of them grow only in Mallorca and the Cabrera archipelago. Most flower in spring and at this time the islands are a blaze of colour. For the rest of the year, the islands are green, but the sun-bleached foliage is no longer quite so lush.

Common broom is typical of Mediterranean flora. Its bright yellow flowers, which blossom in March, can be seen from afar.

Small foxglove, with its distinctive, thimble-like flower, is a highly ornamental plant. It is one of the plants native to the Balearic Islands. Few people realize that the species is also poisonous.

Holm oak is widespread throughout the islands. Its tough, evergreen leaves protect it against water loss.

Coves with sandy beaches are typical of the Balearic Islands' landscape.

Macchia, an evergreen shrub, grows on the rocky mountain slopes.

Fauna of the Balearic Islands

Fauna on the Balearic Islands includes a handful of native species, such as the rare Lilford's wall lizard. The islands are also home to some rare species of birds, including the black vulture, rock falcon and the Balearic shearwater. Several smaller mammals such as rabbits and hedgehogs are commonplace in the lowlands of the archipelago.

The Lilford's wall lizard is one of the few endemic species living on the islands.

The Silver gull is the most common bird inhabiting the coastal regions of the archipelago.

Rabbits have easily adapted to the wide variety of landscapes on the islands, particularly since they have no natural predators.

The Underwater World

Some four million years ago, the Balearic archipelago was joined to the continent. The sinking seabed caused the islands to become separated from the mainland by the Balearic Sea. The coastline is topographically varied, featuring sandy beaches with shallows stretching far out into the sea, and cliffs with distinct layers of rock, full of cracks, niches and caves. Facing them, rising up from the sea, are small rocky islands and solitary rocks created by sea abrasion. In the coastal and offshore waters there is a rich variety of marine life.

Cardinal fish live in small shoals. The tiny red fish can be seen mostly among sea grass or hiding near the entrances to underwater caves and grottoes.

Marine Species

The waters surrounding the archipelago are too cold for coral reefs. The only variety found here is the soft gorgonia. The sea grass meadows are home to a variety of animals, from lugworms to fish. The rocky seabed supports the richest variety of life. Here, you will find varieties of molluscs, starfish, lobster and fish – from the smallest goby to the giant grouper.

Ray fish eggs · Cuttle-fish shells · Sea grass · Shark eggs

Seahorse

Psi shark

The great pipefish hides among sea grass. It feeds on small marine animals, including crustaceans and fry, which it sucks in with its long snout. Pipefish eggs hatch inside the male's pouch.

The cuttlefish is a predator that uses its long tentacles to catch its prey. It hunts while swimming or lying buried in the sand, almost invisible to its victim. The cuttlefish can change its colour to blend in with the background. When threatened, it ejects an inky fluid that disorientates the attacker.

Pinna are huge, long-lived molluscs that dig into the sand with the sharp end of their shells.

Starfish inhabit the coastal regions of the Balearic Islands, up to a depth of 35 m (115 ft). They live mainly on the rocky bottom, and are conspicuous by their red colour.

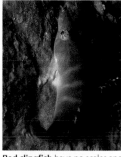

The Balearic shearwater, also known as the "Moresque shearwater", is a common sight. It gathers food by sitting on the water and catching crustaceans, squid and small fish. The shearwater is native to the Balearic Islands and nests in large colonies.

The Lilford's wall lizard can be seen everywhere, even close to beaches, in dry, sunny places. There are 22 known subspecies, which are spread throughout the archipelago.

The Mediterranean monk seal was once a common sight in the archipelago but is now almost extinct.

Red clingfish have no scales and attach themselves to the surfaces of rocks with a sucker situated between their ventral fins.

The Haliotis clam prefers rocky bottoms close to the shore. This primitive snail is highly valued by gourmets.

The species of moray found in the Mediterranean has no venom, but its bite can be dangerous. Hidden amid rocks, it springs surprise attacks, feeding on fish and crustaceans.

Mediterranean scallop

Gorgonia

Link wrasse

Amarela

The slipper lobster is not as common as the cicada lobster, which is twice its size. Its body is covered with a hard shell and is armed with spikes, while its antennae have evolved into short, wide plates.

The Dusky grouper is, despite its fearsome size, a gentle fish. Because of this, and its sheer bulk, it presents an easy target for spear-fishing.

THE BALEARIC ISLANDS THROUGH THE YEAR

The inhabitants of the Balearic Islands are deeply attached to their traditions, a fact that is reflected in the many religious feast days, or fiestas, they celebrate. Fiestas are generally associated with the cult of saints, particularly the patron of the local parish or the island. Though mostly religious, fiestas are an opportunity for people to enjoy themselves, with parades, music and much dancing. The most spectacular of these is the Festa de Sant Joan, which has been celebrated in Ciutadella, Menorca, since medieval times. In the resorts, fiestas are less conspicuous, but elsewhere everybody joins in the fun. During the fiesta, normal life stops and only minimal bus services run. It is also difficult to find hotel accommodation, so book in advance. Tourist information offices can provide details of local fiestas.

Almond blossom in early spring in Mallorca

Spring

With the advent of spring, life in Spain moves out into the streets, and the café terraces fill with guests. This is a very beautiful time of year. Before the arrival of the summer heat, trees, flowers and wild herbs burst into flower. The famous Semana Santa (Holy Week) before Easter is a time of religious processions.

March
Semana Santa On Maundy Thursday in Palma, a procession leaves the church of La Sang at Plaça de Hospital, carrying a crucifix. On Good Friday, solemn processions are held in many towns, including Palma and Sineu (Mallorca) and Maó

(Menorca). The sombre ceremony of laying in the tomb *(Davallament)* is held at the church of Nostra Senyora del Àngels, in Pollença. In Monastir de Lluc the faithful conduct a penitential Way of the Cross.

April
Festa Sant Francesc *(2 Apr)*. The popular feast of St Francis is celebrated throughout the islands, in parishes of which the saint is the patron.
Princess Sofia Trophy *(One week, dates vary)*, Palma. One of the most important yachting regattas in the Balearics.
Festa Sant Jordi *(23 Apr)*. Feast day of the patron saint of many towns and villages, celebrated on all the islands.

May
Festa de Maig *(1st Sun in May)*, Santa Eulàlia, Ibiza. This springtime flower festival is one of the most colourful and beautiful fiestas in the Balearic Islands.
Festa de Nostra Senyora de la Victòria *(2nd Sun in May)*, Sóller and Port de Sóller, Mallorca. Mock battles pit Christian against Moor, and are staged to mark the raid by Turkish pirates, on 11 May 1561.
Eivissa Medieval *(2nd Sun in May)*, Eivissa, Ibiza. A festival to celebrate the declaration of Dalt Vila as a World Heritage Site in 1999, with dancing and concerts.
Festa de Primavera de Manacor *(27 May)*, Manacor. Spring Festival, the most important festival in Manacor, lasting until early June.

Princess Sofia Cup yachting regatta

Average daily hours of sunshine

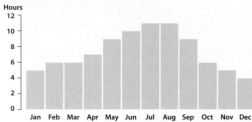

Hours of Sunshine
During July and August, there are nearly 11 hours of sunshine daily. Not surprisingly, these months coincide with the peak of the tourist season. Fewer sunny days occur in November, December and January. At this time of the year the islands are at their least attractive.

Summer

June marks the beginning of the peak tourist season in the Balearic Islands, which will last until September. It is ushered in by numerous cultural events, including concerts, festivals and folk group performances. The latter half of summer features various fiestas associated with gathering the harvest.

Festa de Nostra Senyora de la Victòria in Sóller

June

Corpus Christi, Pollença, Mallorca. The Dance of Eagles, performed in the main square of the town, is followed by a procession.
Sant Antoni de Juny (13 Jun), Artà, Mallorca. A local feast featuring parades of people dressed as horses.
Sant Joan (24 Jun), Ciutadella, Menorca. King Juan Carlos's name day. At its climax the horses rear up and the crowd attempts to support them.
Romeria de Sant Marçal (30 Jun), Sa Cabeneta, Mallorca. A fair where they sell *siurells*. Similar

Beaches of Cala Millor, in Mallorca, crowded with holidaymakers

fairs are also held in Campos, Sineu, Felanitx and Manacor.

July

Día de Virgen de Carmen (15–16 Jul). The feast of the patron saint of sailors and fishermen, celebrated with parades and a blessing of the fishing boats.
Passejada díes Bou i Carro Triunfal (27–28 Jul), Valldemossa, Mallorca. The feast of Catalina Thomàs. A bull is led through the streets of this small town, followed the next day by a procession of carts, with one girl playing the role of St Catalina.

August

Copa del Rey (1st wk in Aug), Palma, Mallorca. International yachting regattas held under the patronage of King Juan Carlos.
Sant Ciriac (8 Aug), Ibiza, Formentera. A feast held to commemorate the Spanish recapture of these islands.
Festa de Sant Lorenç (2nd wk in Aug), Alaior, Menorca. Riding displays in the streets.

Assumption of the Virgin (15 Aug). A festival celebrated throughout Spain.
Sant Bartomeu (24 Aug). Horse races in Capdepera; devil dances in Montuïri.
Sant Agustín (28 Aug). Felanitx, Mallorca. A joyful fiesta in honour of St Augustine, with festivities such as dancing and horse-riding shows.

Busy fruit stalls at Pollença market in Mallorca

Average monthly rainfall

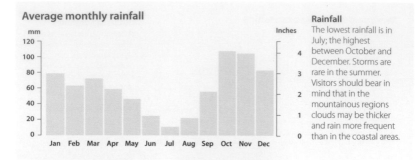

Rainfall
The lowest rainfall is in July; the highest between October and December. Storms are rare in the summer. Visitors should bear in mind that in the mountainous regions clouds may be thicker and rain more frequent than in the coastal areas.

Procession with crops, during Festa des Vermar in Binissalem

Autumn

After the summer scorchers, autumn days bring cool air and rain. With the passing of the peak holiday season, the resorts empty out. Harvest fiestas continue and the wine festivals come to the fore, particularly in Binissalem, Mallorca. The first juice extracted from the grape harvest is blessed and in some places wine is served free.

September

Processió de la Beata (1st Sun in Sep), Santa Margalida, Mallorca. A procession of colourful floats and people dressed in folk costumes honouring Sant Catalina – known as *beata* – the blessed one.
Diada de Mallorca (12 Sep). Commemorates the signing of the Majorcan Statute of Rights by King Jaume II in 1276, with lively concerts, conferences and fun sporting events at sea and in the mountains.

Festa des Vermar (last Sun in Sep), Binissalem, Mallorca. A grape-harvest festival with floats and open-air concerts.
Festa des Meló (first Sun in Sep), Vilafranca de Bonany, Mallorca. Watermelon Festival, marking the end of harvest.

October

Día de la Hispanidad (12 Oct). Spanish National Holiday

Es Vedrà on the coast of Ibiza, shrouded in clouds

celebrating the discovery of the "New World" by Christopher Columbus, in 1492.
La Beateta (16 Oct). Fancy-dress procession in Palma. Fairs in Alcúdia, Campos, Felanitx, Porreres and Llucmajor. Raft races in Porto Portals.
Festa de Les Verges (21 Oct), Palma. Festival where enormous quantities of *buñelos de vientyo* cakes are consumed and young people sing serenades in honour of Santa Ursula and the 11,000 virgins.
Festa d'Es Botifarró (3rd Sun in Oct), Sant Joan, Mallorca. This festival includes dancing and music to accompany the eating of large amounts of sausage (berenada de butifarra) and vegetable pies (coca amb trampó).

November

Todos los Santos (1 Nov). All Saints' Day and the following day – Día dels difunts (All Souls Day) – are a time when people visit the graves of relatives and friends.
Sant Carles (4 Nov), Ibiza. Patron saint's day, celebrated throughout the island.
Dijous Bo (3rd Thu in Nov), Inca, Mallorca. Important agricultural feast in Mallorca, featuring fairs and revelry.
Birthday of Junípero Serra (24 Nov). Celebrated throughout the archipelago as the birthday of this Franciscan monk who founded the cities of San Diego, Los Angeles and San Francisco (see p81).

Average monthly temperature

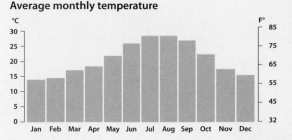

Temperature
Temperatures in the Balearic Islands rarely fall below zero. This happens only occasionally in December and early January. For this reason, many people enjoy out-of-season visits. Summer temperatures may soar to 40° C (104° F).

Winter

The Balearic winter is not particularly severe. Nights are cold, but days are often sunny and mild. Christmas is a time of special celebration throughout Spain, with families gathering to participate in religious festivities.

Working in the fields during early spring

December

Noche Buena *(24 Dec)*. Christmas Eve is celebrated within the family circle, and often includes midnight Mass. Numerous nativity plays and scenes are organized in Palma.

Santos Inocentes *(28 Dec)*. The Spanish equivalent of Britain's April Fool's day.

Festa de l'Estandard *(31 Dec)*, Palma, Mallorca. Feast commemorating the town's conquest by Jaume I, in 1229.

January

Revetlla i Beneides de Sant Antoni Abat *(16–17 Jan)*, Mallorca. Fiesta with bonfires, parades and the blessing of animals. People wander between the bonfires, dressed in costumes, dancing and consuming large quantities of eel and vegetable pies.

Processo dels Tres Tocs *(17 Jan)*, Ciutadella, Menorca. The Procession of the Three Strikes marks the victory of Alfonso III over the Muslims, in 1287.

Festa de Sant Sebastià *(20 Jan)*, Pollença, Mallorca. Procession carrying a banner with the image of the saint and with two dancers, called *cavallets*, mounting wooden horses.

February

Carnival Parades *(Feb/Mar)*. Fancy-dress balls marking the end of Carnival, before Lent. The most spectacular

Carnival in Palma, Mallorca

fiesta, called *Sa Rua* (the Cavalcade), takes place in Palma and its surrounding resorts.

Public Holidays

Año Nuevo New Year's Day (1 Jan)

Día de Reyes Epiphany (6 Jan)

Jueves Santo Maundy Thursday (Mar/Apr)

Viernes Santo Good Friday (Mar/Apr)

Día de Pascua Easter (Mar/Apr)

Fiesta de Trabajo Labour Day (1 May)

Corpus Christi (early Jun)

Asunción Assumption of the Virgin (15 Aug)

Día de la Hispanidad National Day (12 Oct)

Todos los Santos All Saints' Day (1 Nov)

Día de la Constitución Constitution Day (6 Dec)

Inmaculada Concepción Immaculate Conception (8 Dec)

Navidad Christmas Day (25 Dec)

Autumn fishing from a traditional Balearic boat

THE HISTORY OF THE BALEARIC ISLANDS

The Balearic Islands were often a target for conquest and this turbulent history has left behind numerous reminders. Consecutive waves of raiders continually destroyed the heritage of their predecessors and it was not until the conquest of the islands by Jaume I, in 1229, that a period of relative stability began. But even the centuries that followed were not a period of calm.

Earliest Inhabitants

The earliest inhabitants of the Balearic Islands probably arrived from the Iberian Peninsula. Archaeological findings indicate that the islands were occupied by 4000 BC. Archaeological remains include flint tools, primitive pottery and artifacts made of horn, giving evidence that these early settlers were shepherds and hunters. As well as herding sheep, the earliest inhabitants of the Balearic Islands hunted the local species of mountain goat *(Myotragus balearicus),* now extinct. Most archaeological finds were discovered in caves, which were used for shelter and also for ritual burials. The best-preserved complex of caves, developed and extended by the Talayotic settlers, are the Cales Coves discovered near Cala en Porter, in Menorca.

The Beaker ware found in Deià, in Mallorca, represents a style known throughout Western Europe. Beaker People are so named because of their custom of placing pottery beakers in graves. The representatives of this culture were capable of producing excellent bronze tools and artifacts. They appeared in the islands around 2300 BC.

Talayotic Period

The mysterious structures made of giant stones found on the islands date from around 1300 BC. The most typical of the time, which also gave the period its name, is the *talayot* derived from the Arabic word *atalaya,* meaning "observation tower". These structures appear in greatest numbers in Menorca, with somewhat fewer in Mallorca. None has been found in Ibiza. Other common sights are *taulas* and *navetas (see p103).* In southern Europe similar structures can be found only in Sardinia *(nuraghi).*

These early inhabitants of the islands represented a relatively advanced civilization. Some of them lived in fortified settlements, such as Capocorb Vell, Mallorca, where over 30 stone houses and four massive *talayots* have been found.

6000 BC	4000 BC	3000 BC	2000 BC	
	4000 BC Human occupation well established on the Balearic Islands	**2300 BC** Beaker culture flourishes in the Iberian Peninsula	**1300 BC** Beginning of the Talayotic civilization; development of Cales Coves	

Around 5000 BC Probable arrival of man can be dated from finds around Sóller and Valldemossa

Arrowhead dating from the Talayotic era

◄ A painting of Maó harbour, Menorca, in the early 19th century

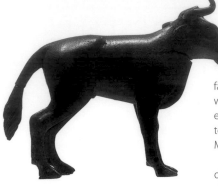

Figurine, 5th century BC, from Torralba d'en Salord

Phoenicians, Greeks and Carthaginians

The Phoenicians arrived in the islands in the early part of the 1st millennium BC. They founded a trading settlement, Sanisera, on the northern coast of Menorca. Two hundred years later, the islands attracted the attention of the Greeks, who were exploring the western regions of the Mediterranean. The Greeks did not settle in the Balearics, as they lacked the metal ores that would have made the islands suitable for colonization. They were also discouraged by the hostile reception from the local inhabitants. But the archipelago owes its name to the Greeks. It derives from the Greek word *ballein* (to throw from a sling). The islanders were famed as outstanding sling-shots and, more than once, made life a misery for various raiders.

The Carthaginians also took an interest in trade in the western region of the Mediterranean. Carthaginian sailors started to explore the Balearic Islands in the early 7th century BC. In 654, they took Ibiza, where they founded the fortified capital of Eivissa (the famous Carthaginian general, Hannibal, was born on Ibiza). After conquering the entire archipelago, they founded new towns, including Jamna (Ciutadella) and Maghen (Maó) in Menorca.

The Balearic Islands played a strategic role during the Punic Wars. Following their defeat at Zama in 202 BC, the Carthiginians were crushed. Soon afterwards, they left Mallorca and Menorca but remained in Ibiza for a further 70 years.

Roman Empire and Byzantium

The Romans conquered Ibiza in 146 BC. Meanwhile, the inhabitants of Mallorca and Menorca, taking advantage of the political upheavals, turned to piracy. This lasted until 123 BC, when the Roman Consul Quintus Metellus occupied the islands. He was awarded the honorary title of *Balearico* for his deeds. Roman rule lasted for over 500 years and the islands were renamed: Balearis Major (Mallorca), Balearis Minor

Ruins of the Christian basilica in Son Bou, Menorca

---

800 BC Twilight of the Talayotic civilization. Greeks visit the islands

654 BC Carthaginians conquer Ibiza

202 BC Carthaginians defeated at Zama

| 1000 BC | 700 BC | 400 BC | 100 BC |

Around 1000 BC Phoenician merchants arrive on the islands

Figurine of the goddess Tanit, 2nd century BC

146 BC Romans conquer Ibiza

(Menorca) and Ebusus (Ibiza). The *Pax Romana* brought prosperity: Roman settlers planted vineyards, built roads and founded Palmeria and Pollentia, a settlement near Alcúdia in Mallorca. They also founded Portus Magonis (Maó) in Menorca, which subsequently became the island's capital and extended the Phoenician port, Sanisera, making it one of the biggest harbours of the empire.

A mosaic from the Calvià library, Mallorca, showing the conquest of Mallorca by Arabs in 904

By the 3rd century AD, the expansion of Christianity had begun on the islands. Roman rule was already in decline when, in 425, the Vandals invaded and destroyed both the Roman and Christian cultural heritages.

Subsequently, the Byzantine army led by Belisarius expelled the Vandal tribes from the Balearic Islands. For over 100 years the islands remained within the sphere of influence of the Byzantine Empire. This ensured their stability until the declining empire came under attack from the Arabs.

The Moors

The conquest of Menorca and Mallorca by the Emir of Cordoba at the beginning of the 10th century marks the beginning of Moorish influence over the islands, which lasted for more than three centuries. During this period the Muslims transformed the Balearic Islands, introducing new irrigation techniques, planting crops like rice and cotton and, on terraced hillsides, oranges, limes and olives. In 1114, Muslim rule was interrupted when an army of 70,000 Italian and Catalan soldiers attacked Ibiza and Mallorca. Supported by the pope, the Christian troops slaughtered most of the Muslims and set sail, filling their ships with spoils. The Moors quickly re-established themselves, however, and flourished once again under the rule of the Almoravids, a Berber dynasty from North Africa. Reminders of Moorish presence on the islands include the agricultural terraces, architecture and designs for embroidery and ceramics.

Arab Bath in Palma, one of few surviving relics of Muslim culture on the islands

Sacking of Pollentia by Vandals

798 Raid by Moorish pirates

1085 Islands gain the status of caliphate ruled by the Almoravids

707 First raids by the Arabs

AD 200   **500**   **800**   **1100**

426 Vandal invasion

533 Beginning of Byzantine rule over the archipelago

859 Vikings raid the islands

902 Mallorca becomes a member of the Cordoba Caliphate

1114 Mallorca invaded, unsuccessfully, by Christian army – "Small Crusade"

Jaume I

In September 1229, on the beach near Santa Ponça, Mallorca, the Catalan King Jaume I, later known as "El Conqueridor", landed with his army, which consisted of 16,000 soldiers and 1,500 cavalry. The pretext for the attack was the seizure of several Catalan vessels by the Emir of Mallorca. In the ensuing battle, Jaume I captured the capital and conquered the entire island. In 1232, he returned to Mallorca with a handful of soldiers. From there he sent delegates to Menorca, who were to negotiate a surrender. Meanwhile, Jaume I built a camp on the mountain slopes near

Cross in Santa Ponça, marking Jaume I's conquest

Capdepera. In the evening he ordered numerous bonfires to be lit, to look as though a large army was preparing to attack. The ruse worked and the Moors surrendered Menorca to the king, who left them to rule the island as his vassals.

In 1230, Jaume I had issued the *Carta de Població* (People's Charter), which encouraged Catalans to settle on the conquered islands, granting them exemption from taxes and guaranteeing equality before the law to all its citizens. Special privileges were granted to Jews, in an effort to stimulate trade. After the king's death, his successors fought for the inheritance, which was finally won by Alfonso III.

Miniature with the image of Jaume I

Alfonso and his Successors

Despite being nicknamed "The Liberal", Alfonso III massacred the rebels of Palma and the remaining fortresses after he had conquered them, a bloody deed that led to his excommunication from the Catholic Church. Worse was to follow. In 1287, Alfonso III's army attacked and conquered Menorca. The Muslim defenders were sold into slavery or slaughtered. Medina Menurqua was renamed Ciutadella and its mosques turned into churches or destroyed. Following the death of Alfonso III in 1291 at the age of 25, Jaume II took control of Mallorca and Menorca. Jaume II, who had been crowned king of Mallorca and

---

1229 Mallorca captured by the army of Jaume I, who is hailed as "El Conqueridor"

1230 Declaration of *Carta de Població* (People's Charter) by Jaume I

1285 Palma conquered by Alfonso III

| 1200 | 1250 | 1300 | 1350 |

1203 The Almohads assume rule over the archipelago

1233 Ramon Llull, philosopher and theologian, father of the Catalan language, is born in Palma

Statue of Alfonso III by the cathedral in Maó, Menorca

Menorca in 1276 before being deposed by Alfonso III, was an altogether more enlightened ruler. He and his successors presided over a "Golden Age" that saw great advances, including the building of the Castell de Bellver and Palau de l'Almudaina, the establishment of a weekly market in Palma and the reintroduction of gold and silver coinage to stimulate trade. The next ruler of the archipelago was Jaume II's son, Sancho, who built a strong fleet to defend the islands against pirates. After his death, in 1324, control passed into the hands of his nephew, Jaume III, whose two-decade reign also marked a period of great prosperity. The "Golden Age" came to an abrupt end in 1344 when an Aragonese conquest, led by Pedro IV, landed on Mallorca and took it in only a week. The islands of Menorca and Ibiza soon suffered the same fate.

Painting of Saint George slaying the dragon, by Francesca Comesa

Decline and Fall

Now part of the kingdom of Aragón, the Balearic Islands found themselves to be outside major politics. The economy soon suffered as a result of high taxes and in 1391 Mallorca was the scene of an uprising by the poorest parts of the community. In Menorca, the rivalry between Ciutadella and Maó ended in armed conflict. The economic position of the Balearic Islands was worsened further by the discovery and colonization of the Americas at the end of the 15th century, which shifted the hub of European trade to the shores of the Atlantic Ocean. This downturn led, in 1521, to a bloody revolt by peasants and craftsmen in Mallorca, which ended in the slaughter of many of the nobility and their supporters.

Throughout the 16th and 17th centuries, there were frequent pirate attacks. Many of the islands' fortifications date from this period including Eivissa's surviving defences and Maó's Fort San Felipe.

Painting of the port in Palma de Mallorca, now at the city's Museu Diocesá

Gothic rosette from a museum in Palma, Mallorca

1521 Armed insurrection of peasants and craftsmen

1531–1558 Devastating raids by Turkish pirates

1400   **1450**   **1500**   **1550**

1391 Insurrection of the poor in Mallorca

1479 Unification of Aragón and Castile

Barbarossa, the conqueror of Maó in 1535

Junipero Serra setting up a mission in California

Under British and French Rule

During the 17th century, Menorca's harbours became the subject of Anglo-French rivalry. In 1708 the British occupied Maó's harbour, and subsequently the whole of Menorca. In 1756, the island was captured by the French, although they soon returned it to the British, in 1763. The government of the island changed hands several more times until, finally, in 1802, Menorca was handed over to Spain. The town of Sant Lluís, founded by the French, stands as a reminder of French rule.

The British colonial legacy on Menorca includes the building of the garrison town of Georgetown (now known as Villacarlos) and major improvements to the roads. The choice of Maó as Menorca's capital is thanks to the British governor, Richard Kane. Reminders of Georgian architecture, including the sash windows in Hanover Street, Maó, can still be seen today.

The 19th Century

The 19th century proved extremely difficult for the islands. The inhabitants were plagued by periods of famine and epidemics, Spanish was declared the official language, and many inhabitants of the Balearic Islands decided to emigrate. During the 19th century the islands acquired scheduled links with Barcelona and Valencia and the situation began to improve. In 1838, Chopin visited Mallorca and in 1867 Archduke Ludwig Salvator *(see p72)* settled here. At the same time, the development of agriculture, particularly almond-growing in Mallorca, and footwear production in Menorca, led to a rise in the standard of living. Catalan culture was also becoming popular and *Modernista* buildings, including designs by Antoni Gaudí, began to appear in Palma and other town centres.

Franco's Dictatorship

During the Spanish Civil War (1936–9), which originated in Morocco, the Balearic Islands were divided. Mallorca

Monument to the pirates defending Ibiza

1652 Islands devastated by horrific plague

1713 Junipero Serra born in the small town of Petra, in Mallorca

1756 Menorca conquered by the French

| 1600 | 1660 | 1720 | 1780 |

Baroque stone tablet from 1672

1708 Menorca conquered by the British

1763 British regain Menorca

1802 Menc passes into hands of the Spar

Monument at Monte Toro for those killed in Morocco in 1925

became an important base for the Fascists, while Menorca and Ibiza declared themselves for the Republicans. In retaliation, Italian planes bombed Ibiza. Menorca was the last stronghold of the Republicans.

Following a peace deal, negotiated with the help of the British, 450 refugees left the island aboard HMS *Devonshire*, and the island was left under the control of Franco. Formentera, which had backed the Republicans, became the site of a concentration camp established by the Fascists, where some 1,400 people were imprisoned. Throughout the entire 40 years of Franco's dictatorship, the Catalan language and culture were suppressed, as elsewhere on the mainland.

Modern Times

After Franco's death in 1975, a process of decentralization began. In 1983, the inhabitants of the islands succeeded in creating the Comunidad Autónoma de las Islas Baleares, and the islands became an autonomous region. This led to the introduction of Catalan in schools and offices and greater control of the local economy. Most of the money earned by the islands now remains here and is reinvested locally.

Initially, the most important factor driving the local economy was tourism. Where the hippies led, others followed. In 1966 Mallorca received one million tourists. By 2012, this number had grown to more than nine million and the islands, so poor until fairly recently, now boast perhaps the highest income per capita in the whole of Spain. This economic achievement has come at a price. Large numbers of foreigners, mainly German and British, have settled here, pushing up the cost of real estate, while the construction of a number of poor-quality resorts has left a blot on the islands' otherwise idyllic landscape. Many jobs on the islands are now seasonal and there has been a general decline in traditional forms of employment. Factors such as these gave rise to a growing environmental movement and the introduction of an "eco-tax" *(see p23)*, designed to sustain the islands' tourism. The tax was scrapped in 2003.

Mallorcan beaches filled with tourists

Archduke Ludwig Salvator

1926 Argentinian poet Adan Diehl opens the Hotel Formentor

1975 Death of General Francisco Franco

1983 Creation of the Autonomous Community of the Balearic Islands

1840 **1900** **1960** **2020**

1867 Mallorca visited by Habsburg Archduke Ludwig Salvator, subsequent promoter of the island

1936–1939 Spanish Civil War

1950 The first charter plane, from Germany, lands in Mallorca

Tourists in a hotel bar

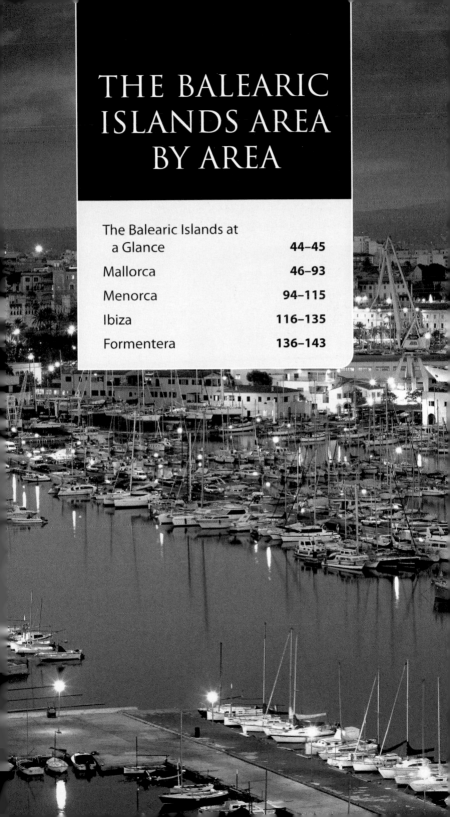

THE BALEARIC ISLANDS AREA BY AREA

The Balearic Islands at a Glance

The hot climate, cooling sea breezes, lively resorts and excellent beaches make the Balearic Islands an ideal holiday destination. Those who want to rave choose Ibiza, with its frenetic clubs and all-night entertainment. Those who prefer a more sedate holiday can find peace and quiet on all the islands, where charming little towns and miles of empty trails are perfect for walking, riding and cycling. Mallorca's caves and grottoes can provide interesting exploration while Menorca's prehistoric structures offer a fascinating glimpse into life on the islands many thousands of years ago.

Palma is the capital of Mallorca and of the Balearic Islands. Full of historic sights and throbbing with life, it is the archipelago's finest city.

Cala Bassa's Blue Flag beach is typical of Ibiza's beaches. Small, with fine, golden sand, it is hidden in a sheltered cove.

IBIZA
(See pp116–135)

Santa Eulària des Riu

Eivissa

Santa Eulària des Riu is one of the loveliest resort towns in Ibiza. It has good restaurants and bars, plenty of shopping and a beautiful beach.

FORMENTERA
(See pp136–143)

Sant Francesc

Platja Migjorn is a narrow sandy beach, stretching over 5 km (3 miles) along the southern coast of Formentera. It is always possible to find an isolated spot.

| 0 kilometres | 20 |
| 0 miles | 20 |

◀ Harbour view of Palma de Mallorca with the La Seu Cathedral glittering in the foreground

Cap de Cavalleria is the northernmost point of the Balearic Islands and one of Menorca's wildest regions. The road to the lighthouse on the headland runs through an undulating area. The steep cliffs here provide a nesting ground for a number of seabirds including, the sea eagle and kite.

Ciutadella

MENORCA
(See pp94–115)

Maó

Alcúdia

Artà

MALLORCA
(See pp46–93)

Manacor

Llucmajor

Colònia
e Sant Jordi

Poblat de Pescadors, Binibeca Vell, Menorca, with its distinctive development of white houses, was purpose-built for holidaymakers to resemble a Mediterranean fishing village.

Aqualand El Arenal, in S'Arenal near Palma, is one of several water parks in Mallorca. With pools, water flumes and plenty of space, it provides a fun day out for the children.

Cap de Formentor is Mallorca's northernmost peninsula. It makes a good destination for a day-long excursion during which you can take in the clifftop views or swim in one of the coves below. At the very tip of the peninsula is a lighthouse, which also serves at a viewing point.

MALLORCA

Mallorca's landscape is incredibly diverse for such a small island, ranging from the fertile lowlands of the central region to the high peaks of the Serra de Tramuntana. Its warm climate, fine beaches and historic capital, Palma, make it one of the main European holiday centres. Venture away from the resorts and you also find picturesque inland villages, pine forests and peaceful coves.

With an area covering 3,640 sq km (1,405 sq miles), and a population of around 846,000, of which nearly half live in Palma, Mallorca is the largest island of the Balearic archipelago. Consisting mainly of limestone, the terrain has a large number of cave systems, particularly in the wild central region of the Serra de Tramuntana and on the east coast. Some of these, such as the Coves d'Artà, can be visited as part of a guided tour. Elsewhere on the island, there is much to enjoy, from stunning nature reserves and charming fishing villages to picturesque ruins and impressive country estates.

The climate here is typically Mediterranean, with dry summers and up to 65cm (26 in) of rainfall during the autumn–winter season. Cold winters are rare. The island has unique flora and fauna, with a wide variety of birds. Native species of flowers and flowering shrubs are also in evidence, though the cultivation of fields, vineyards and olive groves has partly displaced the natural vegetation.

The island has been known since ancient times and traces of Roman and Arab civilizations can still be seen. Once an independent kingdom, Mallorca became part of Aragón in the 14th century, and was later incorporated into Spain. Since 1983, the Balearic Islands have been an autonomous region of Spain.

Much of the island is virtually untouched by tourism. Mallorca offers wonderful beaches and nightlife for visitors who want a lively holiday, and rural retreats, peaceful coves and historic ruins for those seeking quiet.

Crowded beach in Cala Millor, the destination for many sun-seeking visitors

◀ Torrent de Pareis, a major attraction of the Tramuntana mountain range

Exploring Mallorca

Most visitors to Mallorca come in search of sun and make the most of the nightclubs, discos, waterparks and the plentiful supply of clean beaches. Many also enjoy the historic towns and villages, particularly the winding streets of the island's capital, Palma, which has lots to see and a wide range of shops and restaurants. Visitors looking for the best beaches go to the Badia de Palma region or to the northeastern shores of the island.

Locator Map

Historic tram in the main square in Sóller

Sights at a Glance

1 Palma pp50–61
2 Badia de Palma
3 Cala Major
4 Marineland
5 Calvià
6 Andratx
7 Sa Dragonera
9 La Reserva Puig de Galatzó
10 La Granja pp68–9
11 Valldemossa
12 Son Marroig
13 Deià
14 Sóller
16 Jardines de Alfàbia
17 Sa Calobra
18 Monestir de Lluc pp76–7
19 Inca

20 Pollença
21 Cap de Formentor
22 Alcúdia
23 Parc Natural de S'Albufera
24 Muro
25 Sineu
26 Petra
27 Artà
28 Capdepera
29 Cala Rajada
30 Cala Millor
31 Porto Cristo
32 Manacor
33 Vilafranca de Bonany
34 Felanitx
35 Santanyí
36 Parc Natural Mondragó

37 Ses Salines
38 Colònia de Sant Jordi
39 Cabrera Island National Park pp88–9
40 Llucmajor
41 Capocorb Vell
42 Puig de Randa
43 Algaida
44 S'Arenal

Tours

8 Northwestern Coast of Mallorca pp66–7
15 Train from Palma to Port Sóller

For hotels and restaurants in this region see pp148–50 and pp155–9

Getting There

Mallorca has air links with Menorca and Ibiza, as well as with many Spanish towns and cities. However, the majority of visitors arrive by chartered flights. Mallorca's airport is 11 km (7 miles) east of Palma. It is also possible to get here by ferry, from one of the Spanish mainland ports. The high-speed ferry linking Valencia, Ibiza and Palma reduces the journey time considerably. When travelling around Mallorca, you can use its efficient bus service or the one or two railway lines connecting Palma with Sóller and also with Inca, Sa Pobla and Manacor. However, the best way to explore the island is by car.

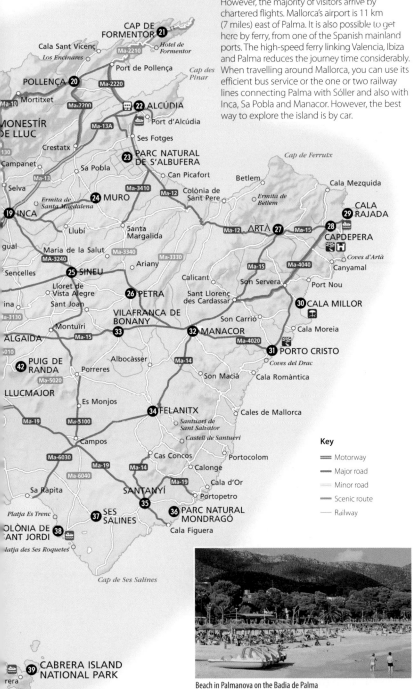

Key

- ▬▬ Motorway
- ▬ Major road
- ▬ Minor road
- ▬ Scenic route
- — Railway

Beach in Palmanova on the Badia de Palma

For map symbols *see back flap*

❶ Street-by-Street: Palma

In 1983, Palma became the capital of the newly created Autonomous Community of the Balearic Islands and transformed itself from a provincial town into a metropolis. Today, it has more than 400,000 inhabitants and captivates all visitors as it once captivated Jaume I, who, after conquering it in 1229, described it as the "loveliest town that I have ever seen". It is pleasant to stroll along the clean, attractive streets past renovated historic buildings. The town and harbour are full of life, while bars and restaurants, busy with locals and tourists, remain open late into the night.

Caixa Forum Palma
Built in 1902, this is the most beautiful 20th-century building in Palma. Formerly the Grand Hotel, it now houses a cultural centre.

★ Palau de l'Almudaina
This former royal residence was the home of Jaume II and was built after 1309, on the site of an Arab fortress.

La Llotja
The elevation of this small Gothic building, which once housed the stock exchange, is decorated with magnificent sculptures.

Key

 — Suggested route

★ Cathedral
The Gothic cathedral, standing near the shore and towering over the town, is built of golden sandstone excavated in Santanyí.

Parc de la Mar

| 0 metres | 100 |
| 0 yards | 100 |

For hotels and restaurants in this region see pp148–150 and pp155–9

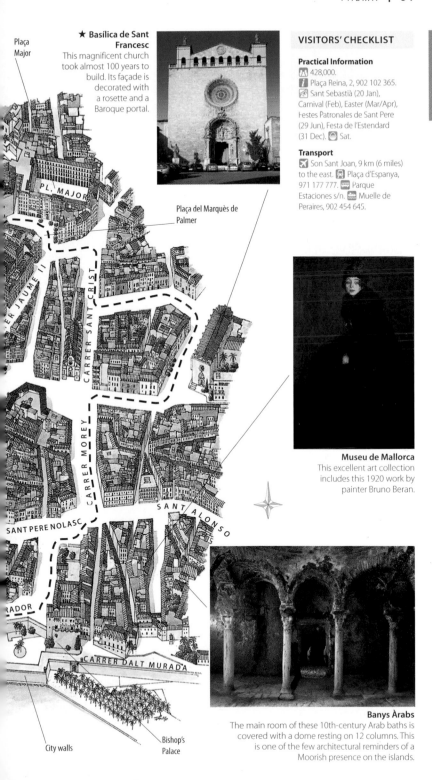

★ **Basílica de Sant Francesc**
This magnificent church took almost 100 years to build. Its façade is decorated with a rosette and a Baroque portal.

Plaça Major

PL. MAJOR

Plaça del Marquès de Palmer

CARRER JAUME II

CARRER SANT CRIST

CARRER MOREY

SANT PERE NOLASC

SANT ALONSO

...RADOR

CARRER DALT MURADA

City walls

Bishop's Palace

VISITORS' CHECKLIST

Practical Information
428,000.
Plaça Reina, 2, 902 102 365.
Sant Sebastià (20 Jan), Carnival (Feb), Easter (Mar/Apr), Festes Patronales de Sant Pere (29 Jun), Festa de l'Estendard (31 Dec). Sat.

Transport
Son Sant Joan, 9 km (6 miles) to the east. Plaça d'Espanya, 971 177 777. Parque Estaciones s/n. Muelle de Peraires, 902 454 645.

Museu de Mallorca
This excellent art collection includes this 1920 work by painter Bruno Beran.

Banys Àrabs
The main room of these 10th-century Arab baths is covered with a dome resting on 12 columns. This is one of the few architectural reminders of a Moorish presence on the islands.

Horsedrawn cabs in Palau de l'Almudaina

Exploring Palma

Of all the Balearic towns, Palma is the richest in historic sights. Christian kings, Arab rulers and Jewish merchants have all left their mark on the Balearic capital and it is a genuine pleasure to stroll through its narrow streets and quiet courtyards.

⬆ Cathedral (La Seu)

Plaça Almoïna s/n. **Tel** 902 022 445.
After the capture of Palma by Jaume I, the town's main mosque was used as its cathedral. Work on the present cathedral *(see pp54–5)*, known in Catalan as La Seu, began in 1230, immediately after the fall of Palma. The main work lasted for almost 400 years and resulted in a monumental Gothic church.

It has three entrances, each framed with a portal. The most beautiful of these is the 14th-century Portal del Mirador, overlooking the Bay of Palma to the south. It is topped with a pediment depicting the Last Supper. Built above the Gothic Portal de l'Almoina is a fortified belfry. The main Portal Major (Great Door), facing the Almudaina palace, has a Neo-Gothic finish and is the least successful of the three.

The splendid interior features 14 slender octagonal pillars supporting the vault. The 44-m (145-ft) central nave is one of the highest in Europe. The eastern rose window, measuring over 12 m (40 ft) in diameter, is made of 1,200 pieces of stained glass.

The cathedral features stalls made of walnut, an interesting stone pulpit and 14 chapels, including Nostra Senyora de la Corona, with statues of allegorical angels.

In the oldest part of the cathedral, hidden behind the altar, is the Trinity Chapel, containing the tombs of Jaume II and Jaume III (not open to visitors). In the early 20th century, Antoni Gaudí removed the Baroque altar and put in its place an alabaster table, with an illuminated canopy symbolizing the crown of thorns.

⬛ Palau de l'Almudaina

Carrer de Palau Real. **Open** 10am–6pm Tue–Sun (to 8pm Apr–Sep). **Tel** 971 214 134. 🅿 🅲
Almudaina means "citadel" in Arabic. This royal residence of Jaume II was built after 1309, using the walls of an Arab fortress. The Gothic palace includes Moorish-style arches and carved wooden ceilings. It is King Felipe VI's official Palma residence. The museum here includes the Santa Ana chapel with a Romanesque portal and a Gothic drawing room, which is sometimes used for official receptions.

⬛ Parc de la Mar

The Parc de la Mar was established in the 1960s in the area between the southern section of the city walls and Ronda Litoral. Its designers, Josep Lluís Sert and Joan Miró *(see p58)*, built the park on several levels and its central points include a man-made lake in which you can see a reflection of the cathedral, and a giant mural by Miró. Nearby **Ses Voltes** is an exhibition space, used for art exhibitions and concerts.

⬛ La Llotja

Plaça Llotja.
This late Gothic building (a former stock exchange) was erected between 1426 and 1456 from plans by Guillem Sagrera – the designer of La Seu's Portal del Mirador. The vault rests on slender spiral pillars, the walls are pierced by tall windows. The entrance is framed by a portal, is adorned with a pediment featuring a statue of the Guardian Angel. La Llotja's interior is open only for special exhibitions.

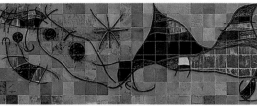

A section of the giant mural by Joan Miró, Parc de la Mar

🏛 Consolat de Mar
Passeig de Sagrera.

This elegant Renaissance-Baroque building, erected in 1614–26, is the seat of the Balearic Islands' government.

The façade features a magnificent covered arcade. The interior has a fine coffered ceiling (1664–9). The Consolat building joins with La Llotja via **Porta Vella del Moll** – a former harbour gate, brought here in the late 19th century.

Train and Bus stations 300 m (350 yards)

🏛 Passeig d'es Born
This is one of Palma's most beautiful corners. In Arab times it featured a moat that guarded access to the walls. Now this wide avenue, which gets its name from the 17th-century jousting tournaments held here, is Palma's main promenade and it forms the axis of the entire city.

At the southern end is **Plaça de la Reina**. The entrance on this side is guarded by stone sphinxes. At the north end is **Plaça del Rei Joan Carles I**, with a stone obelisk resting on bronze turtles standing at its centre. The avenue's most noteworthy house is the **Casal Solleric** residence (No. 27). It was built in 1763 as the home of a merchant who traded in cattle and olive oil and has a beautiful Baroque courtyard. Now a cultural centre, it also has a gallery, café and bookshop.

East frontage of the beautiful Passeig d'es Born

🏛 Avinguda Unió and Plaça Weyler
This lively area is full of shops and there are also numerous cafés in the squares and streets leading off Avinguda Unió. In **Plaça Mercat** two identical buildings stand side by side. These fine examples of *Modernista* architecture were built by banker Josep Casasayas in 1908.

The real gem of the district's architecture, however, is the **Caixa Forum Palma** in Plaça Weyler. The former Grand Hotel was given its present name after the Fundació La Caixa savings bank financed its restoration. It was reopened in 1993 by King Juan Carlos and Queen Sofía. Built in 1903, this early example of Catalan architecture is the work of Lluís Domènech i Montaner. As an outstanding masterpiece of the *Modernista* style, it has been included on the UNESCO World Heritage list and houses, (among other things), a restaurant and exhibition rooms, including a permanent collection of paintings by the important *Modernista* artist Hermengildo Anglada-Camarasa.

Almost opposite Fundació La Caixa is the **Forn d'es Teatre** (theatre bakery). This is a small, eye-catching patisserie where you can buy deliciously flaky spiral pastries *(ensaïmadas)*. Adjacent to the bakery is the **Teatre Principal** (1860). This is one of the most important ballet, opera and theatre venues in town.

Entrance to Forn d'es Teatre

0 metres 200
0 yards 200

Key
Street-by-street map pp50–51

Sights at a Glance

For map symbols *see back flap*

Cathedral – La Seu

Mallorca's cathedral, La Seu, is the most precious architectural treasure of the Balearic Islands and is regarded as one of Spain's most outstanding Gothic structures. Begun by Jaume II on the site of the city's main mosque seven years after the conquest of 1299, the work took some 300 years. In the first half of the 15th century, the building works were supervised by the prominent Mallorcan sculptor and architect Guillem Sagrera. Partly destroyed during the 1851 earthquake, the cathedral was subsequently repaired by Juan Bautista Peyronnet. In the early 20th century, its interior was modernized by Antoni Gaudí. An integral part of the cathedral is its museum, which stores precious works of sacred art.

Belfry
The mighty belfry was built in 1389. The biggest of its nine bells is called *Eloi*.

Mallorca Cathedral
Towering over the former harbour in Palma, the cathedral looks most beautiful when viewed from the sea, or at night, when it is illuminated.

KEY

① **Portal Major (1601)**

② **19th-century pinnacle**

③ **Entrance to the Cathedral Museum**

④ **Flying buttress**

⑤ **The great organs**, built in 1795, stand within a Neo-Gothic enclosure; they were restored in 1993 by Gabriel Blancafort.

⑥ **Stalls made from the dismantled *corro***

⑦ **The Capella Reial** (presbytery) was remodelled by Gaudí during 1904–14.

⑧ **Chapel of the Holy Sacrament (Barceló Chapel)** was designed by contemporary painter Miquel Barceló (b.1957) and boasts a large ceramic mural and stained-glass windows.

⑨ **Portal del Mirador (1420)**

Cathedral Museum
One of the masterpieces on display in the Old Chapter House, now housing the museum, is the reliquary containing wood from the Holy Cross, encrusted with jewels.

★ Giant Rose Window
The largest of the seven rose windows, measuring 12 m (40 ft) in diameter, is filled with 1,200 pieces of stained glass.

VISITORS' CHECKLIST

Practical Information
Plaça Almoïna s/n. **Tel** 902 022 445.
Open 10am–3:15pm Mon–Fri (Apr, May, Oct: to 5:15pm; Jun–Sep: 6:15pm),10am–2:15pm Sat.
Closed pub hols. 🚹 🕐 9am daily; 7pm Sat; 9am, 10:30am, noon, 1pm, 7pm Sun & pub hols.
♿ 🔲 **catedraldemallorca.info**

Trinity Chapel
The chapel, built in 1329, contains the tombs of the Mallorcan kings Jaume II and Jaume III.

★ Baldachin (1912)
Antoni Gaudí's ceremonial canopy with lights and a multicoloured crucifix is suspended above the main altar.

Central Nave
Nineteen metres (62 ft) wide and 44 m (145 ft) high, the central nave, with its vault supported by 14 pillars, is one of the world's biggest.

Museu de Mallorca

The best museum in the Balearic Islands can be found close to La Seu, in Palau Ayamans, a residence built around 1630. The palace was erected on the foundations of an Arab house (12th–13th century), which is still visible in the underground rooms of the museum. Opened in 1968, the museum houses a superb collection of works of art associated with Mallorcan history. The collection comprises several thousand exhibits and includes prehistoric artifacts found during archaeological excavations, stone fragments of fallen buildings, priceless Moorish ceramics and jewellery, and medieval and Baroque paintings.

★ Lar Augustal
From Son Corro Sanctuary in Costixt, this 1st-century-AD bronze statue of a Roman domestic deity was an object of daily worship.

Paris i Helena (c.1665)
Italian painting is represented by this Baroque work by Mattia Preti, whose extensive legacy can also be seen in Rome and Malta.

★ Almohad Treasure
Items of Arab jewellery are among the museum's most precious exhibits. They are kept in the treasury room, behind bulletproof glass.

Key

☐ Vaults
☐ Ground floor
☐ 1st floor
■ 3rd floor

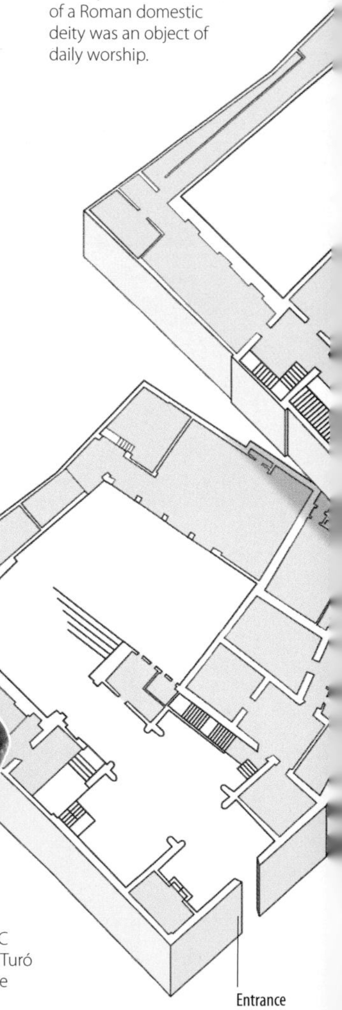

Gallery Guide

The museum's collection is arranged on four floors, in chronological order. The oldest relics, including archaeological finds, are kept in the underground vault. The most recent art, including 19th- and 20th-century paintings, is exhibited on the top floor. The second floor is occupied by offices.

Urna Turó
Dating between the 3rd century BC and 1st century AD, this vase from Turó de Ses Abelles in Calvià imitates the ceramics of the Iberian peninsula.

Entrance

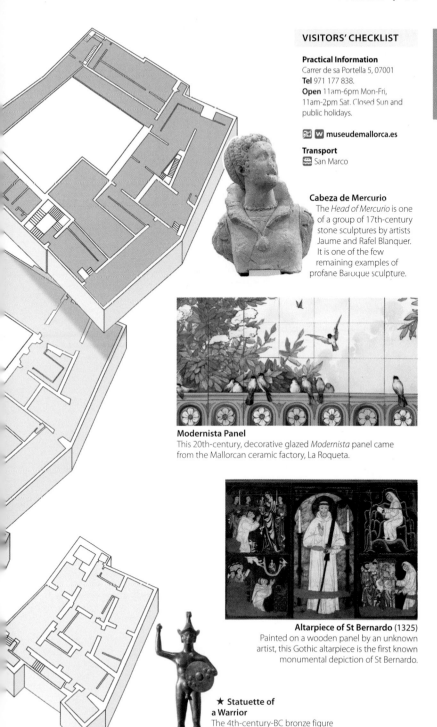

VISITORS' CHECKLIST

Practical Information
Carrer de sa Portella 5, 07001
Tel 971 177 838.
Open 11am-6pm Mon-Fri,
11am-2pm Sat. Closed Sun and
public holidays.

✉ W **museudemallorca.es**

Transport
🚌 San Marco

Cabeza de Mercurio

The *Head of Mercurio* is one of a group of 17th-century stone sculptures by artists Jaume and Rafel Blanquer. It is one of the few remaining examples of profane Baroque sculpture.

Modernista Panel

This 20th-century, decorative glazed *Modernista* panel came from the Mallorcan ceramic factory, La Roqueta.

Altarpiece of St Bernardo (1325)

Painted on a wooden panel by an unknown artist, this Gothic altarpiece is the first known monumental depiction of St Bernardo.

★ Statuette of a Warrior

The 4th-century-BC bronze figure is of a divine warrior from Son Favar and forms part of a series known as *Mars Balearicus*.

Plaça del Marquès de Palmer

This square lies at the end of Carrer Colom – a shopping street running from Plaça Cort, the site of the Ajuntament (Town Hall). It features a five-storey *Modernista* apartment building, Can Rei (20th century). Equally interesting is the nearby building, L'Aguila.

Plaça Major

This pedestrianized 19th-century square has a number of souvenir shops and lively cafés. Many of the square's restaurants have outdoor tables under its arcades.

The centre of the square is given over to stalls that sell a wide variety of handicrafts. There's also a stage that is frequently used by musicians and jugglers who entertain visitors to the city.

The porticoed square was laid out in 1823 following the demolition of the headquarters of the Inquisition. The new square became the main food market until the 1950s. A large underground shopping centre and car park have since been added.

Santa Eulàlia

Plaça Santa Eulàlia. **Open** 8am–12:30pm & 5:20–8:30pm Mon–Fri 8am–12:30pm Sat (Sunday Mass).

The vast Gothic church standing at the end of Carrer Morey was built on the site of a mosque in the 13th century on the orders of Jaume II. It was completed in just 25 years. Renovations in the

Oriel window of Can Rei, Plaça del Marquès de Palmer

19th century involved adding the belfry and remodelling the central nave. The aisle chapels feature magnificent original Gothic paintings, and there is a splendid Baroque altarpiece.

The most precious relic in the church is the crucifix kept in Capella de Sant Crist. Jaume I is supposed to have carried this when he conquered Mallorca in 1229.

Another dramatic event is associated with this church. In 1435, it was the site of a mass baptism of Jews, who converted to Christianity in order to escape being burned at the stake.

Es Baluard Museu d'Art Modern i Contemporani

Plaça Porta de Santa Catalina. **Open** 10am–8pm Tue–Sat (to 3pm Sun) **Closed** 1 Jan & 25 Dec.

Es Baluard is housed in a modern building of concrete and glass, completely and beautifully integrated in the Sant Pere bastion (*baluard* in Catalan) that was part of the Renaissance wall surrounding the city of Palma. It has a wide-ranging collection of works by prominent artists who have converged on these islands from the beginning of the 20th century. The works of Catalans Santiago Rusiñol, Joaquín Mir and Joaquín Sorolla are displayed, while Joan Miró and Pablo Picasso have exclusive rooms dedicated to their works. Contemporary artists are led by the well-known Mallorcan Miquel Barceló, who also painted one of the chapels of the Palma Cathedral and the dome at the UN headquarters in Geneva.

Fundación Bartolomé March

Palau Reial 18, 07001. **Open** Nov–Mar: 10am–6:30pm (to 2pm Sat).

An exhibition space, an auditorium and a library, Fundación Bartolomé March was built in the 1940s as the family residence of financier Juan March Ordinashas. Today, it houses an excellent collection of modern and contemporary sculpture, as well as more than 2,000 pieces of 18th-century Neapolitan nativity crib figures. Spectacular murals by Josep M Sert adorn the dome ceiling over the main staircase and the music room.

Casa Olesa

Carrer Morey 25.

Built in the mid-16th century, this Renaissance residence is one of Palma's most beautiful. The house

Plaça Mayor, the main town square, with live entertainment

Monastery courtyard of Basilica de Sant Francesc

is private but you can admire its courtyard through the wrought-iron gate.

🏛 Basilíca de Sant Francesc

Plaça Sant Francesc. **Open** 9:30am–12:30pm & 3:30–6pm Mon–Sat, 9:30am–12:30pm Sun.

The building of the Gothic church and Franciscan monastery started in 1281 and lasted 100 years. During the Middle Ages, this was Palma's most fashionable church and to be buried here was a major status symbol. Aristocratic families competed with each other by building ever more ostentatious sarcophagi in which to place their dead.

The church was remodelled in the 17th century after being damaged by lightning. Its severe façade, with giant rose window, was embellished around 1680 with a Baroque doorway, decorated with stone statues and the Triumphant Virgin Mary in the tympanum. Next to the Madonna is the carved figure of the famous medieval mystic Ramón Llull *(see p91)*, who is buried in the church.

The dark interior (its Gothic windows have been partially bricked up) contains many fine works of art, which are mainly Baroque in style. Particularly eye-catching (if you can see in the dimness) are the vast altarpiece, dating from 1739, and the organ. The delightful Gothic cloisters, planted with orange and lemon trees, offer light relief.

Standing in front of the basilica is a statue of Junípero Serra *(see p81)*, a Franciscan monk and native of Mallorca, who was sent to California in 1768 and founded Los Angeles and San Francisco.

🏛 Banys Àrabs

Carrer Can Serra 7. **Tel** 637 046 534. **Open** 9:30am–8pm daily (to 6pm Dec–Mar).

The brick 10th-century *hammam* (bathhouse) is one of the few architectural reminders of a Moorish presence on the islands. A small horseshoe-arched chamber, with a dome supported by irregular columns and what would once have been underfloor heating, it has survived in its original form. There's not a lot to see, but the pleasant garden has tables where you can sit and rest.

🏛 Palau Episcopal and Museu Diocesà

Carrer Mirador 5. **Open** 10am–2pm Mon–Sat. **Closed** Sun.

Just behind the cathedral, the Palau Episcopal (Bishop's Palace) is

Sundial from Palau Episcopal

mostly 17th century, though work began in 1238, initiated by Bishop Ramon de Torell. The palace, which is built around a large courtyard, adjoins the city walls. Its façade was completed in 1616.

Two rooms of the palace have been given over to the modest **Museu Diocesà** (Diocese Museum). The little museum has on display items from various churches in Mallorca, as well as a selection of majolica tiles. Particularly noteworthy are a picture of St George slaying the dragon in front of Palma's city gate, painted in 1468–70 by Pere Nisart; Bishop Galiana's panel depicting the life of St Paul (who is portrayed holding a sword); the Gothic pulpit in a Mudéjar (Spanish Moorish) style; and the jasper sarcophagus of Jaume II, which stood in the cathedral until 1904.

🏛 City Walls

The Renaissance city walls were built on the site of earlier medieval walls. This restored section once included a gallery running along the top, from where the city's defenders could fire at besieging enemies. Progress in artillery design meant that the fortifications became lower and thicker. Work on remodelling the walls began in the mid-16th century, but the bastions were only completed in the early 19th century. Today, Palma's city walls feature a walkway that provides a wide view over Badia de Palma, the cathedral and the Old Town.

Restored city walls in Palma's old town

Painting by Pérez Villalta from Fundación Juan March

Further Afield

If you want to relax away from the hubbub of the crowded streets in Palma's Old Town, take a trip to the outskirts of the city. A stroll along the **harbourfront**, or a trip to **Castell de Bellver**, with its lovely view of the city, is always a treat.

🚏 Carrer Sant Miquel

A narrow street that runs north from Plaça Major to Plaça Conquista, Carrer Sant Miquel is closed to traffic and is one of Palma's main shopping streets. Here, you can buy almost anything, though souvenir shops are a rarity. Here, too, you will find the Museu Fundación Juan March (*see below*) and, a little further on, the church of Sant Miquel. Nearby, in Plaça Olivar, stands the large iron structure of the market hall that was built in the early 20th century.

🏛 Museu Fundación Juan March

Carrer Sant Miquel 11. **Tel** 971 713 515. **Open** 10am–6:30pm Mon–Fri, 10:30am–2pm Sat. 🚻.

The museum occupies a Renaissance building that was remodelled in the early 20th century by Guillem Reynes i Font in the *Modernista* style. Purchased in 1916 by Juan March, the building was the first headquarters of Banca March.

The museum's exhibition occupies the first and second floors and features works by contemporary Spanish artists including Pablo Picasso, Joan Miró and Salvador Dalí.

Most of the 50 or so exhibited works are paintings and sculptures by less well-known artists, who nevertheless played an important role in the shaping of Spanish modern art. The museum, which also stages temporary exhibitions, is part of Fundación Juan March, a major cultural foundation.

🏛 Sant Miquel

Carrer de Sant Miquel 21. **Tel** 971 715 455. **Open** 9am–1:30pm & 4–8pm Mon–Sat, 10am–1pm & 4–8pm Sun.

Rose window on the façade of Sant Miquel

This 16th-century church is one of the most popular in town. It was built on the site of a mosque in which the first victory Mass was said after the conquest of Mallorca by Jaume I. The Baroque altarpiece with a picture of St Michael is the work of the Spanish religious painter Francesc Herrera.

La Rambla

Palma's biggest flower market can be found in this shadowy avenue, lined with plane trees. Towards the lower section of the boulevard are two statues of Roman emperors, erected by the Francoists in honour of Mussolini. At La Rambla's northern end stands the vast building of **La Misericordia**, remodelled in the mid-19th century in a Neo-Classical style. It houses, among other things, a conservatoire. Next to it is a botanical garden.

🚏 Plaça d'Espanya

This vast square, containing an equestrian statue of Jaume I, is Palma's main transport hub. The railway stations run services to Sóller and Inca. Most of the town's buses stop here or in the local side streets and many link up with Palma's suburbs and the nearby tourist resorts.

🏛 Nuevo Pueblo Español

Poble Espanyol, s/n. **Tel** 971 737 070. **Open** 9am–8pm daily (Oct–May: to 5pm). 🚻

"Miniature Spain" is located a short way west of Palma's Old Town. It was built in the 1960s on the orders of the Spanish dictator General Franco. Here you can see 20 or so mini versions of outstanding examples of Spanish architecture. They include Granada's Alhambra Palace, El Greco's house in Toledo and Barcelona's Palau de la Generalitat. There's also a craft workshop, restaurants, a bar and a souvenir shop.

Copy of Alhambra in Nuevo Pueblo Español

Arcades surrounding Castell de Bellver's courtyard

Opposite the entrance to Nuevo Pueblo Español stands the monumental **Palau de Congressos**. The congress centre features, among other things, the Roman Theatre and the Imperial Hall.

Castell de Bellver
C/Camilo José Cela s/n.
Tel 971 735 065. 🚌 to Plaça Gomila.
Open Apr–Sep: 8:30am–8pm Tue–Sat (to 1pm Mon), 10am–8pm Sun; Oct–Mar: 8:30am–1pm Mon (to 6pm Tue–Sat),10am–6pm Sun. 🎫 (entrance to the castle is free on Sun). 📷

About 2 km (1 mile) west of Palma's cathedral, on a pine-clad hill, near the entrance to the harbour, stands one of Europe's most beautiful Gothic castles. Though it has, alas, been over-restored, the Castell de Bellver affords spectacular views of the city and bay. Built as a summer residence for Jaume II by Pere Selvà in the early 14th century when Mallorca was an independent kingdom, it was later turned into a prison and remained as such until 1915.

The castle, circular in shape, has an inner courtyard that is surrounded by two-tier arcades.

Three cylindrical towers are partly sunk into the wall. The freestanding Torre de Homenaje is joined to the main building by an arch and was designed to be the final stronghold. The castle's flat roof was built to collect rainwater into an underground cistern.

The entire complex is surrounded by a moat and ground fortifications.

Fishing boats in Palma harbour

A part of the castle has been turned into a museum. It has an exhibition of archaeological finds and Roman sculpture collected in the 18th century by Antonio Despuig – a historian and cardinal who left his collection to the city.

🏛 Museu Krekovic
Carrer de Ciutat de Querétaro 3.
Tel 971 219 606. **Open** mid-Jan–mid-Dec: 9:30am–1pm & 3–6pm Mon–Fri, 10:30am–1pm Sat. **Closed** Aug.

The museum of the Croatian painter Kristian Krekovic (1901–85) opened in 1981. It includes not only works by the artist but also paintings and handicrafts from Spain and Latin America.

🚢 Harbourfront
Palma's harbour, overlooked by the cathedral, bustles with life, as magnificent yachts come and go. Here, at the wharf, you can see fishermen at work. The nearby **Reial Club Nautic** has an excellent restaurant that often plays host to Spanish royalty.

Further on, opposite the **Auditorio** in Passeig Marítim, is a jetty for pleasure boats from where you can take a trip around the harbour. Beyond **Club del Mar**, to the south, is the ferry terminal providing regular services to the other islands of the archipelago and mainland Spain. Nearby, is a naval base. You can see most of the harbour on foot. Alternatively, hire a bicycle or horse-drawn cab. Routes end at the 15th-century **Torre Paraires** or by the lighthouse in **Potro Pi.**

Environs
Five km (3 miles) to the north lies the district of **Establiments**. Its historic sights include an old windmill that now houses a restaurant. Music lovers may be interested to know that it was here, in villa "Son Vent", on the outskirts of town, that Frédéric Chopin and George Sand stopped while on their way to Valldemossa.

Rough waters of the Badia de Palma

❷ Badia de Palma

The Bay of Palma is bounded by Cap de Cala Figuera to the west and Cap Enderrocat to the east. During the tourist boom, in the 1960s–1970s, the bay became surrounded by miles of high-rise hotels and hemmed in by hundreds of restaurants, bars, nightclubs and shops. Today, the eastern part of this beautiful bay is popular with German visitors, while the British tend to congregate to the west.

Platja de Palma, stretching from S'Arenal to C'an Pastilla, is one of the best beaches on the islands if you can ignore the sprawl fringing the shore. The western side is more varied, featuring pine-clad hills, sloping down to the water's edge. The beaches are smaller here, situated in picturesque coves. Along the coast are the popular resorts of Bendinat, Portals Nous, Palma Nova and Magaluf.

Joan Miró (1893–1983)

One of the best-known artists of the 20th century, Miró was a Catalan through and through. Initially influenced by Fauvism, and later by Dadaism and Surrealism, he developed his own style, marked by lyricism and lively colouring. After arriving in Mallorca he became interested in graphics, ceramics and sculpture, scoring significant successes in every art form. His works can be seen in his studio on the outskirts of Palma, where he lived and worked from 1956. He died in Palma in 1983.

Joan Miró, one of modern art's most influential figures

❸ Cala Major

ℹ️ Carretera Andrax 33, Illetes.

The resort area, situated to the west of Palma, is known for its **Fundació Pilar i Joan Miró**. Miró lived and worked on the island for 40 years. After his death in 1983, the artist's wife converted the house and former studio into an art centre. This modern edifice, nicknamed the "Alabaster Fortress" by the Spanish press, is the work of Rafael Moneo, a leading Spanish architect. The new building houses a permanent exhibition of Miró's paintings, drawings and sculptures, as well as a library, auditorium and shop where you can buy items decorated with the artist's colourful designs. The Foundation owns some 140 paintings, 300 graphics, 35 sculptures and over 1,500 drawings

A sculpture by Miró

by Miró. Standing nearby is the **Marivent Palace,** a carefully guarded holiday residence of the Spanish royal family. The main street is lined with *Modernista* villas, which remain from the days when this was a smart resort, visited by the rich and powerful. The **Nixe Palace Hotel** is a throwback to those days.

🏛️ Fundació Pilar i Joan Miró
C/ Joan de Saridakis 29. **Tel** 971 701 420. **Open** 10am–7pm Tue–Sat (summer); 10am–6pm Tue–Sat (winter); 10am–3pm Sun. 🏛️ (free on Sat)

Environs

Some 8 km (5 miles) west of Palma stands the 13th-century **Castell de Bendinat**. Remodelled in the 18th century, the castle is surrounded by pine woods and its imposing walls and towers are decorated with a Baroque frieze. Today, the castle houses a conference centre and is not open to the public. Five kilometres (3 miles) northwest of Palma are the **Coves de Genova**. Discovered in 1906, the caves have some fine formations of stalactites and stalagmites.

Palmanova is famous for its picturesque, though crowded, beaches and lively nightlife. Nearby **Magaluf** is a busy resort with a variety of high-rise hotels and numerous restaurants and English-style pubs where you can order a full English breakfast or fish and chips.

🏛️ Coves de Genova
Carrer de Barranc 45. **Tel** 971 402 387. **Open** 11am–1:30pm & 4–5:30pm Tue–Sun (timings vary in winter). 🏛️

❹ Marineland

Marineland is the only amusement park in the Balearic Islands where you can see performing dolphins and sea lions. This mini zoo also houses a number of aquaria containing sharks and exotic fish. As well as the sealife, there is a good aviary and you can also see exotic animals such as crocodiles and snakes. This is great fun for families with young children.

VISITORS' CHECKLIST

Practical Information
C/ Garcilaso de la Vega 9, Costa d'en Blanes. **Tel** 971 675 125. **Open** end Mar–Oct: 9:30am–5:30pm (last entry: 4:45pm); Jul–Aug: to 6pm. (Note: no food or drink can be taken in.) 🚫 🖥 🚫
Ⓦ **marineland.es**

Transport
🚌

★ Sea Lions
The performing sea lions are well cared for at this fun park.

Entrance
Even on cloudy days there is always a queue at the front gates, with people eager to see the trained animal shows.

Parrots
Parrots can be seen in several places in the park, but shows are staged at a single location.

| 0 metres | 25 |
| 0 yards | 25 |

★ Dolphins
The dolphin shows always attract large crowds of appreciative spectators.

Key

① Entrance
② Sea lions and seals
③ Playground
④ Sharks
⑤ Parrot shows
⑥ Mediterranean fish aquarium
⑦ Dolphins
⑧ Penguins
⑨ Terrarium
⑩ Ray fish
⑪ Museum

For map symbols *see back flap*

❺ Calvià

🚌 ℹ Passeig de la Mar 13, Palmanova, 971 682 365. 🚢 Sant Jaume (25 Jun). ⛴ Mon.
🌐 visitcalvia.com

This quiet little town in the foothills of the Serra de Tramuntana mountains is the administrative centre of Calvià Province, which includes the resorts from Ses Illetes to Santa Ponça.

Standing on a hill in the centre of Calvià is the church of **Sant Joan Baptista**; its forecourt provides a fine view over the surrounding farms and olive groves. The original church was built here in 1245; the present structure dates from the late 19th century. The ceramic tiles lining the walls of the neighbouring public library provide a crash course in the town's history.

Few tourists make it to Calvià, where life proceeds quietly. The bars and restaurants here serve authentic Mallorcan cuisine.

Environs

Santa Ponça is a small port, situated 7 km (4 miles) southwest of Calvià. Nearby are golf courses, good beaches and opulent residences. It was here that Jaume I landed in 1229, freeing Mallorca from Arab domination. The event is marked by the Creu de la Conquesta.

Neo-Gothic façade of Calvià's church

Typical Mallorcan fishing boats in Port d'Andratx

❻ Andratx

🚌 ℹ Av de la Cúria 1, 971 628 019.
🚢 Sant Pere (29 Jun), La Virgen del Carmen (16 Aug). ⛴ Wed.

Andratx has ancient origins and was known as Andrachium by the Romans. It lies in a valley of olive and almond groves, at the foot of the Puig de Galatzó (1,028 m/ 3,400 ft). The local architecture is typical of the inland settlements that used to defend the island against raids by pirates. Old ochre-colour houses with colourful shutters blend well with the narrow cobblestone streets. The main historic sight is the fortified church of **Santa María**, towering over the town. It was built in the 13th century and remodelled in the early 18th century. The main tourist attraction, however, is the local market, which is held on Wednesday mornings.

A visit to the CCA Andraxt, an exhibition space devoted to contemporary art, is a must.

Church tympanum in Andratx

Environs

Some 5 km (3 miles) southwest of Andratx is **Port d'Andratx**. The sheltered bay provides a mooring ground for upmarket yachts. As recently as the 1960s, this was just a small fishing village, which later transformed itself into a swanky resort with luxurious residences built within the woodland setting on the slopes of the La Mola cape, and affording beautiful views of the harbour. The coastal boulevard offers the best place for viewing the magnificent sunsets.

About 5 km (3 miles) east of Port d'Andratx, in **Camp de Mar**, is a vast beach and lovely bathing spot with large hotels situated close to the sea. Neighbouring **Peguera** has many inexpensive hotels. Its pleasant and safe beach is particularly favoured by families with small children and by older visitors. **Cap Andritxol**, between Peguera and Camp de Mar, is a small peninsula with an observation tower at its tip dating back to 1580. It is an excellent destination for walks and offers hikers the chance to see some rare animals and many species of native flora. **Cala Fornells**, a short way from Peguera, is a small, picturesque village and beautiful cove. Surrounded by pine trees, it has great views of the bay. It is also a good place for swimming.

A particularly scenic road runs northwards, from Andratx to Estellencs. The **Mirador de Ricardo Roca viewpoint** and Es Grau restaurant provide good stopping points for a rest en route *(see pp66–7)*.

The delightful hillside village of **S'Arracó** lies 3 km (2 miles) west of Andratx, on the road leading to Sant Elm. The local church has a marble statue of Nostra Senyora de Sa Trapa, brought to the Trappist monastery near Sant Elm in the 18th century.

❼ Sa Dragonera

A narrow rocky island, Sa Dragonera lies at an angle to the coast, about 1km (half a mile) from Sant Elm. It has been a nature reserve since 1988 and is home to a wide variety of birdlife and wild flowers.

According to legend, the island is visited nightly by dragons. However, its name has more to do with its shape than its popularity with mythical beasts.

This wild island is just 4 km (2 miles) long and 700 m (765 yards) wide. A rocky path runs between its two headlands, both marked by lighthouses. Apart from the lighthouse keepers, the only inhabitants of the island are wild goats and birds – the island supports cormorants, Cory's shearwater and many birds of prey including the largest colony anywhere of Eleonora's falcon.

Sa Dragonera can be reached by a ferry from Sant Elm (Feb–Oct), which disembarks to allow you several hours to wander and explore the island. Cruises around the island leave from Sant Elm and Port d'Andratx.

Environs
Sant Elm (San Telmo) is a quiet resort with a fine sandy beach, a wide selection of cafés and restaurants and beautiful scenery. About 4 km (2 miles) northeast of Sant Elm is an abandoned monastery. **Sa Trapa** has a mill displaying some preserved agricultural equipment. A commemorative

Bears in La Reserva Puig de Galatzó

stone stands as a warning against getting too close to the edge of the precipice, which affords a fantastic view over the island of Sa Dragonera.

❽ Northwestern Coast of Mallorca

See pp66–7.

❾ La Reserva Puig de Galatzó

18 km (11 miles) north of Palma, 4 km (2 miles) west of Puigpunyent. **Tel** 971 616 622. **Open** Apr–Oct: 10am–6pm daily; Nov–Mar: Fri-Sun only. 🅿
Ⓦ lareservamallorca.com

This private nature reserve is situated on the eastern slope of the mighty Puig de Galatzó peak, in the southern region of the Serra de Tramuntana. Here, in an area of 250 sq km (100 sq miles), you can sample some of the splendours of nature, as the area features springs and streams, dozens of scenic waterfalls and caves, as well as a

Sign of La Reserva Puig de Galatzó

variety of interesting rock formations. Specially designated pathways lead through the park. Notice boards explain the local flora, the origins of its unusually shaped rocks and the habits of local birds. There is much else of interest, too, including bears, a falcon show, a 1,000-year-old olive tree, *carboneros* (huts belonging to charcoal burners) and the Cova des Moro – Moor's Cave. Real adventures, such as rock climbing, abseiling and archery, are also on offer.

Environs
Set amid lemon groves, 2 km (1 mile) northeast, is the quiet little farming village of **Puigpunyent**, which has a 17th-century church.

Galilea, situated a little way south of La Reserva, is a favourite haunt for artists from all over Europe. It affords a magnificent view of the southwestern coast of Mallorca. The founder of the local church of the Immaculate Conception was Captain Antonio Barceló, a man with a fierce reputation who, in the 18th century, defended Mallorca against pirates. In nearby El Capdella the same captain Barceló founded the church of Virgen del Carmen.

Sa Dragonera, Dragon Island, viewed from Sant Elm

❽ Northwestern Coast of Mallorca

The northern slopes of the Serra de Tramuntana provide some magnificent views and a wonderful sense of isolation. Andratx and Valldemossa have a number of interesting historic sights, but it is the scenery of the rugged coastline, which manages to be both sinister and beautiful, that is most impressive. The route is dramatic, traversing tunnels and gorges, but it is not difficult, except for the approach to Port d'es Canonge and Port de Valldemossa. It can be covered in a single day. If you are fit, you could even cycle.

④ Mirador de Ses Ànimes
The former defence tower, standing on a steep rock, now serves as a viewpoint. The entrance to the tower is narrow and the top terrace is accessible only by stepladder.

③ Estellencs
A small town with old stone houses, an interesting, mostly 18th-century, church and a handful of souvenir shops. The route follows the main street.

② Mirador de Ricardo Roca
This viewpoint is situated on the terrace of the Es Grau restaurant. It affords a spectacular view of the northwestern coastline.

① Andratx
A charming little town with attractive houses and cobbled streets. The market is held on Wednesday and is a time when the usually empty streets teem with life.

0 kilometres 2
0 miles 2

⑤ Banyalbufar
Founded by the Arabs, this small town is surrounded by terraced fields descending to the sea. Until the late 19th century, the district was famous for its vineyards.

⑦ La Granja
Once a country estate, La Granja now houses one of the island's most interesting museums. It stages shows of regional dance, crafts and local winetastings.

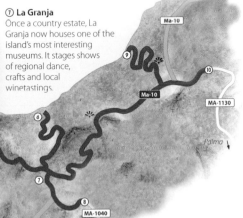

Tips for Drivers
Length: 50 km (31 miles).
Stopping-off points: Most places along the route have a bar or restaurant; the restaurant at Mirador de Ricardo Roca is superb. Accommodation can be found in Andratx and Valldemossa.
Further information:
Valldemossa, Av da Palma 7.
Tel 971 612 019.

⑥ Port d'es Canonge
The road leading to this small fishing port and beach is narrow and winding, but the beauty of the spot makes it worth the trouble. Fishermen's huts and a restaurant are by the beach.

⑧ Esporles
At the centre of this friendly town, far from the tourist haunts, is the shady Passeig del Rei, lined with numerous cafés and restaurants. The nearby church was built in the early 16th century.

⑨ Port de Valldemossa
A small, shingly beach and a few good fish restaurants are the main reasons to follow the winding road from Valldemossa to this pretty hamlet. It offers peace and idyllic scenery, and is visited by only a handful of holidaymakers.

⑩ Valldemossa
Frédéric Chopin wintered here in 1838. It is worth taking a stroll through the town's narrow alleys, after visiting the monastery and the royal palace.

Key
■ Suggested route
= Other road
■ Scenic route

For map symbols *see back flap*

⑩ La Granja

This country house *(finca)* lies in a wooded valley, near Esporles. From the 13th to the 15th centuries it belonged to an order of Cistercian monks, and after this to the Fortuny family. The estate has survived almost unchanged since the 18th century and is now a museum of folklore, full of antique furniture, ceramics and other artifacts. Mouthwatering hams hang in the antique kitchen, peacocks stroll around the beautiful garden, and the local restaurant serves delicious Mallorcan cuisine. In the mornings it is quieter, and you can still see displays of horse dressage and local crafts.

Dye-house
This formed part of the domestic quarters, most of which were situated in basements and cellars.

Park
The estate, situated in a valley, is surrounded by a park to the south and west. Its landscaping includes streams and waterfalls; the house is almost completely hidden by a dense growth of trees.

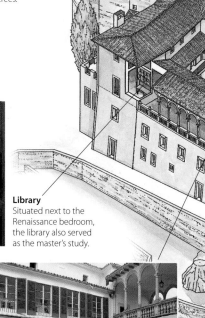

Library
Situated next to the Renaissance bedroom, the library also served as the master's study.

Courtyard
The house is arranged around a courtyard. Don't miss the old carriage that is parked in an open garage. The courtyard has a wide entrance gate to the east.

KEY

① **Restaurant**

② **Gate to the park**

③ **Main entrance**, where the shop and café are located.

★ **Salon**
The formal rooms are situated on the north side. Next to the salon are the games room and a small theatre. From here, French windows open onto the garden.

VISITORS' CHECKLIST

Practical Information
2 km (1 mile) west from Esporles.
Tel 971 610 032.
Open 10am–7pm daily (summer), 10am–6pm (winter).
🏛 🐎 Art & craft exhibition and horse dressage shows: Feb–Oct Wed & Fri 3–4:20pm.
Ⓦ lagranja.net

★ **Garden**
At the centre of the garden is a small fountain; the escarpment hides a grotto.

Corridor
Windows overlook the courtyard. On its east side is a row of smaller rooms, where you can see, among other things, an exhibition of toys.

Exhibitions
Visitors can see an equestrian show with professionals training horses (Wednesday and Friday afternoons from February to October), as well as local artisans working in traditional crafts such as shoemaking, basketwork and embroidery.

Enchanting little alleys of Valldemossa, beckoning strollers

⑪ Valldemossa

🗺 1,750. 🚌 ⓘ Av. Palma 7, 971 612 019. 🚢 Sun. 🎭 Santa Catalina Thomàs (28 Jul), Sant Bartomeu (24 Aug), Chopin Festival (Aug).
🅦 valldemossa.es

The historical records of Valldemossa go back to the 14th century, when the asthmatic King Sancho built this palace in the mountains to make the most of the clean air. In 1399, the palace was handed over to the Carthusian monks, who remodelled it as a monastery. The **Real Cartuja y Palacio del Rey Sancho** (Royal Carthusian Monastery of Jesus of Nazareth) was abandoned in 1835, when the monks were dispossessed.

The composer Frédéric Chopin rented a former monk's cell here in 1838 with his lover George Sand, the feminist French writer, and the monastery is now the town's main tourist attraction. In front of the entrance, in Plaça de la Cartuja de Valldemossa, is a monument to Chopin.

The monastery includes a chapel with a ceiling decorated with late Baroque paintings by Miguel Bayeu, a relative of Goya's. Behind the chapel are rows of shady arcades. The prior's cell, despite its name, consists of several spacious rooms with access to a private garden offering a magnificent view of the valley below. The rooms house an exhibition of religious artifacts and an old pharmacy. The adjacent cells contain mementos of Chopin and George Sand. The 17th-century monastery pharmacy contains a variety of ceramic and glass jars with wonderfully detailed descriptions of their contents (look out for the jar containing "powdered beasts' claws").

The monastery also houses the excellent **Museu Municipal d'Art**, which includes a small collection of works by distinguished Spanish artists including Antoni Tàpies, Joan Miró and Juli Ramis – a Modernist painter and native of Mallorca. There is also a cycle of illustrations by Pablo Picasso, *Burial of Count Orgaz*, inspired by the famous El Greco painting.

On leaving the arcades you can proceed to the **Palau del Rei Sanç** – the Palace of King Sancho. This is the oldest fortified part of the monastery. The main point of interest is the wooden drawbridge connecting the two chambers over the palace's entrance. Once used as a political prison, the palace now serves as a venue for displays of folk dancing and recitals of Chopin's music.

Valldemossa itself is charming and always bustling. Most visitors are keen to see the places associated with Chopin, but a stroll along the town's narrow cobbled alleys is definitely worthwhile.

The modest house at Carrer Rectoría 5 is where the saintly nun Catalina Thomàs was born to a peasant family. The house has been converted into a richly decorated chapel, with the statue of the saint standing in front, holding a jug with flowing water. Nearby is the 15th-century church of Sant Bartomeu, now, unfortunately, partly destroyed.

🏛 **Real Cartuja y Palacio del Rey Sancho**
Plaça de Cartuja de Valldemossa.
Tel 971 612 986. **Closed** Sun in Dec & Jan. 🅿 🅱 🅦 celdadechopin.es

Environs
Port de Valldemossa lies some 6 km (4 miles) north of Valldemossa. This is a small fishing village scenically poised on the shores of a narrow bay and surrounded by rugged cliffs. It is reached by a narrow, hairpin road. The local beach, although small and pebbly, is enchanting and occupies a beautiful location. The demanding journey is rewarded by a number of local restaurants specializing in seafood.

Tile with the image of the Saint, on one of Valldemossa's houses

Santa Catalina Thomas (1531–74)

Catalina Thomàs is the only Mallorcan saint. At the age of 23, she joined an Augustinian order. Known for her humility, she declined the position of Mother Superior, saying that she did not wish to govern but to serve God. She is buried in the chapel of Santa María Magdalena convent in Palma, where she spent many years of her life. She was canonized in 1930.

Frédéric Chopin and George Sand

The great Polish composer Chopin spent four months in Valldemossa's 14th-century monastery *(see opposite)* during the winter of 1838–9. Chopin was accompanied by Aurora Dupin, better known as the French novelist George Sand, and her children. Their arrival here was partly to escape the prying eyes of Parisian society and partly on account of the composer's health. Chopin suffered from tuberculosis, though the weather was so bad during his stay that it made him worse. The short visit to the town by this unusual couple, described by Sand in *A Winter in Mallorca*, has contributed to the popularity of Valldemossa, despite the fact that Sand labelled the locals as "savages".

Garden in front of cell No. 2, in which Chopin's scores and George Sand's manuscripts are held. To this day there is a dispute over which cell Chopin occupied (No. 4). The garden terrace affords a fine view.

Portrait of George Sand
A French writer and journalist, Sand was a highly unconventional figure. She was morally way ahead of her time – she wore trousers, smoked cigars and "lived in sin".

Portrait of Frédéric Chopin, by Italian painter Luigi Calamatta, in the form of a photomontage over an original partiture composed by the musician, displayed in the Royal Carthusian Monastery.

A Winter in Mallorca
George Sand's description of her visit to Mallorca with Chopin has enjoyed lasting popularity.

The Pleyal Piano is the composer's oldest piano, conserved in cell No. 4, where he finished his Preludes, and major partitures on show in the museum.

Rotunda in the garden of Son Marroig

⑫ Son Marroig

3 km (2 miles) northeast of Deià.
Tel 971 639 158. **Open** 9:30am–
6:30pm (to 5:30pm in summer).
Closed Sun. 🐾

This late medieval mansion, perched high above the seashore, was remodelled in the 19th century to become the residence of the Habsburg Archduke Ludwig Salvator. The Austrian aristocrat was fabulously rich and came to Mallorca hoping to escape from the strict morality of the Viennese court. He fell in love with the island, settled here and gave himself over to exploring and promoting the Balearic Islands.

The house is now a museum, dedicated to his life and work and including some of his pen drawings and manuscripts. It is surrounded by a terrace and graced by a rotunda of white marble. From here, the Archduke enjoyed fine views over the wooded shore to the narrow promontory of **Sa Foradada**, where he used to moor his yacht *Nixe*. It takes less than an hour's walk to get there.

Environs
A short way southwest of Son Marroig is the **Monestír de Miramar**. The house was built in 1276 for Ramon Llull but was acquired by Ludwig Salvator in 1827. The Archduke entertained Princess Sisi here during her visit to Mallorca.

🏛 Monestír de Miramar
Tel 971 616 073. **Open** 9am–5:45pm
daily (to 4:45pm in winter). 🐾

⑬ Deià

🏔 700. 🚌 🚂 Sant Joan Baptista (24 Jun). 🆆 deia.info

This lovely mountain town lies at the spot where the mighty Puig d'es Teix meets the sea. Deià is mostly associated with the English novelist and poet Robert Graves *(see opposite)*. Graves settled here in 1929 and for the next 56 years lived and worked here, making the place popular with other artists, including Picasso and the writer Anaïs Nin.

Towering over the town is the modest church of **Sant Joan Baptista** (1754–60). The adjacent building houses the **parish museum**, with a collection of religious objects. Deià also has an interesting **Museu Arqueológic**, founded by the American archaeologist William Waldren, displaying the prehistory of Mallorca.

Hotel La Residencia, in the grounds of a former estate, has attracted many famous guests, including Princess Diana and Sir Bob Geldof.

Environs
A winding road leads to **Cala Deià**, a pretty cove with a shingle beach and clear water.

🏛 Museu Arqueológic
Es Clo Deià. **Tel** 971 639 001. **Open**
Apr–Oct: 5–7pm Tue, Thu & Sun. 🐾

Ludwig Salvator

The Habsburg Archduke Ludwig Salvator was born in 1847. He first visited Mallorca at the age of 19 and became captivated by the island. He settled here permanently, learned the local dialect and created a scandal by marrying a local carpenter's daughter. He was tireless in exploring and promoting Mallorca, producing a seven-volume work devoted to the island's history, archaeology, folklore and topography. It is thanks to him that a 10-km- (6-mile-) long stretch of the coast that he owned has survived intact. In 1910, he was awarded honorary citizenship of Mallorca. He died in 1915.

Hotel La Residencia viewed from the church hill

For hotels and restaurants in this region see pp148–50 and pp155–9

Modernista building of Banco de Sóller, one of Sóller's landmarks

⑭ Sóller

🚌 🚋 ℹ Plaça Espanya 1. **Tel** 971 638 008. ⏰ Sat. 🎭 Festes de Moros i Cristians (2nd Sun in May).

Situated in a valley, Sóller is sheltered by the Serra de Alfàbia mountain massif and overshadowed by the lofty Puig Major (1,445 m/4,740 ft). Its name reputedly derives from the Arabic word *suliar*, meaning "golden bowl" – the valley is famous for its many orange groves.

Arabs, who settled here in the late 8th century, built canals and irrigation ditches and the town grew rich thanks to its plentiful supply of oranges and the vineyards and olive groves, planted on the slopes of the Serra de Tramuntana. In exchange for its oranges and wine, it imported goods from France and links between the town and France remain strong.

Plaça Constitució is a lively square and the centre of Sóller. Mature trees, fountains and lively cafés give the place its unique atmosphere. Notable buildings include the *Modernista* castle-like **Banco de Sóller**, which is the work of Joan Rubió i Bellver, a disciple of Antoni Gaudí, and the Neo-Gothic church of **Sant Bartomeu**, also designed by Rubió. Particularly eye-catching is the vast rosette window on the church façade, carved in stone, and the Baroque sculptures contrasting with the dark interior. To the north of

the square stands **Museu Casal de Cultura**, occupying a renovated building in Calle Sa Mar. Here, you can recapture the atmosphere of old Sóller as you stroll through rooms decorated with antique furnishings, a courtyard and an old kitchen with amusing majolica plates.

Museu Balear de Ciències Naturals (Balearic Museum of Natural Science), on the outskirts of Sóller, was opened in 1992 in a late 19th-century mansion house. Its exhibits include a collection of Mallorcan fossils and rocks and specimens of the local flora. The adjacent **Jardí Botànic** contains plants native to the Balearic Islands. The town's **vintage electric train**, nicknamed the "Red Arrow", which runs between Palma and Sóller, provides a superb

Fountain in Plaça Constitució in Sóller

ride through the mountains. From the Sóller terminus you can hop aboard a **vintage tram**, which takes you on to Port de Sóller (see p74).

Environs

Port de Sóller, situated 5 km (3 miles) from Sóller, is a pleasant although crowded resort with many seafood restaurants next to the harbour and by the beach. Here, you can enjoy a boat trip along the coast, or go for a hike to the nearby lighthouse.

🏛 **Museu Casal de Cultura**
C/ Sa Mar 13. **Tel** 971 631 465.
Open 11am–1pm & 5–8pm (4–7pm in winter) Tue–Fri, 11am–1pm Sat. 🚫

🏛 **Museu Balear de Ciències Naturals and Jardí Botànic**
Ctra Palma–Port de Sóller. **Tel** 971 634 064. **Open** 10am–6pm Mon–Sat, 10am–2pm Sun. 🚫 🚫 ♿

Robert Graves (1895–1985)

Robert Graves was an English novelist, poet and classical scholar. Severely wounded on the Somme during World War I, his frank autobiography, *Goodbye to All That*, earned him enough money to move to Mallorca, where he set up home, accompanied by his muse and mistress, the poet Laura Riding. Here, he wrote two tremendously successful historic novels: *I, Claudius* and *Claudius the God*, which made him world-famous. The outbreak of the Spanish Civil War interrupted his stay but he returned to the island in 1946. He died in 1985 and is buried in the local church of Sant Joan Baptista beneath a simple gravestone. His house is now a museum.

Robert Graves' tombstone in Deià's cemetery

Punta Grosa lighthouse, near Port de Sóller

ⓑ Train from Palma to Port de Sóller

The most enjoyable way to travel from Palma to Sóller is aboard the "Red Arrow", an electric narrow-gauge railway line, which opened in 1912. After passing through farmland, the 27-km (17-mile) route winds its way through the steep peaks and valleys of the Serra de Tramuntana. The line is justifiably regarded as one of the most attractive in Europe, and the narrow-gauge rolling stock, musty carriages and clanking engine only add to the experience.

④ Sóller
After a one-hour ride the train reaches Sóller. From here a vintage tram running through the busy town centre takes you to Port de Sóller.

③ Mirador Pujol d'en Banja
Two special tourist trains, leaving Palma daily at 10:50am and noon, stop briefly at this viewpoint to provide a splendid view of Sóller, the surrounding mountains and the coastline.

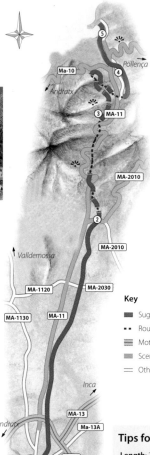

② Bunyola
This is the last stop before passing through the dizzying Serra de Tramuntana mountains. This typical Mallorcan town, towered over by its church, enjoys an idyllic location in a beautiful verdant valley.

⑤ Port de Sóller
The journey from Sóller to Port de Sóller takes 15 minutes. The tram route runs along the beach and ends at the harbour. Trams run much more frequently than the train.

0 km   2
0 miles   2

Key

■ Suggested route
▪▪ Route through the tunnel
▦ Motorway
▨ Scenic route
═ Other road

① Palma
A trip aboard this vintage electric train is a real delight. The line was originally built to transport fruit to Palma from Sóller at a time when the journey by road took an entire day.

Tips for Passengers
Length: 27 km (17 miles).
Stopping-off points: Sóller has many cafés and restaurants.
Information: Eusebio Estada 1, Palma (971 752 051); Plaça d'Espanya, Sóller (971 630 130); or contact Ⓦ trendesoller.com

⑯ Jardines de Alfabia

14 km (9 miles) north of Palma. 🚌
Tel 971 613 123. **Open** Apr–Oct:
9:30am–6:30pm Mon–Sat; Nov–Mar:
9:30am–5:30pm Mon–Fri, 9:30am–
1:30pm Sat. **Closed** Dec–mid Feb.
🅿 W jardinesdealfabia.com

Most visitors come to see the
magnificent Moorish gardens of
this old manor house, set amid
lemon groves. Footpaths shaded
by pergolas crisscross streams
and take you past murmuring
fountains, ivy-clad walls and beds
of splendid roses. The house is
approached via a long stately
avenue of plane trees.

Following the conquest of the
island by Jaume I, the estate
was given to the Moorish
governor Benhabet. Benhabet
had been the governor of
Pollença but supported the king
by provisioning the Catalan
army during the invasion. For
this help, Jaume I gave
Benhabet this land and he set
about planning an estate in the
Moorish style. After his death
the castle became the residence
of the Mallorcan kings. The
origin of the estate's name goes
back to the days of Arab rule,
when it was called *Al-Fabi* ("Jug
of olives").

The house itself, with its
courtyard surrounded by
domestic buildings and shaded
by a giant plane tree, is actually
modest though attractive. Most
notable is the 14th-century oak
throne made for Jaume IV. The
gatehouse features a lovely
Mudéjar (Spanish-Moorish) style
vault, with an inscription
praising Allah.

Sun shining through a pergola in
Alfàbia gardens

Beach at the end of Torrent de Pareis canyon, near Sa Calobra

⑰ Sa Calobra

30 km (19 miles) NE of Fornalutx.

This tiny hamlet occupies a
beautiful cove surrounded by
high cliffs. A busy tourist centre,
its main attraction is the **Torrent
de Pareis** (River of the Twins)
canyon, which is reached by a
coastal walkway, leading partly
through a tunnel.

It is also possible to reach
this impressive canyon from
Escorca, a hamlet on the way
from Sóller to Pollença. This
route is extremely difficult,
however, and requires rock-
climbing skills, ropes and
wetsuits. It takes about six
hours to cover it. During the
winter and spring or after
heavy rainfall, it is virtually

impassable, as the bottom of
the canyon, known as the
"Great Canyon of Mallorca", fills
with torrential waters. Once
upon a time Sa Calobra was
accessible only by boat. Now
there is a twisting road leading
to it, which in view of its
breakneck descents and bends
has been nicknamed *Nus de la
Corbata* ("Knotted Neck-tie").
Two kilometres (1 mile) before
Sa Calobra, you can take a left
turn to the popular resort of
Cala Tuent. Set against the
northern slopes of Puig Major,
the quiet village has a modest
gravel and sand beach. The Es
Vergeret restaurant has a large
selection of fish dishes – its
terrace affords a fine view of
the rocky coast.

Serra de Tramuntana

The northern coast of Mallorca is dominated by the Serra de
Tramuntana (Mountains of the North Wind), which run from Sa
Dragonera in the west to Formentor in the east. The highest peak
of this 90-km (55-mile) stretch is Puig Major (1,445 m/4,740 ft),
though part of this is used by the military and closed to visitors.
The steep slopes are covered with sweet-smelling wild rosemary
and are home to goats, sheep and rare birds. The best way to enjoy
this area is on foot, and a
number of maps are easily
available that list walking
routes through all or part
of the mountain range.
Alternatively, you can
explore the mountains
by car, although great
care should be taken on
the narrow and twisting
roads and frequent hairpin
bends that descend
through steep cliffs to
the sea.

Steep mountain slopes west of Monestír de Lluc

⓲ Monestir de Lluc

The monestir at Lluc is the spiritual centre of Mallorca and has been a place of pilgrimage for over 800 years. The main point of interest is the little statue of the Virgin *(La Moreneta de Lluc)*, which, so the story goes, was found in a cave by an Arab shepherd boy who had converted to Christianity. The image was initially moved to the church but it kept returning to the same spot. A chapel was built to house this miraculous object and this has since been decorated with precious stones. Thousands of pilgrims now arrive here every year to pay homage.

Statue of Joaquim Rosselló i Ferra`
Father Rosselló, who arrived in Lluc in 1891, was the founder of the Sacred Heart Missionary Congregation and the spiritual reviver of the sanctuary.

Statue of Bishop Campins
A patron of the sanctuary, Bishop Pere-Joan Campins commissioned Antoni Gaudí and Guillem Reynés to renovate the basilica and build its Way of the Cross.

KEY

① **Church** The original Renaissance-Baroque church was built during 1622–84 and was designed by Jaume Blanquer. Much of the complex dates from the 18th and 19th centuries.

② **Dormitories**

★ **Museu de Lluc**
Opened in 1952, the museum houses local handicraft, such as *siurells* (whistles) and majolica, as well as works of art, paintings, coins and archaeological finds.

School Grounds
The buildings behind the church belong to the Els Blavets, a school choir founded in 1531. The name derives from the choir's blue cassocks.

VISITORS' CHECKLIST

Practical Information
✝ 12:45pm Mon–Sat, 7:30pm Sat; 11am, 12:30pm, 5pm (winter); 7pm (summer) Sun. Museum: **Tel** 971 871 525. **Open** 10am–5pm daily.
🌿 Botanical Garden: **Open** 10am–1pm & 3–6pm daily. Sa Fonda Restaurant: **Tel** 971 517 022. **Open** 1–4pm & 7– 9:15pm Wed–Mon. **Closed** Mon pm.
📷 Pujol dels Misteris del Rosari (Mar/Apr). **W** lluc.net

Transport
🚌 From Palma.

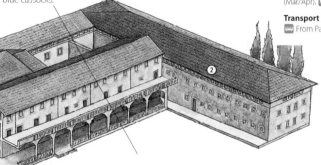

La Dormició de la Verge
The first of the seven steles carved by Miquell Cosquell and Pere Merçol (1399), once standing along the road between Caimari and the sanctuary, now stands in Plaza dels Pelegrins.

★ Els Porxets
The 16th-century building was extended in the early 18th century. It consists of pilgrim quarters on the first floor and stables on the ground floor.

★ La Moreneta de Lluc
The tiny statue of *La Moreneta* ("the little dark One") is just 62 cm (24 in) high. It stands in a niche inside the Royal Chapel, built during 1707–24, at the back of the main altar.

Plaza dels Pelegrins
The drive leading to the monastery is surrounded by greenery and lined with bars, cafés and souvenir shops. It provides a magnificent view of the Serra de Tramuntana.

⑲ Inca

🏙 29,000. 🚉 🚌 🚏 Thu. 🎭 Dijous Bo (3rd Thu in Nov). 🅦 incaturistica.es

Inca, the last stop on the train journey from Palma, is the third largest town on the island. A modern industrial place, visitors come here nevertheless, attracted by the cheap leather goods in Avinguda General Luque and Gran Via de Colon. Thursday, market day, is Inca's busiest time. The stalls lining the streets and squares stretch over several districts of town. Here you can buy almost anything – souvenirs, household goods, flowers and food. Inca is also known for its traditional Mallorcan cuisine, including *caracoles* (snails) and for its wine cellars converted into restaurants *(cellers)*.

Environs

About 2 km (1 mile) past the town, heading towards Alcúdia, is a right turn in the road that leads to the top of **Puig d'Inca** (296 m/970 ft), with a small sanctuary, **Ermita de Santa Magdalena**. For nearly 800 years on the first Sunday after Easter crowds of pilgrims have congregated here. There is a good view from the top over the surrounding fields and mountains. Near the road to Alcúdia are the **Coves de Campanet**, a complex of small but beautiful caves surrounded by tropical gardens. The neighbouring small town of **Sa Pobla** holds one of the best Sunday markets on the island.

🦇 Coves de Campanet

Autopista Palma–Alcúdia, exit 37, 39 km (24 miles). **Tel** 971 516 130. **Open** from 10am daily. 🚫 ✔ 📷

Steps of the Way of the Cross, leading to El Calvari, in Pollença

⑳ Pollença

🏙 17,000. 🚌 ℹ Claustro de Santo Domingo, 971 535 077. 🎭 Sun. 🎭 Sant Antoni (17 Jan), Los Moros y los Cristianos (2 Aug).

Founded by the Romans in the foothills of the Serra de Tramuntana, Pollença has retained much of its old-world charm with narrow, twisting streets, some good restaurants and a lively Sunday market. The remains left by the town's founders include **Pont Romà**, a bridge spanning the banks of the Torrente de Sant Jordi river, at the north end of town.

After 1229, the Knights Templar began the building of the parish church of **Nostra Senyora dels Angels**. Remodelled in the 17th century, the church façade has a fine rosette window, while its dark interior is decorated with paintings and a vast altar that is several storeys high.

The pride of the town is the beautiful **Via Crucis** (Way of the Cross). It leads to the **El Calvari chapel** standing on top of the hills and housing a Gothic statue of Christ. Climbing the seemingly endless set of steps (365 in all), you pass the Stations of the Cross. The chapel may also be reached by walking along the streets. The statue of Christ is carried down to the parish church in a moving torchlight procession every Good Friday, during the *Davallament* (the Crucifixion).

The former **Convent de Sant Domingo** (Dominican monastery) now houses the **Museu Municipal** with its collection of Gothic sacred art, archaeological finds and a small collection of modern paintings.

Colourful stall with souvenirs at Inca's Thursday market

For hotels and restaurants in this region see pp148–50 and pp155–9

To soak up the sleepy atmosphere of Pollença, head for **Plaça Major**, where the locals gather in the cafés and bars.

Environs

The family-friendly resort of **Port de Pollença**, situated 6 km (4 miles) to the east beside a pleasant bay, has a long, sandy beach. Just southeast of Pollença a steep narrow road, then a footpath, climbs 330 m (1,000 ft) to **Puig de Maria**, where a 17th-century hermitage has a rustic restaurant and bar, and simple rooms to let with wonderful views.

🏛 **Museu Municipal**
Convent de Santo Domingo. **Tel** 971 531 166. **Open** 10am–1pm Tue–Sat (also Jun–Sep: 5:30–8:30pm Tue–Sat). 🖼

㉑ Cap de Formentor

6 km (4 miles) from Port de Pollença.

The Formentor Peninsula, at the northern end of the Serra de Tramuntana, is a 20-km (12-mile) long headland of steep cliffs, that is in some places 400 m (1,300 ft) high. The footpath from the road leads to the **Mirador des Colomer** from which you can enjoy spectacular views of the sea and the **El Colomer** rock. There is also a beautiful view of the 16th-century watch tower, **Talaia d'Albercutx**, standing much higher than the viewpoint. Further on, the road passes through the Mont Fumat tunnel and runs among rocky hills, covered with vegetation, up to the **lighthouse** rising to 260 m (850 ft). On a clear day you can see Menorca and its capital, Ciutadella. The rugged cliffs provide nesting sites for thrushes and rock doves, also falcons, swallows and martins.

A spur from the main road leads to the beach of **Cala Pi de la Posada**, which is served by bus from Port de Pollença and gets very crowded in summer. The road ends at one of the oldest, most luxurious resorts on the island – the Hotel

Interior of the Gothic church of Sant Jaume in Alcúdia

Formentor. Opened in 1929, it is noted for its opulence and fashionable clientele (see p149).

㉒ Alcúdia

🏙 19,000. 🚌 ℹ c/Major 17, 971 897 113. 🗓 Tue–Sun. 🎪 Romeria de la Victòria (2 Jul).
🌐 alcudiamallorca.com

The delightful town of Alcúdia, surrounded by 14th-century walls, lies at the base of the peninsula separating Pollença Bay from Alcúdia Bay. Originally, this was a Phoenician settlement. Having conquered the island, the Romans built a town here, called Pollentia, which from the 2nd century was the capital of the island. In 456, it was destroyed by the Vandals. Around the year 800, Moors built their fortress here, naming it *Al-Kudia* (On the Hill). After the Reconquest, Alcúdia

Town hall window in Alcúdia

prospered as a trading centre well into the 19th century. The beautifully restored town is entered through the vast **Porta de Moll** gate. The Gothic church of **Sant Jaume** at the centre is 13th-century. Near the church are a few **remains of Roman houses**. Adjacent to these is **Museu Monogràfic**, which displays objects from Roman times.

On the outskirts of town, along the road to Port d'Alcúdia, is the **Oratori de Santa Anna**. Built in the early 13th century, it is one of the oldest Mallorcan sanctuaries. Nearby are the remains of a first-century BC **Roman theatre** – this is the smallest Roman theatre to have survived in Spain.

Environs

Port d'Alcúdia, 2 km (1 mile) south of the town, is the most popular tourist destination on Mallorca's northeast shores. It has a lovely sandy beach, a marina and a harbour as well as hotels, restaurants and clubs. The road to Es Mal Pas brings you to **Cap des Pinar** where, in 1599, Philip II erected a watchtower, Torre Major. A branch road leads to the **Ermita de la Victòria**. It has a revered 15th-century wooden statue of Victoria, Alcúdia's patron saint.

🏛 **Museu Monogràfic**
Carrer de Sant Jaume 30. **Tel** 971 547 004. **Open** July–Sep: 9:30am–8:30pm Tue–Fri (10am–3:30pm Oct–Jun), 10am–2pm Sat & Sun. 🖼

Lighthouse on Cap de Formentor

The marshes of Parc Natural de S'Albufera, crisscrossed with canals

㉓ Parc Natural de S'Albufera

Tel 971 892 250. **Open** 9am–6pm daily (to 5pm Oct–Mar); Reception Centre (Sa Roca): 9am–4pm daily.

The wetland south of Port d'Alcúdia, occupying the shores of Lake Grande up to C'an Picafort, was once a swamp. Most of it was drained in the 1860s, but a portion remains, which in 1985 become the Parc Natural de S'Albufera. The marshes can be explored on foot, following the marked trails. A major conservation project, this is an excellent place for observing over 200 species of birds, including grey and purple herons, summer osprey and Eleonora's falcon. The park reception is in **Sa Roca** where you can obtain a free map and a list of some of the park's birds.

㉔ Muro

13 km (8 miles) east of Inca. 🏠 7,000. 🚌 🚋 Sun. 🎉 Revelta de Sant Antoni Abat (16–17 Jan).
ⓦ ajmuro.net

The agricultural town of Muro is a pleasant, sleepy place, situated at the centre of the plain, surrounded by cultivated fields. It is full of old mansions built by rich landowners, which give the town its unique charm. Each year on January 16 and 17, Muro is the scene of the *Revelta i Beneides de Sant Antoni Abat* – a big fiesta on the eve of

St Antoni's day. The town's inhabitants and visitors gather around bonfires, drinking wine and eating sausages and *espinagades* – delicious pies made with eels caught in the S'Albufera marshes.

The town is dominated by the church of **Sant Joan Baptista**, remodelled around 1530. This large structure, built in the Catalan-Gothic style, features colourful stained-glass windows and a beautiful rosette on the façade. The interior includes Baroque furnishings and a vast main altarpiece. Adjacent to the church is a huge, seven-storey belfry that once served as a watchtower. The view from the top can be stunning and encompasses all of the surrounding area.

The **Convent des Mínims** and the church of **Santa Ana** are in Plaça de José Antonio Primo de Rivera, once the venue for bullfights. Nearby is the **Museu Etnològic de Muro**, which is situated in an old mansion house. Here, you can see a collection of local furniture, folk costumes, agricultural tools and a series of workshops including a blacksmith's and a cobbler's. The museum also has a collection of *siurells* – whistles.

Baroque cartouche from the museum in Muro

Environs

Some 11 km (7 miles) east of Muro, on Badia d'Alcúdia, adjacent to the Parc Natural de S'Albufera, is the sandy beach of **Platya de Muro** with its stone-pines growing amid the dunes.

About 3 km (2 miles) north is **Sa Pobla**, which has a lovely 17th-century Baroque church and two museums: Museu d'Art Contemporani and Museu de la Jugeta, which has a collection of toys from the 19th and 20th centuries. The town's main square, Plaça Constitució, hosts a busy Sunday market, selling mainly agricultural produce. **Santa Margalida**, situated 5 km (3 miles) southeast, has a history reaching back to Roman times. The views of the mountains and plain are outstanding from here.

🏛 Museu Etnològic de Muro
Carrer Major 15. **Tel** 971 860 647. **Open** 10am–3pm Tue–Sat; 10am–2pm Sun, also 5–8pm Thu. **Closed** Aug.

Multistorey altarpiece in Muro's Sant Joan Baptista

㉕ Sineu

30 km (19 miles) northeast of Palma. 🏠 3,600. 🚌 🚋 Wed. 🎉 Fira Maig (24 Apr).

Sineu is one of the most interesting agricultural towns of the central Es Pla plain and has a rich history. Attracted by its strategic position, at the very heart of the island, Jaume II built his **palace** here. King Sancho came here to benefit from the fresh air and declared the town the centre of Mallorca. Later, Jaume III slept here the night before the battle of Llucmajor, in which he was killed fighting the army of Pedro of Aragón. Today, the palace is occupied by an order of nuns that is known as the *monges del palau* (sisters of the palace).

Adjacent to the former royal residence stands the biggest parish church on the island, **Santa Maria de Sineu**. This Gothic structure was built in 1248 and remodelled in the 16th century. The church has an important collection of Medieval ceramics that can be viewed in the adjacent rectory on Wednesdays. In front of the church, in Plaça de Sant Marcos, stands a statue of a winged lion – the symbol of St Mark the Apostle, the patron saint of the town.

In the neighbouring Sa Plaça square are two excellent restaurants serving traditional Mallorcan cuisine: the Celler Ca'n Font and the Celler Es Grop.

At one time, the Inca–Artà railway line passed through the town. Now, the former station building, dating from 1879, houses a restaurant. Wednesday's market is one of the biggest agricultural fairs in Mallorca and sells local produce and livestock.

Environs
About 4 km (2 miles) north, near the road to Llubia, are the ruins of a Talayotic structure.

Monumental church in Petra, towering over the neighbourhood

㉖ Petra

50 km (31 miles) east of Palma.
🅰 2,900. 🚌 🚍 Wed. 🎉 Santa Pràxedes (21 Jul), Festa de Bunyols (30 Oct). **W** visitpetramallorca.com

This small town is the birthplace of Junipero Serra. Aged 54, the Franciscan monk travelled to America and Mexico, and after a series of arduous journeys on foot, founded missions in California. The old houses lining the labyrinth of narrow alleys have changed little since Serra's time

Stained-glass church window in Sineu

here. The town makes the most of its famous son and all places associated with Junipero Serra are well marked. These include **Casa Natal Fray Junipero Serra**, a humble building in Carrer Barracar Alt, where Serra was born. Next to this is a small but

interesting **museum**, opened in 1955. The exhibition is devoted to his life and work and includes wooden models of the nine American missions established by Serra, as well as a range of memorabilia. At the end of the street in which the Serra family house stands, on the outskirts of town, is the 17th-century monastery of **Sant Bernat**, which has a statue of Serra standing in front of it. The Majolica panels down a side street next to the monastery are a gift from grateful Californians and pay tribute to the famous monk's many achievements.

Environs
Some 7 km (4 miles) west lies the small town of **Sant Joan**. Its 13th-century parish church, remodelled in the 15th and 18th centuries, acquired its present form in the 1930s. If there is time, head for the Santuari de la Mare de Déu de la Consolació, standing on the outskirts of town. Built during the Reconquest period and restored in 1966, it is now a place of pilgrimage.

Ariany, 4 km (2 miles) to the north, is a small agricultural town. Famous during the days of Jaume I, it became the region's capital in 1982. Its houses are dwarfed by the high tower of the Neo-Romanesque church.

🏛 **Museu y Casa Natal Fray Junipero Serra**
C/ Barracar Alt 6–8. **Tel** 971 561 149. **Open** by appointment only.

Junipero Serra
Junipero Serra was born in Petra in 1713 and played an important role in the history of the Spanish colonization of North America. In 1749, he left on a mission to Mexico, and later travelled to California, where he established nine missions and sought to convert the native Indians to Christianity. Some of Serra's missions prospered after his death and became the cities of San Diego, Santa Barbara, Los Angeles and San Francisco. He died in 1784 and was beatified in 1988.

Statue of Junipero Serra in Palma

The medieval fortress of Capdepera

㉗ Artà

🚌 🚶 Wed. 🎏 San Antonio (12–13 Jun), Sa Fira (2nd Sun in Sep).

This hilltop town was built on the site of an Arab stronghold; its name is derived from the Arabic word *jertan* (garden). Much of its medieval walls and fortifications have survived to this day.

The town's most interesting structure is the hilltop **Santuari de Sant Salvador**. It can be reached from the mid-13th-century parish church of **Transfiguració del Senyor** via steps (actually a Way of the Cross) shaded by a line of cypresses.

The chapel and its surrounding walls were built during 1825–32. It contains a revered 17th-century statue of the Virgin with Child. The courtyard affords a lovely view of the town's rooftops.

Madonna from the Artà chapel

Environs
Ses Païsses, a short way to the south, is a 3,000-year-old Bronze Age settlement. The remains include fragments of the defence walls and a huge watchtower. Some of the stone blocks weigh about eight tons. The archaeological findings from this site can be seen in Artà's regional museum. The **Ermita de Betlem**, about 7 km (4 miles) to the north, is built on a hill. Established in 1805, the tiny church has a number of primitive frescoes.

㉘ Capdepera

🚌 🚶 Wed. 🎏 Fiesta Nostra Senyora d'Esperança (18 Dec).

Towering above the town is a castle built in the 14th century to defend the coast against pirates. At the highest point of the castle stands the Gothic church of **Nostra Senyora d'Esperança**. The outside stairs lead to a flat roof from which there is a nice view of the town's terracotta roofscape.

Environs
The **Coves d'Artà**, regarded as one of Mallorca's wonders, are situated some 6 km (4 miles) to the south. Two thousand Arabs were found hiding here by Jaume I during the Reconquest. In the 19th century, the caves were studied by a French geologist and became popular with tourists – Jules Verne is said to have written *Journey to the Centre of the Earth* after visiting them (*see opposite*).

🏰 **Castell de Capdepera**
Tel 971 818 746. **Open** 9am–8pm daily (mid-Oct–mid-Mar: to 5pm). 🐾

🦇 **Coves d'Artà**
Canyamel, Capdepera. Tel 971 841 293. **Open** Apr–Jun & Oct: 10am–6pm; Jul–Sep: 10am–7pm; Nov–Mar: 10am–5pm. **Closed** 1 Jan, 25 Dec. 🐾 📷 only.
🌐 **cuevasdearta.com**

㉙ Cala Rajada

ℹ️ Via Mallorca 36, 971 819 467.

A small seaside resort and bay, Cala Rajada is famous for its beautiful beach shaded by a stone-pine forest. The rocky coast surrounding it is regarded as one of the most attractive in this part of Mallorca. You would hardly guess it but until recently this was just a small fishing village – only the old jetty, which is now used by pleasure boats and sailing yachts, remains.

Above the Cala Gat bay stands **Sa Torre Cega**, a stately home named after its owner, Juan March, a rich tobacco merchant, banker and patron of the arts. Both this palace and its lovely gardens, that have about 40 sculptures by various Spanish artists, are open to visitors through prior appointment.

Environs
From Cala Rajada, it is worth taking a 2-km (1-mile) walk to **Cap de Capdepera**, the easternmost headland of Mallorca. The nearby **Platja de Canyamel** is a small, quiet resort with lovely sandy beaches. There is also a local golf course, and the former watchtower Torre de Canyamel houses a restaurant specializing in tasty Mallorcan cuisine.

🏛️ **Sa Torre Cega**
C/ Joan March 2. **Tel** 689 027 353. 📷 **Closed** Mon–Tue & Dec–Jan.

Fishing boat leaving Cala Rajada's harbour

Mallorca's Caves

Mallorca is famous for its caves, which are carved out of the island's limestone rocks. Many were known by the locals for hundreds of years and they once provided shelter for the early settlers, or served as hiding places from marauding pirates, dens for smugglers or religious sanctuaries. In the 19th century Archduke Ludwig Salvator began to take an interest in them and recruited a French geologist, Edouard Martel, to study them. In 1896 Martel rediscovered the Coves d'Artà. He was amazed by their size (some are the size of a cathedral) and the large number of stalactites and stalagmites.

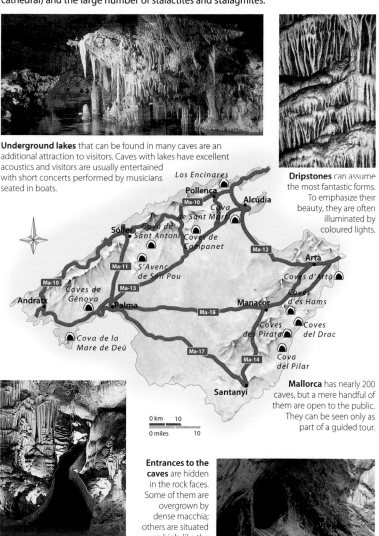

Underground lakes that can be found in many caves are an additional attraction to visitors. Caves with lakes have excellent acoustics and visitors are usually entertained with short concerts performed by musicians seated in boats.

Dripstones can assume the most fantastic forms. To emphasize their beauty, they are often illuminated by coloured lights.

Mallorca has nearly 200 caves, but a mere handful of them are open to the public. They can be seen only as part of a guided tour.

Excursion routes in the caves are arranged so that everybody can see the chambers easily. There are steps and walkways provided in some places.

Entrances to the caves are hidden in the rock faces. Some of them are overgrown by dense macchia; others are situated up high, like the Coves d'Artà, where steps have been built to provide easyaccess for tourists.

Sandy beach of Cala Millor, one of Mallorca's most popular spots

⓪ Cala Millor

Passeig Maritim, 971 585 864.

Cala Millor is one of the most popular resorts on the east coast of Mallorca. The first hotels began to appear here as early as the 1930s, but the real tourist invasion did not start until the 1980s. Similar to neighbouring Cala Bona and Sa Coma, Cala Millor has many beautiful beaches; the main one is 1.8 km (1 mile) long and is quite magnificent. As you would expect, the resort has plenty of bars, restaurants and clubs.

Environs

At the **Safari-Zoo**, a wildlife park 2 km (1 mile) to the south, you can explore by car, miniature road train or as part of a guided coach tour. Free buses go from Cala Millor to the zoo. Some 4 km (2 miles) northwest is **Son Servera**. Not the prettiest of Mallorcan agricultural towns, its prime

feature is the church, which was begun in 1905 by Joan Rubió, a disciple of Antoni Gaudí, and which remains unfinished to this day.

⓪ Porto Cristo

Pl de l'Aljub s/n, 662 350 882.

The ancient fishing port of Porto Cristo is situated at the end of a long bay, where the El Rivet flows into the sea. Today it is a pleasant family resort, but as early as the 13th century this was a seaport for the inland town of Manacor. As the best sheltered harbour on the eastern coast of Mallorca it was also an important naval base, and the lighthouse dates back to 1851. During the Spanish Civil War, Republicans landed here with the intention of taking over the island from General Franco's forces. Despite initial successes, the attack was repelled.

Accessible from the esplanade that takes you along the bay are the spectacular White Caves, which were inhabited by fishermen until the end of the 19th century.

Porto Cristo is one of the few places on the eastern coast of Mallorca where you can find last-minute hotel accommodation during the high season. Among its attractions is the sandy beach.

Environs

Some 2 km (1 mile) south of Porto Cristo are the **Coves del Drac**. The "Dragon's Caves" are one of Mallorca's treasures. Although they have been known for centuries, they were unexplored until 1896. They feature an attractive array of dripstones, as well as one of the world's largest underground lakes, 177 m (580 ft) long, 40 m (131 ft) wide and over 30 m (98 ft) deep. A ride by boat under the stalactite vault is an unforgettable experience. Visits feature a 10-minute concert by a string quartet.

The **Coves d'es Hams**, 2 km (1 mile) to the east, derive their name from the hook-shaped stalactites *(hams)* found here. Boatloads of floating musicians on the underground lake produce an unusual musical ambience.

Coves del Drac
Tel 971 820 753. **Open** Apr–Oct: 10am–5pm daily; Nov–Mar: 10:45am–noon & 2–3:30pm.
W cuevasdeldrach.com

Coves dels Hams
Tel 971 820 988. **Open** daily.
W cuevas-hams.com

Yachting harbour at the end of Porto Cristo bay

For hotels and restaurants in this region see pp148–50 and pp155–9

32 Manacor

🏛 50,000. 🚍 *i* Pl Ramon Llull s/n, 971 847 241. Ⓦ visitmanacor.com

Manacor is Mallorca's second-largest town and boasts a centuries-long tradition of handicraft. It produces furniture and ceramics, including the famous Mallorcan black porcelain, but it is most famous for its simulated pearls. The town is also known for the local speciality – *sobrasada de cerdo negro* – spicy sausage, and sweets called *sospiros* (sighs).

Places worth visiting in Manacor include the church of **Nostra Senyora dels Dolors** in Plaça del Rector Rubi, built in the late 19th century on the site of a former mosque. Its lofty clock tower, resembling a minaret, is a town landmark. The most notable features of the church's interior are the vast wooden door and a figure of the crucified Christ, dressed in white robes, with long flowing hair.

Numerous shops in town sell simulated pearls, which have been produced here since 1890. In order to see them being made visit **Perlas Majorica**, a shop offering free demonstrations. Here, glass beads are covered with consecutive layers of a compound made of fish scale mixed with resin, dried, polished to a high shine and set in silver or gold.

Environs
Sant Llorenç des Cardassar is 9 km (6 miles) to the northeast. The local church has two figures of the Madonna. The first is a wooden statue dating from the 12th or 13th century. The second,

Opulent interior of the Gothic church in Manacor

Music room in the stately home of Els Calderers

carved in stone, was made in the 15th century, probably in France.

Perlas Majorica
Argenters (at the entrance of Manacor from Palma). **Tel** 971 550 900.
Open 9am–7pm Mon–Fri, 9am–1pm Sat & Sun (to 2pm Dec–Jan; 5pm Feb & Nov; 6pm Mar–Jun & Oct.
Closed Sun, Dec & Jan. 🄲

Colourful fruit and vegetable stall in Vilafranca de Bonany

33 Vilafranca de Bonany

🏛 3,000. 🚍 🅿 Wed. 🎉 Festa de Meló (Sep).

The agricultural town of Vilafranca de Bonany lies on the road to Manacor. It is known for its colourful market stalls set along the highway. These sell peppers, sun-dried tomatoes and garlic, as well as fruit and vegetables grown in the local gardens. Also on offer are tiny doughnuts called *bunyelos*. The only historic building in town is the **Santa Barbara church** (1731–8).

Environs
About 2 km (1 mile) northeast, on top of Puig de Bonany (317 m/1,040 ft), is the **Ermita de Bonany** sanctuary. The monastery's stone cross was erected for Junipero Serra, who left from here in 1749 on a mission to California (*see p81*). The sanctuary is 17th century and was built as an act of thanksgiving for a good harvest – *bon any* or "good year". The modern church dates from 1925 and is entered via an imposing gate, decorated on top with ceramic tiles featuring portraits of St Paul and St Anthony. From the church forecourt you can see a splendid panorama of the central plains of Es Pla.

One kilometre (half a mile) northwest of Vilafranca de Bonany is **Els Calderers** – a landed estate established in the 17th century by the Veri family. The stately home is surrounded by fields and farm buildings. Today, parts of the estate are open to the public; these include the private chapel, the granary and the large kitchen. The rooms contain original furniture and are decorated with paintings, family photographs and *objets d'art*, all of which maintain the atmosphere of the former residence. The fire burning in the fireplace and the open piano give visitors the impression that the owners have only just stepped out.

🏛 **Els Calderers**
Tel 971 526 069. **Open** 10am–5:30pm daily. 🄲 Ⓦ elscalderers.com

③④ Felanitx

🏛 18,000. 🛈 Avinguda Cala Marçal 15, Porto Colom, 971 826 084. 🗓 Sun. 🎉 Fiesta San Joan Pelós (24 Jun).

From a distance, the busy little town of Felanitx looks as though it is surrounded by a wall with many turrets. As you approach, it becomes apparent that these are windmills built on the outskirts of town. Felanitx is the birthplace of the outstanding medieval architect Guillem Sagrera (1380–1456) and the highly original 20th-century painter Miquel Barceló.

This small agricultural town has a fine **13th-century church**. Sant Miquel's magnificent Renaissance-Baroque façade, approached by steep stairs, hides a building erected in 1248. It is also worth visiting Felanitx to taste the locally produced *sobrasada de porc negre* – spicy pork sausage – and to buy some of the ceramics made here.

Environs

About 5 km (3 miles) south-east, on top of the 400-m - (1,312-ft -) high hill, are the ruins of Castell de Santueri, an Arab castle remodelled in the 14th century by the kings of Aragón. The view from the ruins is a magnificent panorama of the surrounding area. The Santuari de Sant Salvador stands 4 km (2 miles) east of Felanitx, on top of Puig de Sant Salvador, the highest mountain of the Serres de Llevant.

Huge façade of Felanitx's main church

Giant cactus in the Botanicactus garden, near Santanyí

Founded in the 14th century, and remodelled in the 18th century, the sanctuary is an important place of pilgrimage. The view includes the south-eastern coast of Mallorca.

③⑤ Santanyí

🏛 13,000. 🛈 Perico Pomar 10, Cala d'Or, 971 657 463.

This old town is full of stone houses built from the local honey-coloured sandstone. The same sandstone was used in the building of the cathedral in Palma and Castell Bellver.

One of the old town gates, **Sa Porta**, in Plaça Port is a reminder of medieval times when the town was an important fortress defending southeastern Mallorca, and surrounded by several walls. Towering over the town is the vast church of **Sant Andreu**. The interior of this 18th-century church features a huge Rococo organ brought here from a Dominican monastery in Palma.

Environs

North of town, on top of the Puig Gros hill stands a 16th-century chapel with a beautiful picture of the Madonna. The **Santuari de Consolació** is accessed via stone steps, which have been climbed for centuries by footsore and weary pilgrims. Some 5 km (3 miles) east of Santanyí is **Cala Figuera**, with an unspoiled fishing harbour set in a bay that resembles a fjord.

The adjacent and equally picturesque **Cala Santanyí** bay is situated at the end of a rocky canyon with steep banks, over-grown with trees. Here, rising from the sea, is the **Es Pontas rock**. Six kilometres (4 miles) east is the **Botanicactus**, a garden which has nearly 400 species of cacti.

Rocky coastline in the Parc Natural Mondragó

③⑥ Parc Natural Mondragó

8 km (5 miles) east of Santanyí. **Tel** 971 181 022. **Open** 9am–4pm daily. 🅿 by reservation (971 642 067).

This relatively small, unspoiled area has wonderful footpaths and pretty country lanes and is an ideal destination for walking trips. The routes are marked and are generally easy-going. The coastline itself is rugged, but it is still possible to find small, sandy coves, the best of which are Mondragó, S'Amarador and Caló des Burgit. In the pine forest, which covers most of the park, there are small ponds and dunes.

③ Ses Salines

ℹ Gabriel Roca, 971 656 073.

Ses Salines is a modest little town that is sometimes overlooked by visitors. It owes its origin, wealth and name to the nearby saltworks. The **Salines de Llevant** are large salt lakes and marshes. This area is inhabited by numerous species of birds such as the spotted crane, marsh harrier, kestrel, warbler and hoopoe. During the migration season the marshes are visited by flocks of plover, avocet, tattler, godwit and osprey. There are many paths through the marshes, making them an excellent area for walking and cycling trips, particularly for birdwatchers.

Environs

Cap de Ses Salines is 3 km (2 miles) south of Ses Salines. This is the southernmost promontory of Mallorca. The view from the lighthouse is magnificent and encompasses the entire south coast of the island, as well as Cabrera Island.

Banys de Sant Joan de sa Font Santa lies 4 km (2 miles) northeast of Ses Salines. The local hot springs, with water temperatures rising as high as 38°C (100°F), have been known since the 15th century, when they were used to treat a variety of conditions, including leprosy. The local chapel dates from this period. The present bathhouse was built in 1845. Today, the waters are still believed to be beneficial and are used to treat rheumatism and a variety of respiratory ailments.

Campos, probably founded by the Romans, is situated 12 km (7 miles) from Ses Salines.

The town, rarely visited by tourists, is full of historic remains. The Neo-Classical church of Sant Julià (1858–73) features a painting, *Sant Crist de la Paciència*, by the 17th-century Spanish master Bartolomé Esteban Murillo; the Gothic retable is the work of Gabriel Mògera. The church has a small parish museum. The former Torre de Can Cos, which once guarded the town against pirate attacks, became incorporated into the present town hall in 1649. Markets are held here every Thursday and Saturday.

Some 10 km (6 miles) to the north of Ses Salines is **Ermita de Sant Blas**, which has a restored 13th-century chapel.

Lighthouse at the Cap de Ses Salines headland

③ Colònia de Sant Jordi

52 km (32 miles) east of Palma. ℹ Gabriel Roca, Ses Salines, 971 656 073.

The town of Colònia de Sant Jordi lies on the southern end of the island. It has a handful of modest hotels, a few restaurants, a pretty beach and an interesting harbour. Many people come here with the sole

Sa Ràpita beach, a favourite with windsurfers

purpose of catching a boat to nearby Cabrera Island (*see pp88–9*), which, according to Pliny, was the birthplace of the famous Carthaginian leader, Hannibal. The pleasure boats to Cabrera Island sail daily from May until mid-October.

The town's other main attraction is the nearby salt lake, Salines de S'Avall, from which huge quantities of salt were once extracted – the main source of the town's wealth.

Environs

One of Mallorca's most beautiful beaches is 7 km (4 miles) to the north, in **Es Trenc**, which can also be reached via a shorter route along the coast. This small but constantly developing resort is very popular with visitors to the southern coast of Mallorca. The 4-km (2-mile) stretch of beach can easily accommodate the large numbers of holidaymakers, and is not generally too busy.

Sa Ràpita is a small place near S'Estanyol de Migjorn. The local beach provides good conditions for windsurfing. In summer, the marina is also a popular place. The only historic remains are of the defence tower, which once guarded the coast against pirates. Equally beautiful beaches can be found to the south of Colònia de Sant Jordi. When they get too busy, try **Platja des ses Roquetes**.

🚢 **Excursions to Cabrera**
C/ Explanada del Port. **Tel** 971 649 034. ⬛ excursionsacabrera.es

Beach and harbour in Sa Ràpita, near Colònia de Sant Jordi

⓳ Cabrera Island National Park

Cabrera ("goat island") lies just 18 km (11 miles) from mainland Mallorca. A rocky, bare place and virtually uninhabited, it nevertheless has a rich history. It served as a prison camp during the Napoleonic Wars and was used as a base by Barbary pirates. Since 1991, Cabrera Island, together with an archipelago of 157 sq km (60 sq miles), has been designated a national park. This protection extends not only to rare species of plants, but also includes the surrounding marine life.

Es Castell
The 14th-century castle is one of the few reminders of the island's past. A small museum close to the jetty includes a history of the island.

Cala Santa Maria
In the course of a few hours, you can see the shore areas surrounding the bay. Exploring the interior requires permission from the park staff.

Asteriscus aquaticus
Though this plant is found on all the islands of the archipelago, Cabrera is home to some rare native plant species.

Cap de N'Ensiola
At the island's southwest tip is a lighthouse that can be reached via a winding road. Permission for this must be obtained from the park's office in Palma.

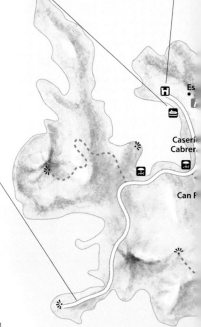

Es
Caseri
Cabrer
Can F

KEY

① **A memorial** was built for the French soldiers abandoned on Cabrera by the Spanish during the Napoleonic Wars. Of the 9,000 prisoners, only 4,000 survived.

0 kilometres   1

0 miles   1

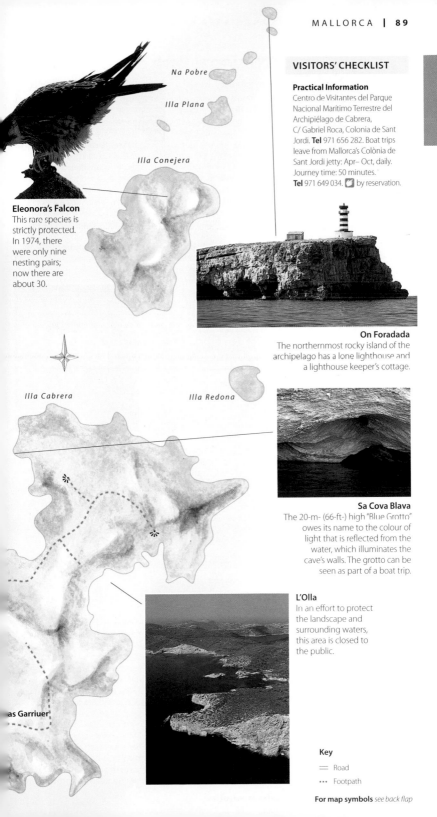

Na Pobre

Illa Plana

Illa Conejera

Eleonora's Falcon
This rare species is
strictly protected.
In 1974, there
were only nine
nesting pairs;
now there are
about 30.

VISITORS' CHECKLIST

Practical Information
Centro de Visitantes del Parque
Nacional Marítimo Terrestre del
Archipiélago de Cabrera,
C/ Gabriel Roca, Colonia de Sant
Jordi. **Tel** 971 656 282. Boat trips
leave from Mallorca's Colònia de
Sant Jordi jetty: Apr– Oct, daily.
Journey time: 50 minutes.
Tel 971 649 034. ⬛ by reservation.

On Foradada
The northernmost rocky island of the
archipelago has a lone lighthouse and
a lighthouse keeper's cottage.

Illa Cabrera

Illa Redona

Sa Cova Blava
The 20-m- (66-ft-) high "Blue Grotto"
owes its name to the colour of
light that is reflected from the
water, which illuminates the
cave's walls. The grotto can be
seen as part of a boat trip.

L'Olla
In an effort to protect
the landscape and
surrounding waters,
this area is closed to
the public.

as Garriuer

Key

═══ Road

••• Footpath

For map symbols *see back flap*

Sunday market in Llucmajor

⑩ Llucmajor

🏛 37,000. 🚌 *i* C/ Trencadors, Cor.
C/ Terral 23, S'Arenal, 971 445 142. 🏠
Wed, Fri & Sun. W visitllucmajor.com

Formerly the main town of the
southern region, Llucmajor has
long been associated with
Mallorca's shoemaking
industry and had a thriving
market in medieval times. It
was just outside Llucmajor's
walls, in 1349, that Pedro IV of
Aragón killed the last king of
Mallorca, Jaume III. The
monument standing at the
end of Passeig de Jaume III
commemorates the event.

The **town hall**, built in 1882,
is in the main square. Nearby is
the 18th-century church of
San Miquel, built over a 14th-
century church. The most prized
historic building in town is the
Franciscan **Església Conventual
de Sant Bonaventura**. This
17th-century church contains
many precious historic objects,
including an impressive
altarpiece (1597) painted
by Gaspar Oms.

⑪ Capocorb Vell

🚌 **Tel** 971 180 155.
Open 10am–5pm Fri–Wed. 🅿
W talaiotscapocorbvell.com

Mallorca has fewer prehistoric
remains than Menorca, but this
Talayotic settlement on a rocky
plateau on the southern coast

of the island is well
worth visiting. The
settlement was probably
established around
1000 BC. Originally, it
consisted of five *talayots*
(stone structures
resembling towers,
covered with a wooden
roof) and 28 smaller
dwellings. It is worth
taking a closer look at
the remains of the
Cyclopean walls,
reaching 4 m (13 ft) in
places, which would
have served as
protection for this
ancient village. Not
much is known about
the inhabitants of the
settlement, and the
function of some of the rooms is
unclear. The narrow underground
chamber, for instance, is too small
to be used for living quarters and
may have served as a ritual site.
A free leaflet, in English, provides
more information on these
fascinating remains and is
available at the site entrance.

The megaliths scattered
through this quiet area, amid
fields and fruit trees, were
declared a cultural heritage site
as early as 1931. Apart from a
restaurant and a small bar, there
are few other traces of modern
civilization here.

Environs
Some 5 km (3 miles) southeast
of Capocorb Vell lies **Cala Pi**.
This is a small cove with an
enticing sand beach. Several

Ruins of the prehistoric settlement in
Capocorb Vell

luxurious villas have sprung up
around here, well hidden
behind pine trees. During the
high season, many yachts drop
anchor here. The area is
dominated by a watchtower
(1659), which provides views of
the entire Badia de Palma.
About 7 km (4 miles) to the
south is **Cap Blanc**, which has a
lighthouse. From here there is
also a splendid view over the
coast towards Cabrera Island. A
large section of the peninsula is
used for military purposes, and
it is therefore important not to
stray from the route that leads
to the lighthouse.

Tree-shaded courtyard of the church at
Puig de Randa

⑫ Puig de Randa

8 km (5 miles) northeast of Llucmajor.
i Santuari de Nostra Senyora de
Cura: 971 660 994.

In the middle of the fertile
plains of Es Pla rises the
distinctive Puig de Randa hill
(549 m/1,800 ft), which provides
stunning views of the whole of
Mallorca. Ramon Llull *(see
opposite)* founded a hermitage
on top of this hill in the 13th
century and it was here that he
trained missionaries bound for
Africa and Asia. Nothing remains
of the original building, but Llull's
legacy has ensured that the site is
an important place for Catholics.

The monastery (the oldest part
of which dates from 1668) is a
popular destination for pilgrim-
ages, particularly those associated
with the blessing of the crops –
Benedición de los Frutos – on
the 4th Sunday after Easter.

Tucked under a steep cliff
face, **Santuari de Nostra Senyora**

de Gràcia is the first of the religious buildings you come to. The interior of the chapel is decorated with beautiful majolica tiles. A little further up the hill is the 16th-century **Santuari de Sant Honorat**. This hermitage houses a courtyard that is filled with ancient trees. The passage to the church is decorated with tiles depicting the sanctuary's history.

The culmination of the pilgrimage is the **Santuari de Nostra Senyora de Cura**, which is on the site where Llull once lived. The gate in the wall surrounding the monastery is 17th-century and opens onto a courtyard built of typical golden Mallorcan sandstone. The monastery, much of which is fairly modern, houses a library and a study centre. The stained-glass windows of the church depict the most important moments of Llull's life.

🅴 Algaida

🚌 🅰 Fri. 🎪 Sant Honorat (16 Jan), Sant Jaume (25 Jul).

Most people pass through the outskirts of this small town on their way to Puig de Randa. If you like churches, however, it is worth stopping here in order to visit the Gothic church of **Sant Pere i Sant Pau**, with its ornamental gargoyles.

Environs
The odd-looking castle on the road from Palma to Manacor dates from the 1960s and

Ceramic sign of Ca'n Gordiola, advertised outside a Palma shop

One of several water slides in Aqualand El Arenal

houses **Ca'n Gordiola**, a glassworks, museum and shop. Here, you can see skilled glass-blowers producing the pale blue and green glass that has been produced on the island for hundreds of years. On the first floor is a museum exhibiting items collected by several generations of the Gordiola family.

Some 9 km (6 miles) to the east is **Montuïri**. The town, built on a hill, is famous for its agricultural produce. Nineteen of the original 24 windmills still stand as testimony to the town's former glory. Just outside Montuïri, on the road that leads to Pina, is one of the best-preserved Mallorcan Talayotic remains – **Son Fornés**. This prehistoric settlement has two *talayots* and includes nine dwellings, which were used up until Roman times.

🅴 S'Arenal

🚌 🛈 C7 Terral 23. **Tel** 971 669 162. 🅰 Thu.

A little to the east of Palma, S'Arenal offers several kilometres of sandy beaches. A tree-lined boulevard runs along the shore, with bars, restaurants, nightclubs and shops. A series of stainless-steel beach bars stretches along the coast. These *balnearios* are numbered: No. 1 is near the harbour, No. 15 is by the Ca'n Pastilla marina (a miniature "tourist train" travels to the marina). In peak season, the resort's narrow alleys throb with life, day and night.

S'Arenal's harbour provides mooring places for yachts. On the outskirts of town is **Aqualand El Arenal**, a children's paradise of pools, water slides and playgrounds.

🅰 **Aqualand El Arenal**
S'Arenal. **Tel** 971 440 000. **Open** May & Jun & Sep 10am–5pm daily; Jul & Aug: 10am–6pm daily 🚲 🆆 **aqualand.es**

Ramon Llull

This prominent Mallorcan was born in Palma to a noble family around 1232. During his youth he lived life to excess. Quite why he changed his ways is

Statue of Ramon Llull in Palma

not known, though legends abound. One story has it that he abandoned court life after seeing a vision of the crucified Christ. At the age of 30 he became a monk and devoted the rest of his days to the Catholic faith. He became a religious scholar, founded a missionary school and wrote over 260 works of theology, philosophy, physics, chemistry and warfare. During the final 30 years of his life, he travelled around the world. He is believed to have been stoned to death in Algeria in 1315.

Mallorca's Beaches

Mallorca has nearly 80 beaches. The best are around Badia de Palma and to the north and northeast of the island. These are great for swimming and sunbathing and are very popular during the peak season. Some of the island's best beaches have been incorporated into larger resorts and include restaurants, fun parks, water sports and beachside bars. It is still possible to find more secluded beaches and coves, however, though these tend to have fewer facilities and may be difficult to reach.

⑥ Ses Illetes

🚌 ⁄⁄ ▢ ▯

This small beach, barely 120 m (390 ft) long, is off the beaten track. Despite that, and the lack of facilities, it remains popular.

④ Palmanova

🚌 ⁄⁄ ▢ 🏠 ♿

One of the best beaches on the Badia de Palma. Nearby buildings are hidden among dense greenery; the Serra de Tramuntana hills can be seen in the distance. It is a good base for family holidays.

⑤ Portals Nous

🚌 ⁄⁄ ▢ ♿

This beach, typical of the Balearic Islands, is on a long narrow cove. The thrills and spills of Marineland are nearby *(see p63).*

③ Magaluf

🚌 ➕ ⁄⁄ ▢ 🏠 ♿

Magaluf's beach has long been popular with visitors, and the town – one of the oldest resorts in Mallorca – is full of restaurants, bars and clubs. Another attraction is the nearby Aqualand Magaluf (shown).

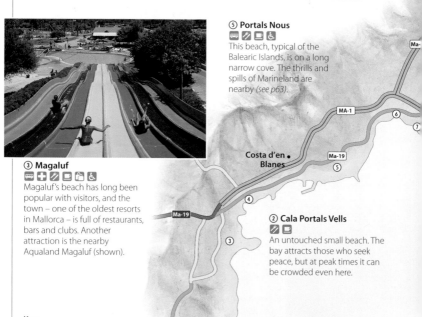

Costa d'en • Blanes

Ma-19

Ma-1

Ma-

② Cala Portals Vells

⁄⁄ ▢

An untouched small beach. The bay attracts those who seek peace, but at peak times it can be crowded even here.

Ma-19

① El Mago

⁄⁄ ▢

This small beach on the bay is favoured by nudists. This is one of three nudist beaches in this part of the bay.

Key

▬ Motorway/highway

▬ Major road

▬ Scenic route

▭ Other road

⑦ **Cala Major**
🚌 🅿 ☐ ♿

This small bay is lined with houses and hotels. The golden beach is hardly secluded, but it is one of the nicest in this area.

⑧ **Palma**
🚌 ➕ 🅿 ☐ 🏠 ♿

Inhabitants of the Balearic Islands' capital make the most of C'an Pere Antoni beach, or other beaches along the Badia de Palma.

⑨ **Ca'n Pastilla**
🚌 ➕ 🅿 ☐ 🏠 ♿

A miniature train runs from here to S'Arenal from March to October. The local beach is similar to Platja de Palma, with umbrellas and deckchairs for hire and a playground.

⑩ **Platja de Palma**
🚌 ➕ 🅿 ☐ 🏠 ♿

At the height of the holiday season this 5-km- (3-mile-) long beach becomes exceptionally crowded. Behind the row of cafés and bars next to the beach are hotels, apartments and clubs.

MA-1130

MA-13

Ma-11

Ma-13A

• Pont d'Inca

MA-3013

Son Ferriol

⑧

MA-19

⑨

MA-6010

Sant Francesc •

⑩

⑪

0 km   1
0 miles   1

⑪ **S'Arenal**
🚌 ➕ 🅿 ☐ 🏠 ♿

S'Arenal lies at the eastern end of Platja de Palma, and is the most popular resort along this part of the coast. Its main attraction, apart from the beach, is Aqualand El Arenal fun park with its pools and rides.

MENORCA

Menorca is the second largest of the Balearic Islands and has low-key, family-friendly resorts and nearly as many beaches as Mallorca and Ibiza combined. Situated furthest from the mainland, it is one of the quieter islands and has escaped most of the side-effects of package holidays. Its small towns and villages appear to be havens of tranquillity, even at the peak of the season.

Travelling across Menorca, the variations in landscape are perhaps less obvious than those of Mallorca. The changes are more gradual, as red-soil and sandstone farmlands become pine-clad ravines, and small, sheltered coves alternate with steep, rocky shores.

Most of the Balearic Islands' megalithic monuments from the Talayotic period are found on this island, including a good number of the cone-shaped towers (talayots) which give the period its name. As with the other islands, Menorca has had its share of visiting conquerors, including the Greeks, the Romans and, during medieval times, the Arabs who defended the island until 1287. During the 18th century, the island was ruled by the English and French in turn, before becoming a Republican stronghold during the Spanish Civil War.

The two oldest and largest towns in Menorca are Maó and Ciutadella; both are full of historic buildings. The island's capital, Maó (often referred to by its Spanish name of Mahón), is the best natural harbour in this part of the Mediterranean. Ciutadella, Menorca's former capital, is situated on the northwestern end of the island and also has a natural harbour. When travelling around Menorca you can appreciate the charm of the island's unhurried lifestyle. Its inhabitants are attached to their traditions and customs – for instance, unlike the rest of Spain, they prefer local gin to wine. Fiesta celebrations are particularly lively.

Colourful traditional folk dancers in Maó accompanied by live music

◄ Brilliant blue waters at Cala Macarella, Menorca

Exploring Menorca

Menorca is sometimes referred to by the locals, jokingly, as "the bit between Maó and Ciutadella". The island mainly attracts those looking for peace and relaxation, such as older visitors and families with young children, who wish to avoid the late-night clubs and bars found elsewhere. The island, proclaimed a biosphere reserve by UNESCO, is also a favourite with nature lovers. It has more than 70 beaches – the south has stretches of white sand, while the north has several inlets. In Fornells you can savour *caldereta de llagosta* – a delicious lobster stew for which the island is famous. Those who enjoy historic monuments can also find much of interest. The vast numbers of Talayotic structures, and the palaces and churches of Ciutadella and Maó, are all worth visiting. One way to explore the island is on horseback.

Locator Map

Lighthouse at Cap d'Artrutx

Getting There

The best way to travel to Menorca is by air. During the high season there are flights from many European countries and other regions of Spain. The most reliable way to travel out of season is via Palma or Barcelona. The airport is near Maó and has good transport links with major towns on the island. You can also travel to Menorca by ferry from Palma or Barcelona. The main road on the island connects Maó with Ciutadella. Minor roads branch from it, running towards the northern and southern coasts. There are no problems reaching large towns and resorts, but some small, attractive places maybe difficult to get to. It is best to travel around the island by hire car, as some of the smaller towns and villages have no bus service.

Sights at a Glance

For hotels and restaurants in this region see pp150–51 and pp159–61

Key

— Major road

— Minor road

— Scenic route

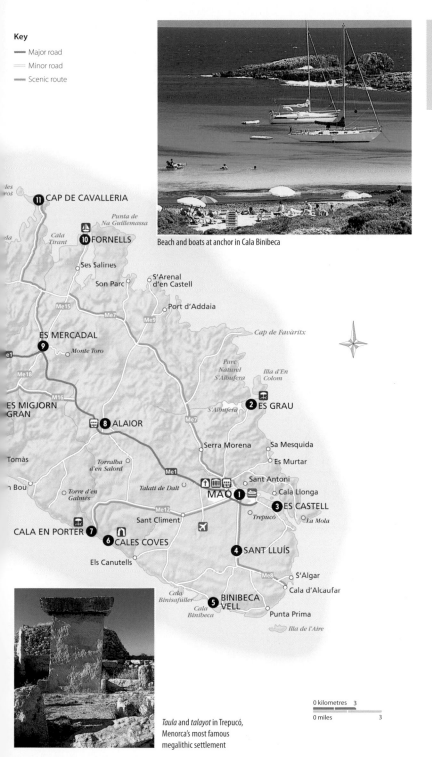

Beach and boats at anchor in Cala Binibeca

11 CAP DE CAVALLERIA

*Punta de
Na Guillemassa*

*Cala
Tirant*

10 FORNELLS

Ses Salines

Son Parc

S'Arenal
d'en Castell

Me15

Me7

Me9

Port d'Addaia

Cap de Favàritx

ES MERCADAL

9

Monte Toro

e1

*Parc
Naturel
S'Albufera*

*Illa d'En
Colom*

Me18

2 ES GRAU

M16

S'Albufera

ES MIGJORN
GRAN

8 ALAIOR

Me7

Serra Morena

Sa Mesquida

Tomàs

*Torralba
d'en Salord*

Es Murtar

n Bou

*Torre d'en
Galmés*

Talatí de Dalt

Me1

Sant Antoni

MAÓ **1**

Cala Llonga

3 ES CASTELL

CALA EN PORTER **7**

Me12

Sant Climent

Trepucó

La Mola

6 CALES COVES

4 SANT LLUÍS

Els Canutells

Me8

S'Algar

Cala d'Alcaufar

*Cala
Binisafúller*

5 BINIBECA
VELL

*Cala
Binibeca*

Punta Prima

Illa de l'Aire

Taula and *talayot* in Trepucó,
Menorca's most famous
megalithic settlement

0 kilometres   3

0 miles   3

For map symbols *see back flap*

❶ Maó

In some respects, Maó (or Mahón in Spanish) is like a small, provincial town. A pretty place, it has a population of almost 30,000 and lies on the steep, southern shore of a bay that is one of the best natural harbours in the world. The remains of the old city walls, several beautiful churches, colourful Spanish mansions and Georgian town houses make it a fascinating place to explore. At the same time, it is the island's capital and is a city of culture – its Teatre Principal was the first opera house in Spain when it opened in 1829.

Exploring Maó

When exploring Maó, it is best to start from Plaça d'Espanya. Here, and around the neighbouring squares, are the town's main historic buildings. The whole district is dominated by the vast Baroque church of **Santa Maria**. For most people, however, the real pleasure is in strolling along the narrow alleys of old Maó and soaking up its unique atmosphere. Some of Maó's streets have restricted car access, turning them into virtual pedestrian precincts. Stopping for a rest in one of the numerous cafés is an experience to savour.

🏛 Església del Carme

Plaça Carme.
This imposing Baroque church began life as a Carmelite convent in 1751. In 1835, the convent was confiscated by the sState and the building was substantially restored in 1941 after being damaged during the Spanish Civil War. The vast interior of the former church, one of the biggest in Maó, is preserved in a Neo-Classical style, but despite its opulence it gives an impression of emptiness. The complex,

Colourful houses built on the high escarpment in Plaça Espanya

mostly closed to visitors, occupies the vast quarter between Plaça Carme and Plaça de la Miranda. The square behind the monastery offers a beautiful view over Cala Sergo.

🏛 Mercat Sa Plaça

Plaça Carme. **Open** 9am–9pm Mon–Sat.
Maó's famous town market (Mercat) takes place in a series of renovated monastery buildings next to Església del Carme. The cool cloister has been turned into a picturesque

fruit and vegetable market, where *queso Mahón*, one of Spain's most delicious cheeses, is much in evidence. Here, you can also buy meat and other food products, as well as souvenirs. The rows of market stalls set under the figures of the saints and other religious symbols provide a strange contrast.

🏛 Museu Hernández Mora

Claustre del Carme 5, Plaça de la Miranda. **Tel** 971 350 597.
Open 10am–1pm Mon–Sat.
The Menorcan historian Hernández Mora (1902–84) donated his collection of antique furniture, sea charts, paintings, engravings and other works of art to the town. The exhibits provide a fascinating slice of Menorcan history during the 18th and 19th centuries, when the French and English ruled the island in turn, as well as information from the 20th century.

🏛 Plaça Espanya

Plaça Espanya is the central square of old Maó. A busy **fish market** occupies a circular bastion on the north side of the square and offers countless varieties of fish, squid, shellfish and other seafood. From here steps lead down to Maó's waterfront.

Fundació Teatre Principal

Costa d'en Deià 40. **Tel** 971 355 603.
W teatremao.com
Maó's theatre opened in 1829, and beats the Liceu in Barcelona and Teatro Real in Madrid to be Spain's first opera house. Built by the Italian singer and architect, Giovanni Palagi, it was often chosen by the big Spanish opera companies to premiere their Spanish tours. Today, it is used mainly as a cinema, but it also hosts some concerts and cultural events, including an annual musical festival in July and August and a week of opera in June and December.

🏛 Santa Maria

Plaça Constitució. **Open** 8am & 7pm Mon–Sat; 8am, 11am, noon, 8:30pm Sun.
This church standing near the town hall was begun in 1287 on

Narrow alleys leading away from Maó's old centre

Façade of the town hall opposite Església de Santa Maria

the site of a mosque, after the defeat of the Moors by Alfonso III. It was rebuilt in a Neo-Classical style in the 18th century and remodelled several times after that, although the large interior has retained much of its Catalan Gothic austerity and is devoid of any ornamentation, with only the transept and the vaults featuring rich Baroque decorations. The most striking features of the interior are the Rococo main altarpiece and the vast organ, built in 1806 by the Swiss maker Johann Kyburz and imported from Barcelona with the help of the British. It is a mighty piece with four keyboards and 3,120 pipes. Look out for the figures of trumpet-blowing angels.

Ajuntament
Plaça Constitució.

The town hall was built in 1613 and its façade *(left)* was remodelled in 1789, giving it a typically Spanish appearance. It features an ornamental clock, presented to the town by Richard Kane, the first British governor of Menorca. Inside, the walls are lined with portraits of local notables, French and Spanish governors and, still hanging to this day, portraits of the British monarch George III alongside Queen Charlotte.

Harbour

The best way to arrive in Maó is by sea so that you catch your first sight of its magnificent natural harbour from the prow of a ship. Several centuries ago the famous Genoese admiral Andrea Doria concluded that June, July, August and Mahón were the best ports in the Mediterranean, by which he meant that outside the safe sailing season of the summer months, it was prudent to seek shelter here.

Today, the tranquil atmosphere of the harbour makes it difficult to imagine a time when this was once a vast British naval base. Tours

of the harbour in a glass-bottomed boat leave regularly from Maó and Es Castell.

Maó, perched on steep slopes, seen from the harbour

Mao

① Església del Carme
② Mercat Sa Plaça
③ Museu Hernández Mora
④ Plaça Espanya
⑤ Teatre Principal
⑥ Santa Maria
⑦ Ajuntament
⑧ Harbour

0 metres 200
0 yards 200

Further Afield

Venturing outside Maó's centre involves a pleasant stroll along narrow avenues lined with quaint houses, and passing all the main historic sights of the town. The most interesting include the magnificent chapel of the Immaculate Conception in the church of **Sant Francesc**, built in an ornamental Spanish Baroque style. The **Museu de Menorca** is also well worth a visit if only for its extensive range of items from the Talayotic period. Another interesting place to see is the **gin distillery**.

For a longer hike, Maó is a good starting point for a walk along the coast – head north to **Cala Llonga**, or south right up to **Port de Malborough**.

Some of the Xoriguer distillery's ancient gin-making equipment

🏭 Xoriguer Distillery

Andén de Poniente 91.
Tel 971 362 197.

Gin production on the island is a legacy of the British occupation, although its local brands taste rather different to the ones currently produced in Britain. You can acquaint yourself with the gin distillation process by visiting the Xoriguer distillery, close to the harbour steps, which was founded in the 18th century.

As well as juniper, which is imported from the Pyrenees, gin contains a number of other aromatic herbs. Menorcan gin is sold only in Menorca and in a handful of restaurants in Mallorca.

The distillery also produces various liqueurs, including the

Gobierno Militar, one of the most magnificent buildings in Maó

hierbas that are believed by some to have therapeutic properties. All these drinks can be tasted on site, and of course bought in the shop.

🏛 Sant Francesc

Plaça d'es Monestir. **Open** 6:30pm daily, 10am, 7:30pm Sun.

The church of Sant Francesc, with its light-coloured Baroque façade (1719–92), stands at the end of **Carrer de Isabel II**.

The church's imposing interior has a vast, dark nave with a soaring Gothic altar at the end of it. The church's most outstanding feature is its octagonal chapel of the Immaculate Conception built in a fanciful Spanish Baroque style and decorated with stucco garlands of vine and roses. This is the most beautiful example of Baroque ornamentation in Menorca. Its creator is believed to be the famous painter, sculptor and architect Francesco Herrara.

Adjoining the south side of Sant Francesc is the monumental structure of the monastery, with an arcaded

Ornament from Sant Francesc

courtyard. Currently it houses the Museu de Menorca.

🏛 Museu de Menorca

Avda Dr Guàrdia s/n. **Tel** 971 350 955.
Open Apr–Oct: 10am–2pm & 6–8:30pm Tue–Sat, 10am–2pm Sun; Nov–Mar: 9:30am–2pm Tue–Fri, 10am–2pm Sat & Sun. **Closed** public hols. 🅿

This museum occupies the former cloisters of a Franciscan monastery. The collection includes works of art and archaeological relics. Many of the exhibits date from prehistoric times, and there is an extensive selection from the Talayotic period, as well as Roman, Byzantine and Arabic artifacts. Among the most interesting exhibits are a bronze statuette of a bull, Punic jewellery and some huge amphorae.

🏛 Gobierno Militar

Carrer de Isabel II. 🖂
The Military Governor's House and army head-quarters are housed in one of Maó's most beautiful buildings. The palace was built in 1768, during the second British occupation. The building is still used by the army and can therefore be seen only from the outside, though the arcaded courtyard is well worth a peek.

🏛 Plaça Bastió

This small, irregular-shaped square has limited vehicle access, and serves as a good place for children to let off steam. Visitors who are fatigued by sightseeing often stop here for a rest.

Courtyard of the former Franciscan monastery

At the north corner of the square stands the medieval **Portal de Sant Roc** which is named after Saint Roch, a 14th-century hermit who was believed to be able to ward off the plague. Flanked by bulky twin turrets and a connecting arch, it is one of the few remaining fragments of Maó's medieval walls and was once the exit point from the city onto the road leading to Alaior. The fortifications did not stop Barbarossa from plundering the town, which he took in 1535, destroying most of the city's defences.

Portal de Sant Roc, viewed from the street leading to the town hall

Plaça Esplanada
Plaça Esplanada, with its flower-beds shaded by pine trees, is the biggest square in the city and was once used as a military parade ground. Now, it provides a popular meeting place for the locals, especially at the weekends. The ice-cream sellers and swings make it equally popular with local children. There is a market on Tuesday and Saturday mornings.

The square is flanked on three sides by low buildings, many of them housing bars, cafés and restaurants. The western section of the square features a huge Civil War memorial erected during the days of Franco. At the back of the square are army barracks built during the first British occupation of the island and now used by the Spanish Army.

Buses on their way to other island towns stop near here.

Mayonnaise
Following his victory over the British, Louis-François-Armand de Vignerot du Plessis, a cousin of Cardinal Richelieu, stopped at a local inn where he was served a tasty sauce. On his return to Paris, he introduced the sauce to the royal court, where the new garnish was an instant hit. Already known on the islands as *salsa mahonesa*, it became known in France as *mayonnaise*.

Ateneu Científic Literari i Artístic de Maó
Rovellada de Dalt 25. **Tel** 971 360 553. **Open** 4–9:30pm Mon–Fri. **Closed** Sat.
Menorca's Centre of Culture and Science has a collection of local ceramics, natural history exhibits (shells, birds, etc.), maps and charts, a library and permanent exhibitions of works by Spanish artists Pasqual Calbó, Màrius Verdaguer and Juan Vives Llull.

Sant Antoni
C/ S'Arraval, 32. **Tel** 971 366 854. **Open** 6–9pm Mon–Fri.
The 17th-century church of St Anthony was closed after it was pillaged during the Civil War. Following its restoration, it is now a venue for cultural events and exhibitions held by the Sa Nosta Foundation.

Es Freginal
The park is a green oasis in the middle of town. During high season it serves as a venue for nightly cultural events. It also provides a stage for musicians taking part in the annual jazz festival.

Environs
About 2 km (1 mile) east of Maó, on the opposite side of the bay, are two swanky suburbs – **Sant Antoni** and **Cala Llonga**. A short distance further, at the end of the headland, stands the vast **La Mola** fortress, guarding the entrance to the harbour. During the days of Franco it was used as a jail for political prisoners.

Near Sant Antoni is the stately home of **Golden Farm** – a beautiful example of Menorcan Palladian architecture. Admiral Nelson is reputed to have first met his mistress Lady Hamilton here, although this is unlikely. Inside is a collection of mementos associated with the couple and an extensive library. The house is not open to the public.

Es Mutar, 9 km (6 miles) to the northeast, is a charming village of white houses standing at the foot of a rocky crag, on the shores of a bay. Neighbouring **Sa Mesquida** lies further along this rocky shoreline. The village is dominated by a well-preserved watchtower.

Plaça Esplanada, where locals come to relax

Lush shores of S'Albufera's Es Grau

❷ Es Grau

6 km (4 miles) north of Maó.

This small fishing village, fringed by dunes and pine forests, lies on the bay with a wide, sandy, horseshoe-shaped beach. Its safe shallow water is perfect for families with young children. At the weekend, the place becomes busier with day-trippers from Maó. From here you can take a cruise boat to nearby **Illa d'En Colom**, which has some nice beaches, the best of them being S'Arenal des Moro.

West of Es Grau is the fresh water lagoon, S'Albufera, the largest stretch of marshland on the island. The **Parc Natural S'Albufera**, where hunting and fishing are prohibited, is a UNESCO biosphere reserve and a magnificent area for hiking or birdwatching.

❸ Es Castell

2 km (1 mile) southeast of Maó.

Es Castell, once known as Villa Carlos, is a former military outpost. Originally called Georgetown, it was established in 1771 by the British and named for George III. The Georgian houses surrounding Plaça d'Esplanada serve as reminders of the British presence. One of the barrack buildings, **Cuartel de Cala Corp**, houses a small military museum with a collection of weapons and uniforms. Another sight is the parish church of **Nostra Senyora del Roser**.

🏛 Museo Militar de Menorca
Plaça Esplanada 19. **Tel** 971 362 100. **Open** varies. 🏛

Environs
Illa Pinto was the site of the main British Navy base on the island, built in the 18th century. The local chapel is dedicated to Virgen del Camen, the patron saint of fishermen and the Spanish Navy. **Illa del Rei** is where Alfonso III landed in 1287 during the Reconquest. **Illa Plana**, the smallest island on the bay, has the remains of a quarantine centre built in 1490 for those arriving at the island. **Illa Llazaret**, the largest of the islands, situated at the entrance to the bay, was once a peninsula, until it was cut off from the mainland by the St George Canal in the early 1900s. On the nearby headland are the remains of **Fort San Felip**, a 16th-century fortress that once guarded the southern entrance to Maó's harbour. In its day, the fortress was one of the most highly advanced systems of defence in Europe and could house an entire garrison of soldiers underground. It was destroyed by the Spanish in 1782 and now only its ruins remain. On the opposite side of the bay, near the village of Sant Esteve, is **Fort Malborough**. Built by the British to back up Fort San Felip, it has since been restored and now

French honeysuckle

houses a museum and has a number of displays (some with loud sound effects) on Menorca's military history.

❹ Sant Lluís

5 km (3 miles) south of Maó.

This quaint little town, consisting of a square, a church and a few dozen whitewashed houses, was built by the French during the Seven Years' War (1756–63), as a quarters for Breton sailors. The French coat of arms on the church façade stands as a reminder of those days.

A windmill, **Moli de Dalt**, at the town's entrance, was built in 1762. Today, it is the only working windmill on the island and serves as the town's symbol. Next to it is a small museum with a collection of farm implements. The road into town bypasses the centre and heads towards the resorts of S'Algar, Cala d'Alcaufar, Punta Prima, Biniancolla, Binibeca Vell and Cap d'en Font.

Environs
Trepucó is a prehistoric site with a well-preserved *taula*. In the seaside villages of S'Algar and Cala d'Alcaufar, hotels stand side by side with fishermen's cottages. **Punta Prima** is the largest local resort. From here you have the view of the uninhabited island of **Illa de l'Aire**, with its lighthouse. West of town is a guard tower built by the Spaniards in the 18th century.

Colourful houses and apartments in Es Castell

Prehistoric Menorca

Menorca is exceptionally rich in megalithic structures. Most of the remains date from the Talayotic period – a civilization that flourished between 2000 and 1000 BC. The period derives its name from the *talayots* (from *atalaya*, the Arabic word for a watch-tower), the stone structures that are dotted around the island, mostly in former settlements. There are various theories as to what their original purpose was – they may have been used as defensive towers, burial sites or storehouses.

Huge *talayot* in the Trepucó settlement

Types of Structures

The ancient stone structures scattered throughout Menorca (and to a lesser extent found in Mallorca) fall into three main categories: *taulas*, *talayots* and *navetas*.

Taulas (table) consists of two slabs of rock, one placed on top of the other in a "T" formation. Some are up to 4.5 m (15 ft) high. Suggestions as to their original function range from a sacrificial altar to a roof support.

Talayots are circular or square buildings. Their purpose is a mystery – they may have been tombs, guard-houses, meeting places or even dwellings.

Navetas, shaped like an upturned boat or a pyramid, were probably built as a sepulchre or a dwelling. At least 10 of them remain in Menorca.

Spectacular 3-m- (10-ft-) high *taula* at Talati de Dalt settlement

Megalithic Sites

Menorca has an estimated 1,600 megalithic sites. Talayotic remains can be seen all over the island, usually in rural areas, but they are more highly concentrated on the plains of the more fertile south.

White houses and steeple in Binibeca Vell

❺ Binibeca Vell

9 km (6 miles) south of Maó.

Binibeca Vell stands out amid the similarity of many of Menorca's southern seaside resorts. Also known as *Poblat de Pescadors* ("Fishermen's Village"), it was built as a resort development in 1972 to resemble a traditional Menorcan coastal fishing village. It has whitewashed, two-storey houses, wooden balconies and a maze of streets that are so narrow you can touch the buildings on both sides with outstretched arms. The blaze of white walls, small patios and lush gardens enhance the Mediterranean atmosphere with a touch of Eastern influence. The "village" even has a church steeple, though no church. Nearby are a number of pleasant coves and beaches, including **Cala Binibeca**, **Cala Binisafúller** and the smallest beach in Menorca – **Es Caló Blanc**.

Environs
The nearby resorts lack any distinguishing features, apart from the beaches and their associated attractions, so it is worth taking a trip to the village of **Sant Climent**, which has a small market and lovely 19th-century church. Sant Climent also has a venue, the Restaurant-bar Casino, which puts on jazz concerts twice a week. These concerts are popular, as long as you can hear the music above the noise from the nearby international airport. Nearby **Torelló**, right on the edge of the airport, has a *talayot* with aircraft warning lights!

❻ Cales Coves

11 km (7 miles) west of Maó.
🚌 Sant Clement.

This complex of prehistoric caves is best seen from the sea. Carved in the cliffs above a picturesque bay, the caves date from the Neolithic era. During the Talayotic period, the caves were used solely as burial chambers. Later they became the site of pagan rituals. On the shore are the remains of a Roman harbour (some of the "newest" caves have Roman inscriptions). Nearby is a small beach.

❼ Cala en Porter

15 km (9 miles) west of Maó.

The seaside resort of Cala en Porter is one of Menorca's oldest holiday towns and is a sprawl of virtually identical holiday villas. Nevertheless, it provides good tourist facilities, including one of the loveliest beaches on the island, which is accessible via winding stairs and suitable for children. Its most unusual attraction is **Cova d'en Xoroi**, a huge cave, situated halfway down a steep cliff, which consists of several large chambers and tunnels. It has now been turned into a nightclub.

Environs
About 15 km (9 miles) northwest is the resort of **Son Bou**, with the ruins of an early Christian basilica (5th–6th century AD). The cliffs hide a number of caves that have been cut into them.

🏴 **Cova d'en Xoroi**
Tel 971 377 236. **Open** timings vary, please check website. 🈯
🆆 **covadenxoroi.com**

❽ Alaior

🚌 🚶 Sant Llorenç (weekend after 10 Aug). 🆆 **alaior.org**

This market town, situated on a hill along the road from Maó to Ciutadella, is famous for its production of exquisite

Cala en Porter, one of the loveliest beaches in Menorca

Restaurant set in an old windmill in Es Mercadal

Menorcan cheeses. This is the dairy capital of Menorca (the island is also famous for its ice cream), with the biggest factories producing the famous *queso Mahón*, a white, half-fat cheese made of pasteurized cow's milk with added sheep's milk that gives it its distinctive flavour.

Besides buying cheese, you could also visit the fortified Baroque parish church of **Santa Eulàlia** (1674–90). The Munt de l'Angel **watchtower** stands on a hill behind the church and provides a beautiful view of the area. The huge fiesta celebrated on the day of St Lawrence includes riding shows, parades and horse races through the streets of the town.

Environs
Torralba d'en Salord, one of Mallorca's biggest Talayotic settlements, is situated along the road to Cala en Porter, about 3 km (2 miles) from Alaior. The local *taula* is one of the best-preserved and the tallest on the island. The rectangular temple has also survived in good condition. A bronze statuette of a bull discovered on this site can now be seen in the Museu de Menorca, in Maó *(see p100)*.

Some 5 km (3 miles) to the south is **Torre d'en Galmés**, another settlement dating from the Talayotic period, which has a range of buildings including three *talayots*.

❾ Es Mercadal
🚗 🏠 Sun. 🎭 Sant Martí (3rd Sun in Jul).

Es Mercadal lies at the very heart of Menorca, along the Maó–Ciutadella road. Founded in the 14th century, the town has been largely overlooked by tourism and earns its keep through farming and a number of local industries. The town itself is charming, with trailing bougainvillea and the pretty 18th-century parish church of **Sant Martí**. Es Mercadal is known for its excellent Menorcan cuisine and you may like to stop for a snack or meal in one of its pleasant small cafés or in

Detail from the façade of Alaior church

Ca n'Aguedet, at Carrer de Lepanto 30, a restaurant that is very popular with the locals.

Environs
Some 3 km (2 miles) east, the convent of **Monte Toro** was built in 1670 on the steep hill of Monte Toro, which at 350 m (1,148 ft) is the highest point in Menorca. Occupied by the nuns of a Franciscan Order, it is regarded as the spiritual centre of Menorca and an ancient centre of pilgrimage.

Inside this 17th-century church is a statue of the Black Madonna – Verge del Toro – set within the main altarpiece, which depicts the Virgin Mary in a golden crown, holding the infant Jesus in her arms.

According to local tradition, the statue of the Virgin Mary has been worshipped here since the 13th century. These days, pilgrims visit Monte Toro, particularly on the first Sunday in May, to participate in the *Festa de la Verge del Toro*. Following mass in the church, the pilgrims then descend the stairs leading to Es Mercadal on their knees.

The old fortress has a military surveillance station. Nearby stands a huge stone statue of Christ, commemorating the Spaniards killed during the colonial war in Morocco.

Some 6 km (4 miles) northeast is **Son Parc** – the only golf course on the island.

Caldereta de Llagosta
This delicious lobster stew is the speciality of the northern regions on Menorca. Fresh lobsters are brought in every morning by local fishermen. The best stews are served in Fornells, which is famous for its seafood. The dish is extremely expensive but absolutely delicious. One popular way to enjoy it is to eat the gravy with bread, treating it as a soup, and have the lobster with mayonnaise as a main course.

Tempting lobster stew

Harbour and yacht marina in Fornells

⑩ Fornells

📧 🎭 Fiesta de San Diego de Alcalá (13 Nov).

A picturesque fishing village, Fornells is situated 10 km (6 miles) north of Es Mercadal. During the summer season luxury yachts moor side by side with the fishing boats. The place has some excellent seafood restaurants. The local speciality is *caldereta de llagosta (see p105)* and it is thought to be so good

here that former King Juan Carlos frequently sailed over in his yacht from Mallorca just to eat in one of the waterfront restaurants. Once Fornells was a major port and you can still see the remains of fortifications built as a defence against Arab and Turkish pirates. At the entrance to the harbour is a huge round watchtower. The village has no beach, but offers excellent facilities for diving, sailing and windsurfing.

In high season there are cruises to the small island of **Illa des Ravells**, with its ruins of an old English fort. Boat trips can also be taken to **Illa dels Porros** and to the cape of **Na Guillemassa**, which has some interesting caves.

Environs
West of Fornells is **Cala Tirant** with a red sand beach. On the

east coast of the bay are luxury villas surrounded by masses of colourful flowers, shrubs and cacti. The view from here extends to Cap de Cavalleria.

Cap de Cavalleria lighthouse rising above the rocks

⑪ Cap de Cavalleria

Cap De Cavalleria is situated 13 km (8 miles) to the north of Es Mercadal. This is the northernmost point of Menorca

Menorca's Beaches

Menorca has fewer easily accessible beaches than Mallorca or Ibiza. The best ones are to be found at the eastern end of the south coast. These are small, sandy beaches, tucked away in coves. There is an increasing number of beaches being developed west of Santa Galdana, and the local resorts of Son Xoriguer and Cala en Bosch are gaining popularity. Beaches on the northeastern coast are also popular.

② **Els Canutells**
A golden beach lies at the end of a narrow bay that cuts deep into the land. Small beaches on the eastern part of the bay are also good places for swimming.

① **Son Bou**
Some 3 km (2 miles) long, Son Bou is the longest beach in Menorca. At its eastern end are the ruins of an early Christian basilica.

③ **Cala Binisafúller**
This 40-m- (130-ft-) long beach is situated next to the road between Cap d'En Font and Punta Prima. It is mainly used by holidaymakers staying at the nearby apartments and bungalows.

Me-20

• Es Migjorn Gran

Me-18

Sant Tomás
•

① • Son Bou

Key

▬ Scenic route

═ Other road

◄ Boats sailing on the idyllic Menorcan waters

and of all the Balearic islands: a tall, rocky headland swept by the northern wind – the "tramontana" – and washed over by the rolling waves of the sea. The steep cliffs provide nesting grounds for peregrine, sea eagle and kite. The road leading to Cap de Cavalleria runs through lovely picturesque areas; however, it is necessary to stop several times on the way to open and shut the numerous farm gates.

At the western end of the peninsula are the remains of **Sanitja**, a Phoenician settlement mentioned by Pliny, which you can visit on a boat trip from Fornells. The Romans built a port on this site, called Sanisera. Nearby is a museum with a modest exhibition of Talayotic and Roman relics. More worthwhile is a trip to the **Torre de Sanitja**, a watchtower built by the British in the late 18th century in order to guard the entrance to this natural harbour.

Magnificent beach in Sant Tomàs near Es Migjorn Gran

Further west is a stretch of barely accessible, unspoiled beaches. The most beautiful of these are **Cala del Pilar**, **Cala d'Alagiarens** and **Cala Pregonda**.

⓬ Es Migjorn Gran

11 km (7 miles) south of Es Mercadal. 🏠 Wed. 🎪 San Cristobal de Ses Corregudes (end Jul or early Aug). 🌐 ajmijjorngran.org

A small, tranquil village set among fertile fields, Es Migjorn Gran has a sleepy, provincial flavour. From here you can take a 5-km (3-mile) walk to the seashore. The road leads through the **Barranc de Binigaus** canyon filled with fragrant wild herbs and flowers. You could stop on the way to see the limestone walls and caves, including the biggest of them – **Cova des Coloms**.

Environs

Some 11 km (7 miles) south is **Sant Tomàs** resort. A dozen or so hotels line its main street, but there are no all-night clubs, and few restaurants. However, there is a great beach.

④ Cala Binibeca
This wide beach is near Binibeca Vell. The beach and the surrounding area have hardly been developed. A restaurant is by the car park.

⑥ Cala Alcaufar
The beach runs along the bay, on the southeast coast. The northern shore of the bay is densely built up.

⑤ Punta Prima
This southernmost beach of Menorca is one of the most popular on the island. The beach overlooks the rocky island of Illa de l'Aire.

Beach on Santa Galdana bay

⑬ Ferreries

📧 C/ Sant Bartomeu. **Tel** 971 363 790 (Maó). 🕐 10:30am–1:30pm & 5:30pm–8:30pm Sat. 🎪 Sant Bartomeu (23–25 Aug).

Ferreries is situated at the foot of the S'Enclusa hill. At 142 m (466 ft) above sea level, this picturesque little town is the highest settlement in Menorca. Its name derives from the many blacksmiths *(ferreries)* who once worked around here. At the heart of the village is the **Plaça d'Espanya**. Here, at a weekly Saturday market, you can buy leather goods as well as produce brought in by local farmers, including vegetables, fruit, cheese and honey. In Plaça l'Església is the parish church of **Sant Bartomeu** (1705) and the town hall. It is also worth stepping into the **Centro de Geologia de Menorca**, to see a selection of the island's natural wonders.

Carrer Fred, close to the main square in Ferreries

Environs

About 6 km (4 miles) north of Ferreries are the ruins of **Santa Agueda** castle. Not much remains of this Moorish stronghold, but the view from the top of the second-highest mountain in Menorca justifies the effort of the 260-m (853-ft) climb.

The strategic advantages of the hill were well-known to the Romans, who, in the 2nd century, chose it as the site for their first fortress. The Moors adapted the site to build a summer residence for the Menorcan governor and improved the surrounding fortifications. The fort was the last stronghold to surrender during the Reconquest. Ferreries is the centre of the leather industry. Along the road to Maó are several shops selling Menorcan sandals.

Festa de los Roselles in Ferreries

🏛 **Centro de Geologia de Menorca**
C/ Mallorca 2. **Tel** 971 374 505.
Open May–Sep: 10am–2pm & 6pm–8pm Tue–Sat, 10am–2pm Sun.

⑭ Santa Galdana

5 km (3 miles) south of Ferreries.

The only way to get to Santa Galdana is by car from Ferreries or on foot, along the d'Algendar canyon. Situated on a beautiful bay, the town's popularity is growing, and a number of high-rise hotels have begun to pop up. Most of the other buildings are villas, set among the trees. The main tourist attraction is the beach, with its white sand and turquoise water, sheltered from the wind by high cliffs and a pine forest.

It is worth taking a walk west from here to the charming **Macarella cove**. The adjacent **Macarelleta cove** has a nudist beach. Both beaches are well established and can be accessed by steps carved into the rock.

Further west is **Cala Turqueta**, probably the most beautiful bay on this part of the coast. Another beach, situated in a charming cove east of Santa Galdana, is **Cala Mitjana**, which is a lovely spot, though it can get busy in summer.

Gin in Menorca

One legacy of the 100-year rule of Menorca by the British is the tradition of producing and drinking gin, which was a popular drink with the many British sailors stationed here. Unlike the rest of Spain, where wine is the most popular tipple, Menorcans have taken to gin in a big way. The production process can be seen in the 18th-century Xoriguer distillery, next to the landing stage in Maó *(see p100)*. The gin produced by the Xoriguer distillery is the most popular brand on the island and is sold in *canecas* – ceramic bottles reminiscent of the clay jugs that were once used by British sailors.

Gin from the distillery in Maó

⓫ Western Coast of Menorca

The region between Ciutadella and Cap d'Artutx is excellent for exploring. Whether walking, cycling or driving, you can enjoy the best of the island, including a nature reserve near Son Xoriguer, the Son Olivaret megalithic remains and the churches and museums of Ciutadella, the former capital of Menorca. Parts of this unspoiled region can even be explored on horseback.

⑤ Sa Caleta
Near the beach, at the entrance of Cala Santadria bay, is a former defence tower, Es Castellar.

④ Cala Blanca
This small beach is tucked away between bungalows, villas and a cluster of narrow streets. Visited mainly by locals, it is uncrowded and has safe swimming.

③ Son Olivaret
The two sets of megalithic structures – Son Olivaret Nou and Son Olivaret Vell – include both *talayots* and *taulas*.

② Cala en Bosch
This harbour, situated in a sheltered bay, has a landing stage for pleasure boats. Next to the harbour there is a shopping centre.

Cala Morell

Cala En Blanes

Me-1

Maó

Torre-Saura

Santandria

Me-24

⑥ Son Oleo
On the outskirts of Ciutadella is a small beach, lying at the end of a long narrow bay. It is fairly quiet and used mainly by the locals.

⑦ Ciutadella
Take at least one day to explore the former capital of Menorca. From here you can make trips north to Cala en Blanes or to Cala Morell.

Tips for Drivers

Length: 16 km (10 miles).
Stopping-off points: Stop off for refreshments at one of the restaurants in Cala en Bosch or Ciutadella. A good place for swimming is Cala Blanca, halfway along the route.

0 km 1
0 miles 1

Key

▬ Suggested route
= Other road

① Son Xoriguer
Son Xoriguer is also the starting point for trips on horseback to the neighbouring reserve. The route leads past two beaches and then along the seashore.

⑯ Ciutadella

A picturesque town with narrow, winding streets, handsome palaces and a busy harbour, Ciutadella has always competed with Maó. In the days of Arab rule it was the island's capital, and in 1558 it was invaded by the Turks, who killed many of its inhabitants and carted off some 3,500 more to slave markets in Istanbul. Of its buildings, only the cathedral remained. Those who survived were determined to rebuild Ciutadella. Most of the Menorcan aristocracy continued to make it their home, even after Maó became the capital.

Neo-Gothic canopy above the Cathedral altar

Plaça d'es Born, the town's principal square

Exploring Ciutadella

Though there are few traces of Arab rule, Ciutadella has much to offer in the way of architecture. Numerous opulent palaces and Gothic and Baroque churches reveal just how successful the restoration of Ciutadella in the 17th and 18th centuries was. The main square in town is Plaça d'es Born, a characterful area close to the Gothic cathedral. The Museu Diocesà, housing sacred art objects that document the cultural and religious life of the island, is well worth a visit.

🏛 Plaça d'es Born

This is a former Arab military drill ground and was rebuilt in a Neo-Renaissance style in the 19th century. It is considered to be one of Spain's most beautiful squares. At its centre stands an **obelisk** marking *Any de la Desgràcia* – the "Year of Calamity", when Turkish corsairs invaded Ciutadella. The square is lined with historic buildings, including the **town hall**, a former palace of the Moorish governor, as well as the late 19th-century **Teatre Municipal d'es Born** and 19th-century

palaces with Italian-style façades. The most imposing of these is the early 19th-century **Palau de Torre-Saura**. The adjacent **Palau Salort**, dating from the same period, is Ciutadella's only aristocratic residence that is open to visitors during the summer. The opulent Hall of Mirrors and the majestic painted ceiling in the ballroom make this handsome house well worth visiting. The square is also worth seeking out for its restaurants and open-air cafés and bars.

🏛 Cathedral

Plaça de la Catedral. **Open** 10am–4pm Mon–Fri, 10am–2:15pm Sat

Work on the cathedral began towards the end of the

13th century on the site of a mosque. Although it suffered fire damage, it escaped much of the destruction during the Turkish raid but was heavily remodelled after 1558. During the Civil War the workers' militia destroyed most of its furnishings.

One of the oldest parts of the cathedral is the Gothic south entrance that bears stone carvings of weird creatures and the heraldic crests of the Menorcan knights and nobility. The main Neo-Classical entrance dates from the early 19th century. The dominant feature of the interior is the Neo-Gothic canopy hanging over the main altar.

🏛 Capella del Roser

C/ Roser.

The façade of this small church includes a beautiful 17th-century Spanish Baroque-style doorway. Destroyed during the Civil War, the church was rebuilt and is now used as a municipal exhibition hall.

🏛 Can Saura and Palau Martorell

C/ Santissim.

These two adjacent palaces were built in the 17th century. Their

Cafés spilling onto the pavements at Plaça Nova

distinctive façades reflect the character of the town's noble mansions built during that period.

🏛 Museu Diocesà de Menorca

C/ Seminari 7. **Tel** 971 481 297. **Open** 10am–4pm Mon–Fri, 10am–2:15pm Sat.

The Diocese Museum occupies a former Augustinian convent and cloister. Its collection of prehistoric and modern artifacts includes a miniature statuette of a bull and a bronze casting of a mermaid. It also has a collection of Catalonian paintings, and some sacred objects made of precious metals, including chalices and Communion cups. Next to the monastery is the Baroque **Església de Socors**.

⛪ Sant Crist

Near the bank building that was formerly the house

Ses Voltes' arches line the walkway leading to the Cathedral

of Menorcan aristocrat, Joan Miquel Saura, stands the Baroque Capella del Sant Crist, built in 1667. Its fanciful façade is decorated with stone carvings of fruit garlands and masks. The statue of Christ above the high altar is said to have dripped with sweat in 1661 and became the

VISITORS' CHECKLIST

Practical Information
Plaça Catedral, 5 🄰 29,000.
Tel 971 382 693. 🄰 Fri & Sat.
🄰 Festa Sant Joan (23–24 Jun)
🅆 ajciutadella.org

Transport
🚌🚌

object of a folk cult. Standing near the chapel is a column topped with a bronze figure of the Lamb of God, the work of local artist Matias Quetglas.

⛲ Plaça Nova

This small square is the site of the town's most popular cafés and bars. Ses Voltes, an arcaded walkway which runs from here to the cathedral, is one of the main streets of the Old Town. The Moorish vaulted arches that line the street hide a good selection of patisseries and souvenir shops.

⛲ Plaça Llibertat

This charming square situated at the rear of the former Augustinian monastery is well-known to all who shop for food. Its two covered markets, selling fresh meat, fish, fruit and vegetables, are popular with the locals.

Arcades of the covered market in Plaça Llibertat

Ciutadella

① Plaça d'es Born
② Catedral
③ Capella del Roser
④ Can Saura and Palau Martorell
⑤ Museo Diocesà de Menorca
⑥ Sant Crist
⑦ Plaça Nova
⑧ Plaça Llibertat

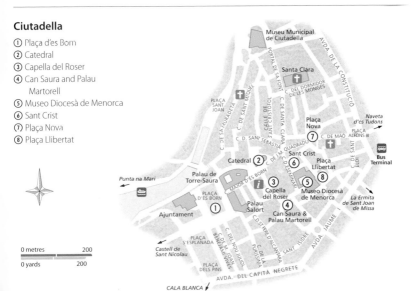

0 metres 200
0 yards 200

Further Afield

The Old Town boundaries are defined by the wide avenues of Avda del Capità Negrete, Avda del Jaume I and Avda de la Constitució. Outside these limits there are a few interesting sights, including the **Castell de Sant Nicolau**, the remains of the city fortifications and the harbour. A stroll along the north coast of the bay will take you to **Punta na Mari**. Ciutadella, situated on Menorca's west coast, makes a good base from which to explore the area. From here you can get to **Cala Morell** in the north, or **Cap d'Artrutx** 10 km (6 miles) to the south.

Statue of a horse, the star of the Festa de Sant Joan

🏛 Santa Clara

Portal de Sa Font, 2. 🕐 10am–1:30pm & 5–7pm Mon & Tue (11am Sat & Sun).

The original church and convent of Santa Clara was founded in 1287 by Alfonso III. Destroyed during the Turkish raid in 1558, it was rebuilt in the 17th century only to be destroyed again during the Spanish Civil War. A community of nuns still lives here. The wood carving depicting the *Adoration of Shepherds*, seen in the convent, was stolen by the Turks and taken to Istanbul but subsequently recovered.

🏛 Museu Municipal de Ciutadella, Bastió de sa Font

Plaça de sa Font s/n. **Tel** 971 380 297. **Open** 10am–2pm Tue–Sat (from 6–9pm May–Sep). 🎫 (free on Wed)

The museum occupies the bastion of the former town fortifications built in 1677. This is the only

preserved fragment of the town's fortifications. Founded in 1995, the Museo Municipal has a good collection of Talayotic, Roman and Muslim artifacts, most of which are kept in a large, vaulted room. There are crafted beakers and tumblers, bowls and jugs, bronze weapons and jewellery (with a distinct Phoenician influence). There is also an odd collection of human skulls, showing the damage caused by the practice of trepanning.

🏛 Plaça Alfons III

This modest square is on the outskirts of the Old Town, by Avda de la Constitució. Several cafés and restaurants shelter under the trees. The square can be seen from some distance and you can't miss the old windmill, now housing a tourist office. This is a good place to sit or pick up a souvenir.

🏛 Plaça de s'Esplanada and Plaça dels Pins

These two adjacent green squares are the lungs amid the historic buildings of Ciutadella. The many bars and restaurants provide pleasant places in which to relax and the peace is broken only by the screech of brakes from the nearby bus garage. In the evening there are jazz concerts here.

An alley leading to Santa Clara

Windmill and tourist office in Plaça Alfons III

🏛 La Ermita de Sant Joan de Missa

Carrer de Comte Cifuentes. The chapel situated southeast of the town centre is an important venue for the Festa Sant Joan celebrations. Vespers are sung here on the evening of 23 June. The nearby road, which leads to Macarella, Macarelleta and Cala en Turqueta beaches, is transformed into a racecourse during the two days of celebrations *(see box)*.

🚢 Harbour

Moll Comercial. Ciutadella's shallow harbour was the main reason the British moved the island's capital to Maó. Today, the harbour has been dredged and can accommodate large ferries linking Ciutadella to Barcelona, as well as the many yachts and fishing boats that moor here.

Having descended from Plaça d'es Born to the ferry terminal, it is worth taking a walk along the bay to soak up some of the harbourside activity. Early in the morning you can see fishermen returning with their catch, the first bars opening and the town waking up to a new day.

From **Punta na Mari**, at the entrance to the bay, you can see Castell de Sant Nicolau. On the other side of the harbour bay, about 500 m (1,640 ft) further on, is

Cala des Degollador's tiny beach. The beaches of **Platja Petita** and **Sa Platja Gran** are several hundred metres further on.

A phenomenon peculiar to Ciutadella bay is the mysterious *rissaga* wave. No one is able to predict when this event will take place, but it can cause flooding of the port to a height of several metres. The last big *rissaga* occurred in 1984 and left the harbour under 2 m (7 ft) of water.

Fishermen in the harbour preparing their nets

🏰 Castell de Sant Nicolau

Plaça Almirall Farragut.

The 17th-century Castell de Sant Nicolau was built as a watchtower to protect the harbour. You can still enter the stronghold via a drawbridge and in the evening the castle remains open to provide a vantage point for the spectacular sunsets over the harbour. It also serves as a venue for temporary exhibitions.

Standing near the castle is the statue of a four-star admiral of the United States Navy, David Farragut, hero of the American Civil War and son of an immigrant from Menorca. The admiral is depicted in his uniform with epaulettes, holding a telescope. When he returned to Menorca in 1867, he was awarded honorary citizenship and a huge crowd turned out to greet him.

Environs

Naveta d'es Tudons, 5 km (3 miles) east of town, is Menorca's best-preserved prehistoric ruin. The Bronze Age

Festa de Sant Joan

This midsummer festival (23–24 June) has provided the citizens of Ciutadella with an opportunity to go wild since the 14th century. St John's Day begins with Mass in the cathedral, but fireworks, jousting and the carrying of a live sheep through the streets are also part of the fun. For most, the highlight of the day is the *caixers* (horsemen). Representing the medieval social classes, they ride among the noisy crowds.

Prancing horse in the streets of Ciutadella

structure, built of stone blocks, is 7 m (23 ft) high and 14 m (46 ft) long and was used as a burial chamber. When it was excavated, in the 1950s, more than 50 bodies were discovered. In **Torre Llafuda**, about 3 km (2 miles) away, amid the shade of olive groves, stands one cracked *taula* and a well-preserved *talayot*. The pleasant setting and the surrounding fertile farmland make this a good place to stop and relax. Travel southeast of Ciutadella and you find a number of beautiful beaches hidden in small coves. These include **Cala des Talader**,

dominated by a stone watchtower. Along the road leading to **Son Saura** is Son Catlar, Menorca's biggest prehistoric settlement. Its wall is several metres high and built of enormous stone blocks. Inside, amid the sea of ruins you can distinguish one *taula* and five *talayots*.

A short way to the north are two large resorts – **Cala en Blanes** and **Los Delfines** (which has a small aqua center). Eight kilometres (5 miles) northeast is the tourist village of **Cala Morell**. The man-made prehistoric caves are dug into rocks and were used for burials in the late Bronze and Iron Ages. They are now open to the public.

🏊 Aqua Center

Urb los Delfines. **Tel** 971 388 705. **Open** mid May–Sep: 10:30am–6:30pm daily. 🅿 🅦 aquacenter-menorca.com

Castell de Sant Nicolau guarding the entrance to the harbour

IBIZA

Despite its reputation as a party island, Ibiza has maintained much of its rural charm. Fields of almonds and figs, olive groves, the relentless munching of the flocks of sheep – all are part of modern-day Ibiza. Yet there is no denying that the island is a magnet for clubbers, who flock here every summer attracted by the music, lovely beaches, lively nightlife and extraordinary tolerance of the locals.

The closest of the Balearic Islands to mainland Spain, Ibiza is intersected by a modest range of mountains and surrounded by scores of islets and protruding rocks. Its 200-km- (125-mile-) long coastline is extremely varied, with small coves hiding beautiful beaches and mysterious caves.

Together with Formentera and a number of outlying islets, Ibiza belongs to the group of islands dubbed by the Greeks as the Pitiusas, or "pine tree islands". Besides the Greeks, Ibiza's visitors included the Phoenicians, the Carthaginians and the Romans. The last big invasion took place in the 1960s, when the island was "discovered" by hippies, and subsequently began to appear in all the European holiday brochures. Tourism took a firm and rapid hold on the economy, and during the 1990s Ibiza gained entry into the *Guinness Book of Records* as the entertainment island of the world. Famous for its nightlife, thousands of visitors fill the resorts, and big-name nightclubs offer a wealth of DJs and dancing.

Away from the clubs, the north of the island is a rural patchwork of almond, olive and fig groves. The most distinctive features of the southern region are the vast salt lakes where sea salt is extracted to this day.

Dalt Vila, the old part of Eivissa, is one of the best-preserved medieval towns in Europe, despite its influx of pleasure seekers. For many locals time still moves at a gentle pace on the island.

An alley in Sa Penya, in the old district of Eivissa

◄ Pedestrians shopping on a sunny morning at Calle de Santa Cruz

Exploring Ibiza

Ibiza has much to offer holidaymakers. It is the Mediterranean's club capital and the majority of visitors come here to enjoy the delights of over 50 local beaches in sheltered coves, as well as to revel in the nightclubs of Eivissa and Sant Antoni. Everyone should visit Dalt Vila, Eivissa's Old Town, for its Gothic cathedral and to see and be seen in one of the many swanky restaurants and chic bars. Those in search of tranquillity can head for the island's interior, where the hilly countryside is peppered with old stone cottages. For the energetic, the rugged coastline to the northwest provides excellent walking.

Locator Map

Platja d'en Bossa near Sant Jordi

Getting There

Ibiza has fewer scheduled flights than Mallorca. Most visitors arrive by charter flight. During the holiday weekends, Ibiza's airport becomes one of the busiest on the planet. The planes landing here are mainly from the UK, bringing tourists for a week or two of partying. Barcelona and Madrid also have frequent flights to the island. Ferries from Eivissa and Sant Antoni de Portmany harbours sail for Mallorca and Formentera, as well as to Barcelona and Dénia.

Cala d'en Ferrer seen from the top of Sant Miquel, near Na Xamena

Sights at a Glance

1 Eivissa pp120–23
2 Sant Jordi de Ses Salines
3 Ses Salines
4 Sant Josép de sa Talaia
6 Sant Antoni de Portmany
7 Santa Agnès de Corona
8 Els Amunts
9 Sant Joan de Labritja
10 Portinatx
11 Sant Vicent de Sa Cala
12 Santa Eulària des Riu
13 Jesús

Tours

5 West Coast of Ibiza pp130–31

Plaça des Parque below Dalt Vila in Eivissa

Key

— Major road
= Minor road
— Scenic route
△ Summit

For map symbols see back flap

❶ Street by Street: Eivissa

Attracted by the hilltop site and sheltered harbour, the Phoenicians founded Eivissa in the mid-7th century BC. The Puig de Molins necropolis dates from those days. Dalt Vila (Upper Town) is the oldest remaining part of Eivissa and since 1999 has been a UNESCO World Heritage Site. Strengthened by fortifications begun by the Emperor Charles V, it once guarded the entrance to the bay. Sa Penya, at the end of the harbour under Dalt Vila, was once the fishermen's quarter and is still one of the more colourful parts of town. La Marina, stretching out along the waterfront, is the place to go for night-time entertainment.

★ Portal de ses Taules
A broad paved drive leads from Sa Penya to Portal de ses Taules – the main town gate.

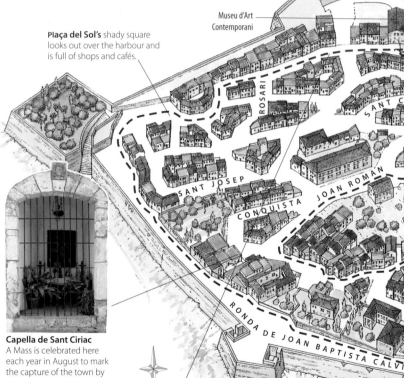

Plaça del Sol's shady square looks out over the harbour and is full of shops and cafés.

Museu d'Art Contemporani

Capella de Sant Ciriac
A Mass is celebrated here each year in August to mark the capture of the town by Jaume I in 1235.

Plaça de la Vila
The main square of Dalt Vila is lined with shops, restaurants and cafés to tempt passing visitors.

Key
— Suggested route

Dalt Vila
The Upper Town, built on a hill, is best seen from the harbour shore where its strategic importance is obvious.

VISITORS' CHECKLIST

Practical Information
49,500.
Tel 902 404 704. Passeig Vara de Rey, 1, 971 301 900. Mon–Sat (summer). Sant Joan (23 Jun), Sant Cristòbal (10 Jul), Nostra Senyora de les Neus (8 Aug), Sant Ciriac (5 Aug).

Transport
Es Codolar, 8 km (5 miles) to the southwest.

Museu Arqueològic

City walls

SA CARROSSA

IGNASI RIQUER

G. BALANSAT

PERE TUR

CARRER DE PONENT

PLAÇA DE LA CATEDRAL

Sa Carrossa
Quiet by day, Sa Carrossa is popular with Eivissa's gay visitors and is a hip night-time hangout in the summer.

Castell Almudaina

Reial Curia
The modest house of the former Royal Tribunal of Justice, standing near the cathedral, has a fine Gothic doorway.

★ Cathedral
The cathedral, dedicated to Our Lady of the Snows, was completed in 1592. It is Dalt Vila's most impressive building.

Vast city walls surrounding Dalt Vila

Exploring Eivissa

Eivissa is the largest and most beautiful town on the island. To avoid the crowds, visit early in the morning. For a romantic stroll, visit after dark, when it is a bit cooler. In Sa Penya and Sa Marina, the harbour district, you can take a break and see evidence of present-day Eivissa. The place is full of bars, restaurants, clubs and market stalls. As night falls, the streets outside Dalt Vila become one huge dance floor.

⌂ Cathedral

Plaça de la Catedral.
The Cathedral Church of Santa María de las Nieves (Our Lady of the Snows) stands at the highest point in Dalt Vila, near the severely dilapidated medieval castle (Castell).

Ibiza's consecutive rulers used this place as the site for their temples in Punic times. In AD 283, on the orders of the Roman Emperor Marcus Aurelius, a temple was built here and dedicated to the god Mercury. Following the conquest of the island by the Catalans, work began to build a Christian church, which was completed in 1592. The only remains of the original Gothic structure are the tower and the vestry portal. In the 18th century, the cathedral was remodelled in a heavy Baroque style. The vestry houses a small museum with a collection of beautifully embroidered chasubles (priestly garments), as well as Gothic and Baroque paintings. On the first floor is a collection of altar pieces in silver and gold plate.

⌂ Fortifications

The present city walls surrounding Dalt Vila were erected in the 16th century during the reign of Felipe II, according to plans by the Italian architect Giovanni Battista Calvi. In 1585, with the completion of the impressive Portal de ses Taules (decorated with the coat of arms of Felipe II and replicas of ancient Roman statues), the city's defences were in place.

The view from the northern bastion of Santa Llucia encompasses the new town, the harbour docks and the nearby island of Formentera.

🏛 Museu Arqueològic

Plaça de la Catedral 3.
Tel 971 301 771. **Open** Apr–Sep: 10am–2pm & 6–8pm Tue–Sun; Oct–Mar: 9am–3pm Tue–Sun. 🌣
W maef.es

The archaeological museum houses a collection of

prehistoric artifacts and relics dating from the times of the island's Carthaginian, Roman and Moorish rulers. On display are tombstones, statuettes and coins, as well as glass and ceramic objects. The museum building is itself impressive, and was the home of Ibiza's government for 300 years.

🏛 Museu d'Art Contemporani

C/ Ronda Narcis Puget. **Tel** 971 302 723. **Open** timings vary, please check website. **Closed** public holidays.
W mace.eivissa.es

The Modern Art Museum in Portal de ses Taules consists of two underground galleries of the former arsenal, built within the city walls. The museum was founded in 1969 and includes several hundred works by artists living in Ibiza. Some works are for sale, but prices can be rather steep.

Replica Roman statue at Portal de ses Taules

🏛 Plaça de Espanya

The **Ajuntament** (town hall) dominates this square and occupies a building that was once a Dominican monastery and a school for the town's poor. Adjacent to it is the church of Santo Domingo *(see p123),* with its later Baroque façade (entrance from Carrer Balansat). The local *chiringuito* bar, open 24 hours, serves Balearic snacks and specialities. Carrer Pere Tur features splendid 18th-century

Fresh fruit at a stall in Es Mercat Vell

Sa Torre bastion guarding the harbour

mansions. Among them is **Casa Riquer**, once home to Antoni Riquer, the most famous buccaneer in Ibiza.

Santo Domingo
Carrer Balansat.
Below the city walls is the late 16th-century church of Santo Domingo, commonly known as El Convent.

It is worth visiting this to see the lovely paintings covering the vaulted ceilings, and the ceramic tiles lining the walls and floors. The Capella del Roser has an interesting Baroque altar.

Es Mercat Vell
Plaça de la Constitució.
The old market building lies north of Portal de ses Taules. The hall, resembling an ancient Greek temple, was built in 1873. Every morning it is packed with vendors selling fresh fruit and vegetables. A short distance further on is the **Sa Peixateria** fish market.

Sa Penya
The Sa Penya district, situated between Dalt Vila and the harbour, was once inhabited mainly by fishermen and has always been a fairly "picturesque" part of town. Even today, it does not enjoy a good reputation and when venturing here you should take extra care of your wallet and any valuables you might have. During high season, the streets get very crowded. The place is full of cafés, bars and clubs. Life in Sa Penya only starts in earnest after dark.

Sa Marina
Like Sa Penya, Sa Marina was originally a working-class district and sprang up as overcrowding in Dalt Vila forced many people to live outside the city walls. Now the area around the harbour provides ferry links to mainland Spain and is packed with restaurants, cafés, bars and shops. Its narrow alleys are full of stalls selling clothes and souvenirs. Many of these offer items reminiscent of the days when the island was a favourite with hippies.

Sa Torre
A small military defence tower stands at the end of Carrer Garijo. The bastion was restored in 1994 and is a relic of the fortifications that once guarded the entrance to the harbour. Today, it affords a view over the entire bay and the harbour and on to Formentera.

Monument als Corsaris
Passeig des Moll.
In the early 19th century, the inhabitants of Ibiza, tormented by constant pirate raids, enrolled the help of Antoni Riquer, a buccaneer who fought battles with the pirate ships that brazenly attacked the passing merchant vessels.

His struggles with Novelli, a buccaneer in the pay of the British who commanded the large brig *Felicity*, became the stuff of legend. Despite being hugely outgunned by Novelli, Riquer sank the enemy vessel after a fierce battle, for which the grateful Ibizans erected this monument. It is believed to be the world's only monument that is dedicated to a pirate.

Teatro Pereyra
C/ Comte Rosselló 3.
Built in 1898, this was the first theatre in Ibiza. Now the Neo-Classical building houses the Teatro Pereyra café, which is worth dropping into in the evening for live music or stand-up comedy.

Passeig de Vara de Rey
Eivissa's main street is named after General Joachim Vara de Rey, a Spanish general who perished in Cuba during the Spanish-American war in 1898. The street's many bars and restaurants are very popular in the evenings.

Puig des Molins
Via Romana 31. **Tel** 971 301 771.
Open Oct–Mar: 9:30am–3pm Tue–Sat, 10am–2pm Sun; Apr–Sep: 10am–2pm & 6–8pm Tue–Sat, 10am–2pm Sun.

Many of the objects associated with Punic culture on display in the Museu Arqueològic were unearthed from this ancient burial site. The "Hill of the Windmills" was one of the Mediterranean's top burial sites and the remains of the nobility would have been brought here from all over the Carthaginian empire. Ibiza, being free of snakes and scorpions, was attractive to the Carthaginians, whose religion specified a burial site free of poisonous creatures.

Neon sign of Teatro Pereyra café

Environs
There are several beaches near Eivissa served by local buses. **Playa de Talamanca** is not large, but is nearest to the town. On the opposite side of the capital, at its southern end, is **Platja de ses Figueretes. Es Cavallet**, a short way down the coast, is very popular, especially with gay visitors. **Ses Salines**' beach, a little further on, is favoured by many people staying in Eivissa, and has regular bus links to the city.

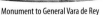

Monument to General Vara de Rey

Nightlife in Ibiza

In the early 1960s, Ibiza became a popular haunt of hippies who were drawn to this isolated Spanish outpost by the beauty of the scenery and the relaxed way of life. They brought with them valuable foreign cash and the local bars, shops and businesses started to prosper. At times, though, even the islanders' legendary tolerance was strained and in 1968 the loud music, drugs and sex on the beach resulted in the deportation of 41 people. Where hippies led, however, the rest have followed and Ibiza is today the club capital of the world.

Scantily clad podium dancer – a big feature of many Ibiza clubs

Foam party, popular in the clubs of Ibiza

Birth of Club Culture

The pioneers of clubland were **Pacha** and **Amnesia**, which opened in the early 1970s. The Ku club, currently known as **Privilege**, joined the scene shortly afterwards. Banking on the popularity of the party scene at the time, they offered their own more stylish and restrained version. Gradually, word spread and the clubs became fashionable with the rich and the famous.

The 1980s and 1990s heralded the emergence of DJs who decamped to Ibiza for the summer and forged a new type of dance music. Some became stars in their own right, performing to crowds of 3,000 or more. From then on, the club scene in Ibiza gained its own momentum and it is now a major part of the island's economy.

Clubs

There are eight major clubs on the island, each capable of accommodating several thousand people. The biggest of them, Privilege, can host

parties for up to 10,000 guests. Every night they offer new attractions, including parties in foam, Brazilian nights, ghost nights and "Flower Power" balls. In addition, the clubs make their premises available to other promoters that operate on the continent. On Mondays from June to September, the best party is Circoloco at **DC10**. Admission charges are high and may be anything up to €50. Drinks are also expensive.

Smaller clubs are cheaper. They do not offer such elaborate entertainment, but have their own unique charm. They tempt their guests in with free drinks and various fun gimmicks. In the Sa Penya and La Marina districts of Eivissa, revellers often end up partying on the streets. During high season, special night-bus

services run between Eivissa and Sant Antoni, where most of the clubs are concentrated.

Clubbers

People of all ages can be found in Ibiza's many clubs because there are no age limits, although young people prevail. Many come to party, others are drawn by sheer curiosity. For some, the Ibiza club scene is simply a way of life. The clubs are most frenetic during summer weekends, when they are invaded by clubbers from all over Europe. The rule is to visit several clubs each night. As is usual at such hectic events, there may be an occasional petty theft or scuffle. You may also come across drug dealers and con artists offering various goods at bargain prices to drunken passers-by. Nevertheless, generally speaking, the clubs have tight security and are safe places.

Neon sign of a club in Eivissa

Coloured lights and laser beams at El Divino

Music and Dancing

Dancing in the local clubs is led by some of the world's top DJs. They include Fatboy Slim, Paul van Dyk, Mark Spoon, Carl Cox and John Digweed, to mention but a few. These DJs dictate which music will later find its way into the clubs of London, Paris and Berlin. Each year they try to surprise their fans with something new.

As the party season ends in Ibiza, most of the seven top clubs and their associated DJs go on worldwide tours, promoting their latest music. Individual clubs also produce CDs of last season's hits.

Although many kinds of music can be heard in Ibiza, the clubs have become famous for their summer anthems and for a unique Balearic Beat that is a fusion of electronic music with Latin and funk rhythms. Much of it is based on drum machines pounding out four beats to the bar, but Ibiza is known for its eclectic tastes and has produced a more subtle sound often branded as "chillout".

No one style of dancing prevails in the clubs and you will often see a free-form frenzy. Many people just copy the podium dancers.

DJ Sonique at the decks in Es Paradis Terranal

Before and After

Most clubbers do not wait until midnight to begin partying. After a day spent relaxing on the beach, many people start their evening in cafés, bars and pubs. The first to open their doors are the small clubs. By the time **El Divino** or **Amnesia** open their doors, the party on the island is already in full swing. Even at dawn, it is common to still see people dancing in the streets of Eivissa. Some beaches have daytime dance cafés and clubs, such as Bora-Bora opposite the flamboyant **Space** club on Platja d'en Bossa (Space hosts a party that begins at 8am!).

Gaudy poster advertising Space

Clothes

It is not necessary for people to wear any special clothes to be admitted to an Ibizan club, the exception being theme parties, when you are expected to wear appropriate costume and come dressed as a "Flower Child" or astronaut, for example.

Clubbers who are playing in foam or jets of water tend to be scantily dressed. Regular clubbers are usually fashionably dressed, with clothes that are often provocative and sexy. As with the music, club fashions change every year.

Dancing crowds at Amnesia enjoy a sudden deluge of foam

DIRECTORY

The Best Clubs in Ibiza

Amnesia, Sant Rafael.
Tel 971 198 041.
W amnesia.es

DC10, Ctra Las Salinas., km 1, Sant Jordi.
Tel 971 393 405.

El Divino, Puerto Eivissa Nueva s/n, Eivissa. **Tel** 971 318 338.
W eldivino-ibiza.com

Es Paradis, C/ Salvador Espriu 2, Sant Antoni. **Tel** 971 346 600.
W esparadis.com

The Forgotten Club, C/ Cala de Bou, Sant Antoni de Portmany.
Tel 971 620 664.

Gatecrasher, C/ Salvador Espriu s/n, Sant Antoni. **Tel** 971 805 439.
W gatecrasher.com/ibiza

KM5, Ctra Sant Josep, km 5.6.
Tel 971 396 349.
W km5-lounge.com

MOMA, C/ Murtra 5, Platja d'en Bossa.
W momaibiza.com

Pacha, Avinguda Ocho de Agosto s/n, Eivissa.
Tel 971 313 612.
W pacha.com

Privilege, Sant Rafael.
Tel 971 198 160.
W privilegeibiza.com

Sankeys, C/ Alzines 5, Platja den Bossa.
W sankeysibiza.com

Space, Platja d'en Bossa.
Tel 971 396 793.
W spaceibiza.com

❷ Sant Jordi de Ses Salines

4 km (2 miles) southwest of Eivissa.
🚌 Sat.

The small village of Sant Jordi de Ses Salines lies along the road leading from Eivissa to the airport. It was established in the 15th century, but there is not much evidence left of its ancient pedigree. The most important local sight is the modest white church of **Sant Jordi** that stands surrounded by a high wall. A quirky Saturday market takes place here from 8am and has a good mix of cheap jewellery, clothes and second-hand books.

Environs

A little further on is **Platja d'en Bossa**. The local beach is popular with young people, especially the southern end where a dynamic club scene has developed. Much of this is based around Space, a huge club that opened in 1988 *(see pp124–5)*. Close to this is Bora-Bora, a club-bar where parties spill out onto the sand.

Children have not been forgotten here. Behind the beach is a large waterpark, **Aguamar**, with numerous pools and slides.

A short way south of Sant Jordi is a hippodrome where you can bet on trotting races, popular throughout the Balearic Islands.

🏊 Aguamar

Platja d'en Bossa. **Tel** 971 396 790.
Open May–Oct: 10am–6pm daily. 🏊

Ses Salines, a haven for many species of bird

❸ Ses Salines

10 km (6 miles) southwest of Eivissa.

Situated at the southern end of Ibiza are the saline lowlands – Ses Salines. These natural saltpans are extremely important for the local wildlife and were known as the "Salt Gardens" in Phoenician times.

They are sheltered to the north by the Serra Grossa hills that rise up to 160 m (520 ft) in some places; to the south they are flanked by the wooded areas of Faló and Corbari. In 1992, the area was given special protection as a nature reserve.

For centuries, the revenue from the local salt production provided a large chunk of the island's income. Until quite recently, the place was served by a narrow-gauge railway carrying salt to La Canal – a

small port at the southern end of the peninsula. Salt production still continues here, though not on such a grand scale – some 70,000 tonnes of the stuff are exported each year.

Built between the salt lakes is the village of **Sant Francesc de S'Estany**, where some salt workers still live. It has a small picturesque church. The asphalt road that passes the church leads to a 16th-century watchtower, **Torre de sa Salt Rossa**, 2 km (1 mile) away. From here there is a fine view over nearby Illa Sal Rossa island, the wide beaches of Figueretes lying to the south of the capital and Dalt Vila in Eivissa.

Ses Salines' beach, **Platja de Ses Salines**, is one of the island's most fashionable spots. One section of this beautiful, long sandy beach has been set apart for nudists.

❹ Sant Josep de sa Talaia

👥 25,000. 🚌 ℹ️ Plaça Església s/n, 971 801 627. 🎉 Sant Josép (19 Mar).

The small town of Sant Josep de sa Talaia, 13 km (9 miles) west of Eivissa, is the municipal capital of the southwestern region and is off the beaten track. Its pace of life is slow. It is worth visiting the local traditional tavern, Bernat Vinya, where men gather to play cards and chat over a glass of wine. The only historic relic to visit is the **church**, built in the typical island style.

Environs

The town lies at the foot of Ibiza's highest mountain, **Sa Talaiassa** (475 m/1,558 ft). Keen walkers can make the two-hour hike to the peak along a well-marked trail that starts in Sant Josép. From the top there is a magnificent panorama of the

Slides in Aguamar, near Sant Jordi

For hotels and restaurants in this region see p151 and pp161–3

district, including the rocky islet of **Es Vedrà**. In order to take a closer look at Es Vedrà you need to drive along the coast up to the sandy bay of **Cala d'Hort**, with its pleasant sandy beach and several terraced restaurants.

According to legend, Es Vedrà was once the home of the sirens who lured Odysseus. Sailors and divers experience a strange magnetic anomaly here, and some believe the island to have been a landing site for aliens. This lofty rock, now inhabited only by birds and flocks of wild goats and sheep, makes an extraordinary impression. Occasionally, in calm weather, it even blows off a plume of steam.

Some 5 km (3 miles) from Sant Josép, situated to the right of the road that leads to Eivissa, is **Cova Santa**. The main attractions of this cave, which is the largest in Ibiza, are its huge stalactites, some of which are a dozen or so metres long.

Fountain in Passeig de ses Fonts in Sant Antoni de Portmany

Plaça de Església, was built on a hill, away from the harbour, and served as a shelter for the local population during pirate raids. Originally, there were defensive guns positioned on the church roof.

The bustling fishing harbour is popular with visitors. A palm-fringed promenade runs along the bay. At one end is a large flowerbed with sculptures made in Sant Rafael, including the ingenious *Columbus' Egg*. The famous entertainment district between Carrer de Mar and Carrer Ample comes to life only after dark. The local clubs, including Es Paradis, are among the island's best *(see pp124–5)*.

Of the nearby beaches, **Cala Bassa** and the blue-flag **Cala Conta** are probably the best. **Port d'es Torrent** is also popular, especially with families *(see p131)*.

❼ Santa Agnès de Corona

8 km (5 miles) northeast of Sant Antoni de Portmany.

Santa Agnès de Corona has maintained its old-world atmosphere. There is not much here apart from a small quaint church, a shop and a bar where you can quench your thirst and enjoy a plate of tapas. You can take a walk from here to the nearby summit of **Es Camp Vell** and on to the neighbouring village of **Sant Mateu d'Aubarca**.

Environs
Southwest of Santa Agnès de Corona is an original early Christian chapel of **Santa Agnès**, discovered in 1907 in a grotto. Local legend says that a sailor was saved from drowning by St Agnes during a fierce storm, and built a chapel to her on the spot where he was washed up by the waves. On St Agnes's Day, local people make a pilgrimage to this site.

❺ West Coast of Ibiza

See pp130–31.

❻ Sant Antoni de Portmany

🗺 23,000. 🚌 ⛴ ℹ Passeig de Ses Font s/n, 971 343 363. 🎭 Sant Antoni (17 Jan), Sant Bartolome (24 Aug).

The second-largest town in Ibiza was known as Portus Magnus by the Romans. The large bay that provided a natural harbour for ships now boasts yacht marinas and a ferry terminal. Once upon a time this was a small fishing village, until it was transformed in the 1960s into a busy, commercialized summer resort with scores of hotels. Regular bus services run from here to Eivissa and Santa Eulària des Riu. Amid the sea of high-rise hotel buildings stands the 14th-century church of **Sant Antoni Abat**. This fortified parish church, now standing in

Columbus' Egg in Sant Antoni

Village church in Santa Agnes de Corona

❺ West Coast of Ibiza

The main attraction of Ibiza's west coast is its magnificent beaches, many of which are tucked away in small coves and offer family-friendly facilities and safe bathing. Some of the resorts have become built up in recent years, but the west coast remains one of the island's most beautiful areas, with a romantic coastline, pristine waters and remote mountains clad in pine trees. The mysterious islet of Es Vedrà *(see p127)*, just off the coast, is a remarkable sight and featured in the film *South Pacific* as Bali Ha'i. The route suggested here cuts across the Serra de Sant Josep in the south and bypasses the highest peak on the island, Sa Talaiassa (475 m/1,558 ft).

Illa Sa Conillera

Illa de s´Esparta

⑥ Cala Molí
This small resort is flanked by steep cliffs and consists of modest villas and pensions surrounded by green pine trees. Its beach *(right)* is regarded as one of the most beautiful on the island.

⑤ Cala Vedella
This little resort is slowly becoming fashionable. Situated at the mouth of a narrow inlet, it has a wonderful beach and plenty of low-rise hotels and apartments. The resort is unlikely to be spoiled as there is no room for large hotels.

③ Mirador des Savinar
The best way to reach nearby Torre de Pirata, a former watchtower and now a viewpoint, is on foot. A drive over the bumpy road may damage your car. The point provides the best view of Es Vedrà.

Illa Vedranell

Illa es Vedrà

④ Cala d'Hort
This is the southernmost resort on the western coast. Many visitors come to this beach, far from the main resorts and towns, to admire the view of Es Vedrà, others to enjoy the exquisite local paella.

② Cap Llentrisca
The rough track leading along the craggy cliffs is fairly difficult, but from here you can see the entire south coast of the island.

⑦ Cala Tarida

Another beautiful cove, Cala Tarida has golden beaches and a number of family-friendly hotels. Until recently a quiet corner of the island, it is beginning to get busy, especially during high season.

Sant Antoni
de Portmany

Sant Antoni
de Portmany

PM 803

• **Sant Agustí
des Vedrà**

**Sant Josep
de sa Talaia**
PM 803

Eivissa

Vista Alegre

⑧ Port d'es Torrent

Here you can join an organized canoe trip to Illa Sa Conillera and Cala Bassa. Several of the nearby villas are owned by the rich and famous, including Claudia Schiffer.

⑨ Cala Bassa

One of the most beautiful and popular beaches in the region of Sant Antoni de Portmany; it can be reached by bus. Numerous cruising boats visit the local harbour.

① Es Cubells

This village has a beautifully simple church and a modest restaurant. It offers a magnificent view over Cala d'Es Cubells. On a clear day you can see Formentera from here.

Key

- Suggested route
- Other road
- Scenic road

0 kilometres 2
0 miles 2

Animals grazing around St Mateu d'Aubarca

❽ Els Amunts

Ibiza's spectacular mountain range, Els Amunts, is situated in the northern part of the island and stretches from Sant Antoni de Portmany in the west to Sant Vicent de Sa Cala in the northeast.

Rarely visited by tourists, the region has maintained its unspoiled charm. Pinewood hills are interspersed with fertile valleys full of olive, almond and fig groves, as well as the occasional vineyard. The shore rises steeply and the roads leading to the water's edge are narrow, unmade and rugged, presenting a challenge even to four-wheel-drive vehicles. The area is a hiker's paradise; walking around you are likely to meet only the local shepherds.

Except for the small resorts, such as Port de Sant Miquel, Portinatx or Cala de Sant Vincent, the inland towns, including Sant Joan de Labritja and Santa Agnès de Corona (see p127), have maintained their traditional, rural character. A good example of this is the little village of **Sant Mateu d'Aubarca**, where you can see flocks of sheep and goats grazing in the orchards.

Near Sant Llorenç lies the fortified settlement of Balàfia. Believed to be the island's only surviving Moorish hamlet, the whitewashed interlocking houses with flat roofs and amber-coloured watchtowers once acted as fortresses during pirate attacks.

❾ Sant Joan de Labritja

16 km (10 miles) north of Eivissa. 🚌 🚢 Sant Joan (24 Jun), Santa Maria (5 Aug).
W sanjuanibizatravel.com

This quiet little town in the north of the island lies in the shadow of the Es Fornàs mountain (410 m/1,345 ft). The only buildings of note in town are the **Ajuntament** (town hall) and a small 18th-century **church**. The local cafés and restaurants are well worth visiting. Sant Joan was popular with hippies in the 1960s, and you can stock up on beads, Roman sandals and magically endowed crystals at the New Age Bazaar.

Environs

About 7 km (4 miles) west of town is the small village of **Sant Miquel de Balansat**. It has an impressive 16th-century fortress-church that provided shelter during the frequent raids by pirates, who once ventured deep into the island's interior in search of loot and slaves. Every Thursday at 6pm from May to October, there is a music and dance show performed by a local folklore group in front of the church. Dressed in traditional costumes, they entertain people with lively dances to tunes played on traditional instruments, including drums and local flutes (xeremia).

Hibiscus flower in full bloom

Port de Sant Miquel is 4 km (2 miles) north of Sant Miquel. It has a fishing harbour and a handful of hotels. The resort is popular with families and has facilities for water sports as well as a diving centre. Nearby, on top of a hill, stands one of the island's most exclusive hotels – Hacienda Na Xamena. The top of the 200-m- (656-ft-) high cliff provides a magnificent view over the surging waves below.

To the north of the town is the **Cova de Can Marça**. This cave, which was used by tobacco and liquor smugglers, is one of the most beautiful of its kind on the island, and is on a par with the caves found in Mallorca. There is an entrance fee which buys you a sound and light show and a 40-minute guided tour.

East of Port de Sant Miquel is **Cala de Benirràs**. It gets very busy in the evenings, when visitors arrive to admire one of the most beautiful sunsets on the island. At other times it is relatively quiet. On Thursday nights it becomes a venue for hippy concerts and dances.

🏞 Cova de Can Marça
Port de Sant Miquel. **Open** 10:30am–1:30pm & 2:30–8pm daily (Nov–Apr: 11am–5:30pm). 🅿 ✉ 🎟

❿ Portinatx

8 km (5 miles) north of Sant Joan de Labratija. 🚌

The northernmost holiday village of Ibiza was built as a family resort. It consists solely

Lighthouse on Punta de Sa Galera, near Portinatx

Coastal boulevard in Cala de Sant Vincent

of hotels, apartments, souvenir shops, restaurants and numerous cafés.

It is an attractive, quiet place with four beaches – Sa Torre, S'Arenal Petit, S'Arenal Gran and Es Portitxol – separated from each other by rocky protrusions. It can become busy during high season, but instead of baking on a beach you may prefer to go water-skiing or take a trip in a glass-bottomed boat to admire the life lurking beneath the clear waters.

Environs

Nearby, just 4 km (2 miles) west of Portinatx, is **Cala Xarraca**, a beautiful beach with views along the north coast. The beach provided the setting for the film *South Pacific*.

⓫ Sant Vicent de Sa Cala

8 km (5 miles) east of Sant Joan de Labratija.

Sant Vicent de Sa Cala lies along the main road leading from Sant Joan de Labratija to the east coast of Ibiza. Running to the south of it is the range of the Serra de Mala Costa mountains. The only local historic building is the modest 19th-century **parish church**, open only during service hours.

Sant Vicent de Sa Cala is nevertheless worth visiting for a different reason. The passage of time seems almost to have ground to a halt here. The locals work on the land using age-old methods and tools, and they

have neither telephones nor any other modern conveniences. The island authorities set up the **Camp d'Aprenentatge** here, where pupils from local schools learn about the old ways of rural life and about Ibiza's natural environment.

Environs

About 3 km (2 miles) east of town is **Cala de Sant Vicent**. This beautiful cove has become a modern resort, with quiet hotels and good restaurants. Visitors love the beach with its clean water and rugged scenery, surrounded by green pine forests.

From here, signposts point towards the famous **Cova d'es Culleram**, discovered in 1907, which was a temple to the goddess Tanoit during the days of the Carthaginian rulers. The caves can be visited and the finds unearthed here can be seen in the Museu Arqueològic at Dalt Vila, in Eivissa *(see p122)*.

Another interesting destination for a walk is **Punta Grossa** – a headland situated a little way to the east, which has a lighthouse. The view from here includes the **Illa de Tagomago** and the eastern cost of the island. **Tagomago** island lies 6 km (4 miles) southeast of Cala de Sant Vicent. It is uninhabited and has no regular ferry links with the main island but it is often visited by cruise boats and yachts. The clear waters around the island are popular with scuba divers.

🦋 **Cova d'es Culleram**
Open Apr–Dec: Tue–Sun. 🚶

Hippies

Hippies began arriving in Ibiza in the 1960s, attracted by the beaches, the people and the unhurried lifestyle. It soon became the "in" place and tour operators were quick to catch on. Most of the hippies moved on long ago, but the hippy style has found its way into the island's culture. A small number of hippy families still live on the island; one community is near Balàfia.

Hippy stall selling jewellery

Fortified church at the top of Puig de Missa in Santa Eulària

⑫ Santa Eulària des Riu

🏔 35,000. 🚌 ℹ️ C/Mariano Riquer Wallis 4, 971 330 728. 🚩 Santa Eulària (12 Feb).

Ibiza's third-largest town stands on the banks of the island's only river, the Riu de Santa Eulària. The town's main shopping street is Passeig de s'Alamera. This **Ramblas** connects the main street with the coastal promenade. During the day, the palm trees provide welcome shade. At night there are many lively clubs, restaurants and cafés to enjoy.

You can escape the town by by walking up nearby **Puig de Missa** (67 m/219 ft). At the top is a 16th-century **fortified church**, regarded by many as the loveliest and best-preserved example of its kind in Ibiza. This whitewashed building, once used by the town's inhabitants as a shelter from pirates, is surrounded by a handful of picturesque local houses and a small cemetery. The adjacent flat-roofed building houses the modest **Museu Etnològic**. Just a short walk away is the **Museu Barrau**, which has a collection of paintings, furniture and drawings by the Spanish Impressionist Laureá Barrau.

Environs
Es Canar, a popular resort 4 km (2 miles) north of Santa Eulària des Riu, lies on the shore of a pine-fringed bay with a beautiful beach. The local hippy market (Apr–Oct:

Wed) is the best known and biggest in Ibiza. Held in the grounds of the Punta Arabi club, it attracts large crowds. Here, you can buy jewellery and unusual clothes and T-shirts, though much of the stuff on sale is not made locally. Nearby are two large camp sites and a couple of beaches – **Cala Nova** and **Cala Llenya**. During the summer there is a daily boat trip to Formentera.

Anita's Bar in **Sant Carles de Peralta**, a little town 8 km (5 miles) northeast of Santa Eulària, was the cradle of the island's hippy culture and still remains popular. Two kilometres (1 mile) south of Sant Carles is a hippy bazaar, Las Dalias. On Saturdays and Sundays, the colourful stalls display everything from beads and bangles to bongos and intricate water pipes. There is also a café-bar here.

About 5 km (3 miles) south of Santa Eulària is **Cala Llonga**. This is one of the most popular resorts on the southeastern shores of the

Town hall in Plaça de Espanya

island. Its beautiful sandy beach makes it an ideal place for families with young children.

🏛 Museu Etnològic
Puig de Missa. **Tel** 971 332 845. **Open** Apr–Sep: daily; Oct–Mar: Tue–Sun.

🏛 Museu Barrau
Puig de Missa. **Tel** 971 330 072. **Open** 9:30am–1pm Tue–Sat.

Arcaded entrance to a church garden in Jesús

⑬ Jesús

2 km (1 mile) north of Eivissa. 🚌

This modest village is situated near Eivissa, on the road to Santa Eulària. The church of **Nostra Mare de Déu de Jesús** has a unique early 16th-century Gothic-Renaissance altar of the Virgen de los Angeles. Painted by the Valencian artists Pere de Cabanes and Rodrigo de Osona, it illustrates scenes from the life of the Virgin Mary, Christ and the Apostles. There are a couple of cafés opposite the church.

Environs
A short way to the south and within walking distance of Eivissa is **Talamanca**. Its main attractions, beside the 2-km (1-mile) sandy beach, are the Aqualandia waterpark and some good fish restaurants.

Ibiza's Beaches

Apart from the clubs, Ibiza's main attraction is its beaches. There are over 50 of them, adding up to over 50 km (30 miles) of stunning coastline. Many of the most popular ones are on the southeast coast, between Santa Eulària des Riu and Cala de Sant Vicent, and have excellent facilities. It is still possible to find a quieter spot. The delightful Cala d'en Serra, for instance, near Portinatx, has a *chiringuito* ("refreshment shack") and little else.

① Cala es Figueral
A long, sandy beach with small, rocky islets near the shore. The northern portion is used as a nudist beach.

② Cala Boix
Surrounded by green hills, this beach remains relatively deserted even during high season. It is situated near Punta Prima, offering a view of Illa de Tagomago.

Es Figueral ●
①

Sant Carles de Peralta

La Joya

②

0 km   1
0 miles   1

PM 810

③

● S'Argamassa

④

Santa Eulària des Riu

PM 810

⑤

Key
▬ Major road
▬ Scenic route
═ Other road

PMV 810-1

⑥

③ Platja des Canar
This popular resort has a small beach, situated near the pleasure-boat harbour. The surrounding area is full of shops, bars and restaurants.

④ Platja des Niu Blau
This pine-fringed beach in a cove with shallow water is a particular favourite of families.

⑥ Cala Llonga
Situated between Puig de ses Torretes and Punta Roja, on a 300-m- (1,000-ft-) wide bay, Cala Llonga is a friendly resort and attracts hundreds of holidaymakers.

⑤ Platja del Pinos
The beach, close to Santa Eulària, is situated at the mouth of the seasonal Riu de Santa Eulària that dries up in the summer.

FORMENTERA

The tiny island of Formentera, 4 km (2 miles) south of Ibiza, is just 85 sq km (32 sq miles) in area, including its two satellite islets, Espardell and Espalmador. A sense of peace and tranquillity pervades the island. The beaches are secluded, the grassy farmland is serene and the tiny clusters of whitewashed houses that make up the island's villages are positively slumberous.

It is the very lack of high-profile tourist facilities that attracts visitors. Its beaches are some of the emptiest and cleanest to be found anywhere in Spain, high-rise hotels are nowhere to be seen and the main means of transport on the island are bicycles and scooters – the tourist office will encourage you to cycle rather than hire a car.

The Greeks called it Snake Island (although snakes are rarely seen), but never settled here. The more practical Romans left settlers on the island to grow cereals and other crops, and named it *Frumenteria* (Wheat Island), giving rise to its present name.

Following the fall of the Roman Empire, the island became a refuge for outlaws and pirates. For two centuries it was ruled by the Arabs. Throughout the Middle Ages, Formentera remained practically deserted. The second major wave of settlers arrived in the late 17th century. It was at that time that several defensive watchtowers were built, although only a handful of them survive today.

Ever since that time, Formentera has managed to maintain its unique character as a virgin island. The quiet farmsteads and villages appear to have remained unaffected by modern living, and the loveliest corners of the island are only reached by rough, unpaved roads. For the peace-loving visitor, it is a tranquil idyll. Even so, the island's economy is entirely dependent upon its summer visitors, most of whom come for day trips. Each summer the island's population doubles, but there are still plenty of quiet spots to be found.

A popular beach party in Es Pujols

◀ Beautiful coast of Formentera

Exploring Formentera

With few hotels and plenty of seclusion on offer, Formentera is a paradise for those seeking a quiet holiday, free from distractions. The coastline is stunning, with crystal-clear turquoise waters and pristine beaches. The nightlife is calm and unhurried in the bars and restaurants of Sant Francesc – the island's tiny capital. Es Pujols is the main resort. It too is small-scale, but it is a lively, fun place to be with some good bars and a couple of laid-back clubs. For a little gentle sightseeing, the island has a handful of ancient defensive towers, pretty village churches and some prehistoric ruins in Ca Na Costa.

Lonely lighthouse at the end of the road on Cap de Barbària

Sights at a Glance

1. Sant Francesc
2. Cap de Barbària
3. La Savina
4. Illa Espalmador
5. Ses Salines
6. Ca Na Costa
7. Es Pujols
8. Platja Migjorn
9. El Pilar de la Mola

Catamarans with sails aloft on the beach in Es Pujols

For hotels and restaurants in this region see p151 and p163

Key

— Major road

═ Minor road

Locator Map

Platja Migjorn, the longest beach on Formentera

Quiet beach in Cala Saona, used by the guests of the only hotel

Getting There

There is no airport on Formentera, but the island has good sea links with Ibiza. Most services run between La Savina and Eivissa. The voyage takes about one hour (fast ferries take 25 minutes), although journey times can vary. Santa Eulària des Riu also has ferry links with Formentera and with Dénia during the summer. Buses from La Savina harbour go to various parts of the island, but the best way to travel is by scooter or bicycle. The main road cuts across the island, connecting La Savina to Punta de sa Ruda. There are also good roads leading to Es Pujols, Cala Saona and Cap de Barbària.

Plaça de la Constitució in Sant Francesc

❶ Sant Francesc

🏔 3,400. ℹ C/ Calpe, Port de la Savina, 971 322 057. 🎉 Sant Francesc Xavier (3 Dec).

Formentera's tiny capital is a mere 3 km (2 miles) from La Savina harbour and contains most of the island's historic buildings. In Plaça de la Constitució is an imposing **fortified church** dating from 1729, which was used by the many of the island's inhabitants as a shelter from the frequent pirate raids that ravaged the island. Now it houses the local government offices and a post office. Nearby is the **Museu Etnòlogic**. Carrer de Jaume I and its adjacent streets are full of market stalls selling clothes and souvenirs. Among them, you can find hippy stalls offering jewellery.

The oldest building in town is the 14th-century **Capilla de sa Tanca Vell**, a stone structure with no windows and covered with a barrel roof, which was also often used as a refuge from pirates. Also worth visiting is the local restaurant, Es Pla, situated along the road to Cala Saona, which is famous for its Indian cuisine and large selection of beers.

Environs
Some 3 km (2 miles) to the east is **Sant Ferran**. This modest village with a lovely church was once the centre of alternative culture, taken over by large numbers of hippies. The legendary Fonda Pepe bar and the library, run by an American called Bob, were hippy meeting places in the 1960s. It is worth going there

for a drink, just to savour the hazy atmosphere of "flower power" nostalgia.

Not far from Sant Ferran is **Cova d'en Xeroni**, a limestone cave, discovered by accident in 1975. The cave has been illuminated with 1970s disco lights, which only adds to the charm of the guided tour.

🚇 **Cova d'en Xeroni**
Ctra Sant Ferran–La Mola, 6 km (4 miles). **Open** May–Oct: Mon–Sat. Call 971 328 214 to arrange a visit. 🗂

❷ Cap de Barbària

8 km (5 miles) southwest of Sant Francesc.

A bumpy road leads from Sant Francesc southwards, across an area of wild desert, to the distant Barbària headland. This is the southernmost point of Formentera and it features an 18th-century defence watchtower, **Torre des Garroveret**, as well as a lighthouse warning passing ships of the numerous rocks that jut from the sea at the island's tip. Nearby are the unearthed

Torre des Garroveret in Cap de Barbària

remains of a fortified megalithic settlement. The area is also rich in sculptures built of stones placed one by one by passing visitors. The most typical and eye-catching features of this windswept desert are pine trees twisted into weird shapes by the wind, and rocks eroded by centuries of wind and water.

Environs
Travelling from Sant Francesc, you pass the little road leading to **Cala Saona**. Here, positioned in a small cove, are a beautiful sandy beach, a handful of restaurants and a solitary hotel.

Moored boats in the Estany d'es Peix lake

❸ La Savina

3 km (2 miles) north of Sant Francesc. ⛴

The only harbour in Formentera providing ferry links with Ibiza is situated in the northern part of the island. Apart from when visitors are spilling on or off the ferries, La Savina is a fairly sleepy, unassuming place. Nevertheless, it is possible to find several shops and supermarkets here, as well as car, scooter and bicycle hire. Buses to Sant Francesc, El Pujols and other villages depart from stops behind the ticket offices. There is also a taxi stand here. In view of the small distances involved, cab rides are not very expensive. La Savina adjoins the protected saltwater lagoons of **Estany Pudent** and **Estany d'es Peix**. The latter has a fishing harbour that is always full of boats seeking shelter in the shallow, calm waters of the lagoon; drying nets can be seen hanging along the shore.

The southern coast of Illa Espalmador as seen from Formentera

❹ Illa Espalmador

This small, 3-km- (2-mile-) long island is situated between Formentera and Ibiza. There is no regular ferry service; however, during high season the island is visited by pleasure boats sailing from La Savina.

The tiny island is popular with day-trippers from Ibiza, who flock here for the chance to sunbathe on the shores of s'Alga, a large natural harbour situated at the southern end of the island. This is also a favourite spot for yachts cruising the archipelago. A short walk north of the beach is a **sulphurous mud pool** where you can indulge in a bath of warm, sticky ooze (get there early to avoid the rush). The island's only monument is the **Torre de sa Guardiola**, an 18th-century defence tower that has recently been restored.

At low tide, some people attempt to walk across the sound to Formentera, although this is prohibited by the notice boards displayed at the tip of the **Es Trucadors** peninsula – the only traces of man's presence on this spit of white sand are the fragments of boats, nets and buoys washed ashore by the sea.

❺ Ses Salines

3 km (2 miles) north of Es Pujols.

The flat, salty marshes found along the road leading from La Savina to Es Pujols are famous for their birdlife. The most common species include the heron and the fen-duck. During the summer season, the grounds are also visited by flamingoes. Until recently it was commercially viable to produce salt here, but in 1955 the area was declared a listed zone in view of its ecological importance. Now the area including Ses Salines, Estany Pudent and the Punta de sa Pedera headland to the west of La Savina island forms a nature reserve.

Situated to the north of Ses Salines are **Platja de ses Illetes** and **Platja de Llevant**, which are considered to be among the loveliest beaches the Balearic Islands have to offer. The adjacent 200-year-old saltmill now houses a restaurant.

Salt was valued for centuries, not only as a condiment but also as legal tender. Even today it is still being produced in the traditional way in many places throughout the Balearic Islands. Seawater floods the shallow lagoons and then evaporates when heated by the sun, leaving behind pure salt. This creates a specific environment on which salt-loving flora and fauna thrive. Salty shrimps are the favourite food of many birds, including the black-winged stilt.

❻ Ca Na Costa

1.5 km (1 mile) north of Es Pujols.

Situated close to the Es Pujols resort is the megalithic burial chamber of Ca Na Costa (1800–1600 BC), a circle of seven vertical limestone blocks. The simplicity of the stone ring belies its historical importance, as it is the only structure of its kind in the Balearic Islands and the most precious historic relic on Formentera. It is also the only evidence of prehistoric human habitation remaining on the island.

The excavations were begun in 1974 and unearthed a number of objects, including ceramic and bronze vessels and axes, which are now on display in Eivissa's Museu Arqueològic (see p122).

Picturesesque Ses Salines

Popular beach in Es Pujols

❼ Es Pujols

7 km (4 miles) northeast of Sant Francesc. 🚌 🎭 Virgen del Carmen (16 Jul).

The small resort of Es Pujols is the island of Formentera's main holiday centre. It is a low-key, relaxed kind of place with a small marina at the eastern end of the town. Some of the island's best beaches are within easy walking distance, and the nightlife in the bars, restaurants and clubs, for otherwise sleepy Formentera at least, is quite lively.

Environs
A short way east of Es Pujols, standing on a peninsula, is a 17th-century watchtower – **Torre de Punta Prima**; next to it is one of the best hotels on the island – the luxury Punta Prima Club. A little further along the coast, among the rocks, is **Cova de ses Fumades Negres**.

❽ Platja Migjorn

This lovely beach is a 5-km- (3-mile-) long stretch of fine sand, with pale turquoise waters. It is fringed by pine forests and is the longest beach on the island. At its eastern end is the **Torre d'es Català**; at its western end are the **Cova d'es Ram** caves. The holiday village of **Maryland** in the east and **Es Ca Marí** in the west have numerous hotels and apartments tucked away in the woods. The central section of the beach is the most pleasant and secluded. A handful of bars and restaurants are set back

from the beach and are more easily accessible by car. The most popular of them, the Blue Bar, doubles up as a low-key nightclub.

Platja Migjorn in the vicinity of Es Arenals

❾ El Pilar de la Mola

11 km (7 miles) southeast of Sant Ferran. 🚌

Situated at the heart of the La Mola plateau, El Pilar de la Mola is a fairly sleepy little place and makes a good stopping-off point on a trip to Formentera's 19th-century lighthouse, **Faro de la Mola**. El Pilar de la Mola's most interesting historic building is the

whitewashed church of **Nostra Senyora del Pilar** (*see below*), built in 1784. The town is best known for its craftsmen, whose workshops are open to visitors. The popular Wednesday and Sunday markets sell jewellery, good-quality leather goods and excellent local cheese (which goes perfectly with a glass of the local dry red wine).

Environs
Es Caló is a small fishing village on the north coast of the island. Unusually, it has no harbour and the boats have to be pulled ashore on special rails. When travelling from here towards La Mola, it is essential to stop at the **El Mirador** bar, which offers a magnificent panoramic view of Formentera. Some 2 km (1 mile) north of El Pilar de la Mola rises the 133-m- (436-ft-) high Ferrer hill. A little further on, to the west, is the **Cova d'es Fum**, a large cave where the locals hid their treasures during a Viking raid in 1118. Unfortunately for them, the Viking pirates discovered the hiding place and, having smoked them out, slaughtered the defenders and made off with the loot.

Travelling 3 km (2 miles) east, you arrive at **Punta de sa Ruda** – a rocky crag that drops steeply towards the crashing sea, over 100 m (320 ft) below. The views of the island from here are stunning. The Faro de la Mola lighthouse, built in 1861, is situated at the edge of the crag and was the inspiration for "the lighthouse at the end of the world" in Jules Verne's *Journey Around the Solar System*.

The village church in El Pilar de la Mola

Formentera's Beaches

In terms of beauty, the beaches of Formentera can easily rival those of Ibiza. The unspoiled natural environment, magnificent sand and clean waters attract an increasing number of visitors. Most have no hotels or clubs nearby and only a few feature bars or restaurants, which for many people only adds to their charm. The roads leading to some of the beaches (even the popular ones) can be quite rough and, as a consequence, they are never as busy as elsewhere on the Balearic Islands.

① Platja de ses Illetes
The most popular beach in Formentera. Stretching to the north of it is the Es Trucadors peninsula.

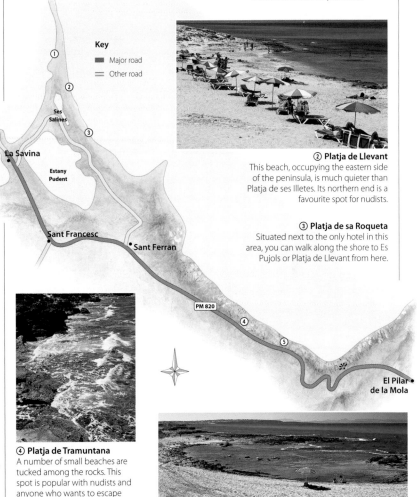

② Platja de Llevant
This beach, occupying the eastern side of the peninsula, is much quieter than Platja de ses Illetes. Its northern end is a favourite spot for nudists.

③ Platja de sa Roqueta
Situated next to the only hotel in this area, you can walk along the shore to Es Pujols or Platja de Llevant from here.

④ Platja de Tramuntana
A number of small beaches are tucked among the rocks. This spot is popular with nudists and anyone who wants to escape the bustling atmosphere of Illetes and Platja Migjorn.

⑤ Es Caló de Sant Augusti
Several beaches are situated to the west of town. They can be reached via the footbridges that cross the thicket covering the dunes.

Key

- ▬ Major road
- ═ Other road

Ses Salines

La Savina

Estany Pudent

Sant Francesc

Sant Ferran

PM 820

El Pilar de la Mola

0 kilometres 2
0 miles 2

TRAVELLERS' NEEDS

WHERE TO STAY

The Balearic Islands are one of Europe's most popular holiday destinations. Their magnificent climate, fine beaches and close proximity to mainland Europe mean that visitors arrive in thousands between June and September. Unsurprisingly, a large number of hotels have been developed to cater for the demand. Until recently, this has meant that much of the accommodation has been fairly formulaic, although a rise in rural tourism has seen a boom in bright B&Bs away from the coast. Mallorca has the best-developed hotel facilities while, Formentera has the fewest hotels. Visitors should also note that many hotels close down during low season.

The exclusive La Residencia in Deià, Mallorca

Hotels

Most hotels on the Balearic Islands are situated along the coast, around the old town centres and harbours, and are usually within easy reach of the beaches. There are more hotel beds in the Balearics than in the whole of Greece. Even so, at the height of the season it can be difficult to get a room unless you have booked well in advance. The most popular resorts are so densely packed that finding a quiet hotel with a sea view is virtually impossible. As an alternative, some historic buildings have been turned into luxury hotels, particularly in the major towns. These offer a higher standard and bags of old-world charm but often at a higher price.

Many hotel developments are located in remote spots. Most provide a range of attractions. These include evening entertainment as well as recreation facilities such as tennis courts, swimming pools and gymnasiums. It is certainly advisable to check in advance to find out whether these facilities are included in the basic price.

Fincas and Casa Rurales

As elsewhere, rural hotels and apartments are becoming popular on the Balearic Islands, especially with those seeking quiet, out-of-the-way places. This type of holiday is offered by *fincas* and *casas rurales*. These are hotels that occupy former country mansions or farmhouses, predominantly in the island's interior. Mostly found in Mallorca, they are not necessarily a cheap option

Traditional bungalows on Ibiza

but can provide a degree of authenticity not found elsewhere. Rooms are mostly furnished with period furniture, which accentuates the character of the place.

Some *fincas* are very high-class, and cater for the wealthy. Others are in ordinary country houses and may be surrounded by holiday bungalows and apartments. When choosing to stay in a *finca*, you should bear in mind that they are typically far from the beaches and town nightlife. All tourist information offices have lists of organizations offering this type of service. Details can also be found on the Internet.

Camp Sites

Those who enjoy camping or caravanning will have difficulties in the Balearics. There are few camp sites and those that do exist are generally situated in unattractive locations. Before travelling, check the facilities on the island you intend to visit. Camping on unauthorized sites is allowed with some limitations. You are not allowed to pitch a tent in town, on military grounds, tourist sites or within 3 km (2 miles) of an official camp site.

Historic Hotels

The Balearic Islands do not have the equivalent of the state-run parador hotels that can be found elsewhere in Spain, but along with *fincas* it is possible to find

The elegant Formentor, a favourite of the rich and famous

accommodation in places with more history, such as convents and monasteries. This is mainly true of Mallorca, where the most popular hotel of this type is the Monestir de Lluc. These inexpensive rooms are intended for people who are prepared to put up with a certain lack of luxury (it is a monastery after all). However, they are very popular with visitors and you may have problems finding a room during the high season.

The lovely pool in Hotel Son Granot

Prices

The price you pay for a hotel room depends on the season. Although the main holiday season coincides with the summer months, prices only peak during the month of August. Out of the tour operators' peak season, rates are generally much lower. When enquiring about prices, you should remember that hotels can quote their tariffs in a variety of ways. Some are per room; others, per person, per night. Always check what is included in the price. In many cases, breakfast has to be paid for separately. Many resorts offer an all-inclusive service, in which all meals and soft drinks are included in the price.

Most of the Balearic Islands' hotels and apartments are block-booked in advance by travel agents and tour operators.

Booking this way can prove much cheaper than trying to book directly with the hotel. You should also note that some smaller *pensiones* may not accept credit cards.

Booking

Accommodation may be booked in writing or via the hotels' websites. Obviously, you can also book over the phone, but it is always preferable to have a piece of paper to confirm your reservation. It is relatively easy to find accommodation off-season, even at short notice. If you are visiting during the peak season, you should book well in advance.

Some hotels require a deposit or even full payment at the time of booking, in which case you should take your receipt with you. Despite the set price lists, try haggling over the price, particularly out of season.

Recommended Hotels

In this book we have chosen hotels that we believe stand

The charming patio of the Hotel Born, Palma

out from the rest. Many of these may not adhere to the commonly accepted criteria of what makes a "good hotel", and instead may brim in history, great service or be the type of place where location rules over mod cons and designer details.

The best of these have been given a DK Choice symbol. In a geographical area that is dotted with world-class accommodation, these represent the most outstanding. They generally carry four or five stars and range from boutique urban boltholes to chic rural retreats. Do book well ahead, as for many people a stay at these destination hotels is the main reason to visit.

Where to Stay

Mallorca

ALCÚDIA: La Victoria Petit Hotel €
Historic
Carretera Cabo Pinar, km 6, 07400
Tel *971 549 912*
Ⓦ lavictoriahotel.com
Simple and comfortable rooms in a renovated hermitage that dates back to the1400s.

ANDRATX: Son Esteve €€
Historic
Cami c'as Vidals 42, 07150
Tel *655 572 630*
Ⓦ sonesteve.com
Rustic rooms in rolling countryside, that can be explored on horseback. Stylish contemporary suites.

BANYALBUFAR: Sa Baronia €
B&B
C/Baronia 16, 07191
Tel *971 618 146*
Ⓦ hbaronia.com
A rambling extension to an old 17th-century watchtower on the fabulous northwest coast.

CALA BLAVA: Cap Rocat €€€
Historic
Ctra. d'enderrocat, s/n, 07609
Tel *971 747 878*
Ⓦ caprocat.com
An atmospheric hotel in what was once an old fortress standing guard over the bay.

CALVIÀ: Hotel Roc Illetes Playa €
Resort
Paseo Illetes 62, 07181
Tel *971 402 411*
Ⓦ roc-hotels.com
Seafront hotel with access to a spectacular beach. Large, airy rooms and two pools.

CALVIÀ: Hospes Maricel & Spa €€€
Boutique
Crta s'Andratx 11, 07181
Tel *971 707 744*
Ⓦ hospes.com
Modern, understated rooms, some with sea views. Enjoy the fabulous, sea-facing infinity pool.

CAPDEPERA: Casas de Son Barbasa €€
Boutique
Cala Mesquida, 07580
Tel *971 565 776*
Ⓦ sonbarbassa.com
Smart rooms retaining a rustic charm. Beautifully situated in Parque Natural de Llevant.

DEIÀ: Hotel La Residencia €€€
Luxury
Son Canals s/n, 07179
Tel *971 636 046*
Ⓦ hotellaresidencia.es
With an award-winning spa, this is a popular celebrity getaway. Spacious and well-decorated bedrooms.

INCA: Finca Son Vivot €€
Boutique
Ctra Palma–Alcúdia, km 30, 07300
Tel *971 880 124*
Ⓦ sonvivot.com
Fourteenth-century country house with period decor but modern facilities.

LLUC: Sanctuari de Lluc €
Historic
Plaça Pelegrins, 1, 07315
Tel *971 871 525*
Ⓦ lluc.net
Tranquil rooms within a sanctuary that dates back to the 13th century. Wonderful views of the Tramontana mountains.

MANACOR: Finca Es Rafal Roig €
B&B
Ctra. Manacor–Can Picafort (Colonia) km 8, 200, 07500
Tel *971 557 109*
Ⓦ esrafalroig.com
Traditional *finca* with a large pool. Admire the stunning countryside on horseback.

MANACOR: Son Amoixa Vell €€€
B&B
Ctra Manacor–Cales de Mallorca, km 5.4, 07500
Tel *971 846 292*
Ⓦ sonamoixa.com
This restored 16th-century finca is set amid lush green trees. Eat from an a la carte menu and enjoy the extensive wine list.

MURO: Grupotel Amapola €
Resort
Urb. Las Gaviotas s/n, Circuito Del Lago 49, Playa del Muro, 07458
Tel *971 890 551*
Ⓦ grupotel.com
Next to a lake in the S´Albufera region. Excellent for family holidays.

PALMA: Hotel Born €
Historic
C/Sant Jaume 3, 07012
Tel *971 712 942*
Ⓦ hotelborn.com
Spacious rooms set around the leafy patio of what was originally a medieval mansion.

PALMA: Brondo Architect Hotel €€
Boutique
C/C'an Brondo 4, 07001
Tel *971 720 507*
Ⓦ brondoarchitect.com
Lovely bohemian decor and private balconies in a medieval townhouse.

PALMA: Hotel Feliz €€
Boutique
Avinguda Joan Miró 74, 07015
Tel *971 288 847*
Ⓦ hotelfeliz.com
Charming hotel with small but inviting rooms with an eclectic 1970s ambience.

PALMA: Hotel San Lorenzo €€
Historic
San Lorenzo 14, 07012
Tel *971 728 200*
Ⓦ hotelsanlorenzo.com

Outdoor seating area of Hotel La Residencia, Deià

Quaint hotel with a rooftop pool and terrace, besides a separate swimming pool. Excellent views.

PALMA: Hotel Santa Clara €€
Boutique
C/San Alonso 16, 07001
Tel 971 729 231
W santaclarahotel.es
A historic mansion tastefully converted into a smart urban hotel. Spa and views of the bay.

PALMA: Hotel Tres €€
Boutique
C/Apuntadores 3, 07012
Tel 971 717 333
W hoteltres.com
With parts of a 16th-century palace within, Hotel Tres has superb views over the old town.

PALMA: Puro Hotel €€
Boutique
C/Montenegro 12, 07012
Tel 971 425 450
W purohotel.com
Chic hotel with a faux-Asian decor. Popular with young people and groups.

PALMA: Hotel Can Cera €€€
Luxury
C/San Francisco 8, 07001
Tel 971 715 012
W cancerahotel.com
Gothic and Renaissance architecture with lavish interiors. Spacious and bright bedrooms.

PALMA: Hotel Calatrava €€€
Boutique
Plaza Llorenç Villalonga 8, 07001
Tel 971 728 110
W boutiquehotelcalatrava.com
Complete with a spa and terrace-café, this hotel sits on Palma's lovely waterfront.

PALMA: Hotel Convent de la Missió €€€
Luxury
C/de la Missió 7a, 07003
Tel 971 227 347
W conventdelamissio.com
Elegant 17th-century convent, imaginatively converted. The crypt now houses a spa!

PALMA: Palacio Ca Sa Galesa €€€
Luxury
C/Miramar 8, 07001
Tel 971 715 400
W palaciocasagalesa.com
Majestic 16th-century mansion with 12 individually-designed rooms. Excellent spa and wellness facilities.

DK Choice

PALMA: Portixol Hotel €€€
Boutique
C/Sirena, 07006
Tel 971 271 800
W portixol.com
In the small fishing port of Portixol, this outstanding hotel offers a splendid choice of rooms, impeccable service and a great Scandinavian vibe.

PALMA: Reads Hotel and Spa €€€
Luxury
Santa María, 07320
Tel 971 140 261
W readshotel.com
An old manor house converted into a rural retreat of great comfort and high repute.

POLLENÇA: Hotel Desbrull €
Boutique
C/Marqués Desbrull 7, 07460
Tel 971 535 055
W desbrull.com
Period architecture, avant garde decor combined with innovative technology.

POLLENÇA: Posada de Lluc €€
Boutique
C/Roser Vell, 11, 07460
Tel 971 535 220
W posadalluc.com
Classic 15th-century building with modern amenities and a pool. Rooms are cheerful and bright.

POLLENÇA: Son San Jordi €€
B&B
Calle Sant Jordi 29, 07460
Tel 971 530 389
W hotelsonsantjordi.com
Four-poster beds, an outdoor pool and full kitchens. Ideal for families.

DK Choice

POLLENÇA: Son Brull €€€
Boutique
Crta. Palma–Pollença PM 220, km 49.8, 07460
Tel 971 535 353
W sonbrull.com
Sophisticated spa-hotel with 23 luxurious rooms, located in a sensitively-restored 12th-century monastery. The restaurant serves creative organic fare.

PORT D'ALCÚDIA: Condes de Alcúdia €
Resort
Avda de la Platja 4, 07410
Tel 971 545 920
W hotelesglobales.com
Excellent family getaway, with rooms large enough for a couple and two children.

Vibrant, colourful interiors of the dining area in Portixol Hotel, Palma

PORT DE POLLENÇA: Hotel Sis Pins €
Resort
Passeig d'Anglada Camarassa, 77, 07470
Tel 971 867 050
W hotelsispins.com
Waterfront location and classy interiors with traditional furniture.

PORT DE POLLENÇA: Hotel Formentor (Barceló) €€€
Resort
Playa de Formentor s/n, 07470
Tel 971 899 100
W barcelo.com
Once a celebrity haunt, this elegant retreat has the beach at its doorstep.

PORT DE POLLENÇA: Hotel Illa d'Or €€€
Resort
Paseo Colón 265, 07470
Tel 971 865 100
W hotelillador.com
Waterfront hotel with indoor and outdoor pools. Cosy bedrooms.

PORT DE SÓLLER: Citric Hotel Soller €
Resort
Cami del Far s/n, 07108
Tel 971 631 352
W citrichotels.com
Modern-themed hotel on the water's edge with a large terrace overlooking the bay.

DK Choice

PORT DE SÓLLER: Hotel Espléndido €€€
Resort
Es Traves 5, 07108
Tel 971 631 850
W esplendidohotel.com
Perched on the water's edge at Sóller, this stunning destination hotel has a vintage decor. Excellent spa facilities and an intimate bistro.

For more information on types of hotels see page 147

PORTO CRISTO: THB Felip Class €
Resort
Burdils 41, 07680 Porto Cristo
Tel *971 820 594*
[w] thbhotels.com
Hundred-year-old hotel on the seafront. The rooms have attached balconies.

PUIGPUNYENT: Gran Hotel Son Net €€€
Historic
C/Castillo de Sonnet s/n, 07194
Tel *971 147 000*
[w] sonnet.es
A getaway fit for royalty, replete with gardens and mountain views.

SANT LLORENÇ: Hotel Son Trobat €€
B&B
Carretera Manacor–Sant Llorenç, km 4.8, 07530
Tel *971 569 674*
[w] sontrobat.com
A handsome *finca* surrounded by orange and lemon groves.

SINEU: Hotel Son Cleda €
Boutique
Plaça es Fossar 7, 07510
Tel *971 521 027*
[w] hotelsoncleda.com
Originally a 16th-century townhouse, the hotel has a terrace overlooking the village square.

SÓLLER: Hotel La Vila €
Historic
Plaza Constitución 14, 07100
Tel *971 634 641*
[w] lavilahotel.com
Pretty *fin de siécle* architecture and great personalised service.

SÓLLER: L'Avenida Hotel €€
Boutique
Gran Via 9, 07100
Tel *971 634 075*
[w] avenida-hotel.com
Cosmopolitan ambiance in a rural setting. The hotel offers beautiful mountain views.

SÓLLER: Finca Can Coll €€
B&B
Camí de Can Coll 1, 07100
Tel *971 633 244*
[w] cancoll.com
Stylish little hotel with an outdoor pool and lovely views of the countryside.

SÓLLER: Finca Ca N'Ai €€€
B&B
Camí Son Sales 50, Vall de Sóller, 07100
Tel *971 632 494*
[w] canai.com
Nicely-renovated, 300-year-old country mansion surrounded by orange groves.

Exterior of Son Granot, Es Castell

SÓLLER: Gran Hotel €€€
Luxury
C/Romaguera 18, 07100
Tel *971 638 686*
[w] granhotelsoller.com
Spacious rooms that look out over the town and surrounding countryside.

DK Choice

SON SERVERA: Finca Son Gener €€€
Luxury
Ctra. Vella Son Servera, Artà km 3, 07550
Tel *971 183 612*
[w] songener.com
Spanish architect Toni Esteve converted this 18th-century farmhouse into one of the best hotels in Mallorca. Rooms have terraces with great views of the surrounding almond and olive groves.

VALLDEMOSSA: Cases de C'as Garriguer €€
Boutique
Ctra Valldemossa a Andratx, km 2.5, 07170
Tel *971 612 300*
[w] vistamarhotel.es
The ancient Son Olesa country estate is now a peaceful rural hotel with antique furnishings in the bedrooms.

Menorca

CALA EN PORTER: Sa Barrera €€
Boutique
Carrer Sa Barrera 12, 07712
Tel *971 377 126*
[w] hotelsabarrera.com
Moroccan-influenced decor, elegant rooms and a lovely bay just a short walk away.

CIUTADELLA: Hotel Sa Prensa €
B&B
Carrer Madrid, 70, 07760
Tel *971 382 698*
[w] saprensa.com
Great port views from the terraces of some rooms. Situated just a stone's throw from the seafront. Book ahead.

DK Choice

CIUTADELLA: Agroturisme Biniatram €€
Boutique
Ctra Cala Morell s/n, Cala Morell, 07760
Tel *971 383 113*
[w] biniatram.com
This small, family-run finca offers apartments with self-catering facilities as well as rooms with balconies. The beach is within walking distance.

CIUTADELLA: Hotel Rural Sant Ignasi €€
Historic
Ronda Norte s/n, Ciutadella, 07760
Tel *971 385 575*
[w] santignasi.com
A grand country mansion with vast grounds, gardens and vineyards. Traditionally decorated rooms.

CIUTADELLA: Hotel Tres Sants €€
Boutique
C/Sant Cristofol 2, 07760
Tel *626 053 536*
[w] grupelcarme.com
Chic interiors, an enticing rooftop terrace and a Turkish bath. Apartments are also available.

CIUTADELLA: Morvedra Nou Ciutadella €€
Historic
Camí de Sant Joan de Missa, km 7, 07760
Tel *971 359 521*
[w] morvedranou.es
This classy rural hotel was a cottage in the 1600s. Set in gorgeous grounds.

DK Choice

ES CASTELL: Son Granot €€€
Luxury
Carretera de Sant Felip s/n, 07720
Tel *971 355 555*
[w] songranot.com
A lovely 18th-century Georgian home with a delightful entrance staircase, this hilltop hotel has interiors that combine period detail with modern elements.

ES MERCADAL: Hostal Jeni €
B&B
C/Mirada del Toro 81, 0740
Tel *971 375 059*
w hostaljeni.com
Charming town-centre hotel
with a terrace garden which
includes a jacuzzi and pool with
a retractable roof.

MAÓ: Posada Orsi €
B&B
C/Infanta 19, 07702
Tel *971 364 751*
w posadaorsi.es
Brightly furnished rooms, shared
kitchen and a rooftop patio

SANT LLUÍS: Binlaroca Hotel
Rural €€
B&B
Camí Vell 57, 07710
Tel *971 150 059*
w binlarroca.com
Run by a local artist, this private
cottage has a nice garden and
antique-filled rooms.

Ibiza

DK Choice

EIVISSA: Ibiza Gran Hotel €€€
Boutique
Paseo Juan Carlos I, 17, 07800
Tel *971 806 806*
w ibizagranhotel.com
This fashionable hotel offers
chic rooms and terrific wellness
facilities: a spa, pool, gym and
wetdeck. Visiting celebrities are
often seen working on their tans.

EIVISSA: Mirador de Dalt
Vila €€€
Historic
Plaza. España 4, Ibiza, 07800
Tel *971 303 045*
w hotelmiradoribiza.com

Deck chairs lining the outdoor swimming
pool at Ibiza Gran hotel, Elvissa

Fabulous 19th-century palace
with elegant rooms and suites.

PORTINATX: Cas Mallorqui €
B&B
Cala Portinatx s/n, 07810
Tel *971 320 505*
w casmallorqui.com
Comfortable rooms with
panoramic views of the beach.
Ideal for watersports and
diving enthusiasts.

SAN MIGUEL: Hotel Hacienda
Na Xemena €€€
Luxury
Urbanización Na Xemena, 07815
Tel *971 334 500*
w hotelhacienda-ibiza.com
A superb retreat for an
unparalleled Balearic life-
style experience.

SANT GERTRUDIS DE FRUITERA:
Cas Gasi €€€
Boutique
Camino Viejo de Sant Mateu s/n, 07814
Tel *971 197 700*
w casgasi.com
Built in 1880, this mansion has
a large pool in the gardens,
and a private yacht available
to guests.

SANT JOAN: The Giri
Residence €€€
Boutique
C/Principal 3–5, 07810
Tel *971 333 345*
w thegiri.com
This hotel offers Morroccan
interiors with a pleasing
Mediterranean ambiance.

SANT JOAN DE LABRITJA:
Finca Can Marti €€
B&B
Venda de Ca's Ripolls, 29, 07810
Tel *971 333 500*
w canmarti.com
A finca and working farm that
offers an eclectic, apartment-
style stay.

SANT JOSÉP DE TALAIA: Ses
Pitreras €€€
Boutique
C/Valladolid 1–3, 07839
Tel *971 345 000*
w sespitreras.com
A delightful, compact hotel
with plush rooms, set in a
1970s building.

SANTA EULÀRIA DES RIU:
Aguas de Ibiza €€€
Resort
C/Salvador Camacho 9, 07840
Tel *971 319 962*
w aguasdeibiza.com
Premium resort on the
beachfront. Offers spa and
wellness facilities.

Formentera

EL PILAR DE LA MOLA: Es Ram
Resort €€€
Boutique
Camino Es Ram, Route de la Mola
Tel *971 948 427*
w esramresort.com
Independent mini-villas with
charming terraces, set between
pine forests and the beach.

DK Choice

ES CALO: Hostal Entre
Pinos €
B&B
Ctra La Mola, km 12.3, 07872
Tel *971 327 019*
w hostalentrepinos.com
Close to the fabulous beaches
of Es Caló and Arenal, this
family-run hotel has a lovely
terrace-bar, pool and garden.
The outdoor spaces are great
for children.

LA SAVINA: Hostal Bellavista €
B&B
Puerto de La Savina, 07870
Tel *971 323 324*
w hostal-bellavista.com
A no-frills but economical option
in front of the port of La Savina.
Some rooms have balconies with
views and most of the restaurants
can be found in the area.

LA SAVINA: Hostal
La Savina €
B&B
Avenida Mediterránea 20–40, 07870
Tel *971 322 279*
w hostal-lasavina.com
Lovely, fourth-generation,
family-run hotel with whitewashed rooms. Located right
on the water's edge. Gorgeous
sea views.

PLATJA MIGJORN: Riu La
Mola €€€
Resort
*Playa de Mitjorn s/n, San Francisco
Javier, 07860*
Tel *971 327 000*
w riulamola.com
Family-friendly resort on the
incredible, mystical Migjorn
beach. Good amenities,
including a spa.

SANT FERRAN DE SES ROQUES:
Hostal Illes Pituïses €
B&B
*Avda Juan Castelló Guasch 48, Sant
Ferran, 07871*
Tel *971 328 189*
w illespituises.com
En-suite rooms with balconies or
terraces. Pleasant gardens.

For more information on types of hotels *see page 147*

WHERE TO EAT AND DRINK

The resorts and large town centres found in the Balearic Islands offer a good selection of restaurants, able to satisfy even the most demanding of palates. While the resorts do, of course, cater to visitors who have come for the beaches rather than the food, good-quality local cuisine is always available. Restaurants serving local specialities can be easily spotted (not having an "international" or photo menu is a good rule of thumb) and many are open all year.

The Stay restaurant in Port de Pollença, Mallorca

Local Cuisine

A number of the Balearic dishes are Catalan in origin. *Ensaimadas*, delicious spiral pastries that are dusted with icing sugar, are commonplace. So, too, are the spicy pork pâtés (*sobrasadas*). Rustic "one-pot" dishes and soups are also popular. The best known of these is *caldereta de llagosta (see 105)*.

With the exception of cheaper varieties such as sardines, the price paid for local fish and seafood is the same as elsewhere on the Peninsula, though you'll always find a cheaper daily special.

When to Eat

As with the rest of Spain, lunchtime in the Balearic Islands is usually between 1:30pm and 3pm. It may be that restaurants are full and you may have to wait a long time to be served. Outside traditional mealtimes, the menu selection can be limited. Some restaurant kitchens may be closed after 3pm. As an alternative, bars can provide a good variety of food and snacks while beachside restaurants are good for snacks at any time of the day.

Dinner on the islands usually starts after 9pm, when the temperature drops. This is when the restaurants, cafés, gardens and bars fill up. For Spaniards this is a time to meet with friends. Restaurants also tend to fill up for Sunday lunch and booking is essential at this time.

Places to Eat

There is a boundless choice of places to eat in the Balearic Islands. This is especially true during the high season, when many restaurants that are

A modest restaurant in Estellencs

closed during the other months of the year open. In the cheaper bars it is worth trying *tapas* or *raciónes* (small plates), as these are most likely to be freshly prepared (a *ración* is often enough for two). When venturing into a bar that is popular with the locals, you should try the set price *menú del día* (menu of the day). This is a full three-course meal, accompanied by a drink. Often these menus are very good value and may cost as little as €10.

Many visitors prefer to use their hotel's restaurant for breakfast and dinner, and take their lunch in bars and restaurants close to the beach. Some hotels have wonderful restaurants; others are merely adequate. One point in hotel restaurants' favour is that they can offer a wide selection of food, low prices, fast service and a friendly atmosphere. Most of them serve a safe, international cuisine and you are likely to see paella, pizza, fish and chips, roast chicken and curry all on the same menu. These restaurants successfully compete with the popular fast-food chains. Restaurants that are near or on less crowded beaches tend to offer much better food, but the choice may be limited.

Vegetarians

The food of these islands tends to be on the heavy side and is based mainly on pork and fish, but it also has a lot to offer vegetarians. It is easy to make a meal of *tapas* consisting of vegetables such as artichokes, broad beans, aubergines, peppers, tomatoes or *tortilla española* (Spanish omelette). One of the simplest vegetarian dishes is *tumbet* (a tomato-rich vegetable stew). Local vegetarian cuisine worth recommending includes *eggs al modo de Sóller* and Mahón-style beans. Most restaurants offer some vegetarian dishes. If there are none on the menu you can always ask for a salad (specify that you don't want meat or fish in it) or a *macedonia* (fruit salad), or even a *gazpacho* (the traditional Spanish cold tomato soup). Local cheeses are also great. Try the creamy, nutty *queso mallorquín* and the cured cheese from Maó.

The elegant interiors of Simply Fosh, run by renowned chef Marc Fosh

Booking

There are a large number of restaurants on the Balearic Islands and there should not be any problem in finding a table. Nevertheless, it is worthwhile booking a table in advance to avoid disappointment, particularly when you want to dine in reputable rural restaurants such as those attached to hotels, or those in a remote location.

Disabled Persons

New restaurants are obliged to have disabled access, but many of the rest are not; they may not have wheelchair ramps and the tables tend to be placed close together. The most accessible are the bars and small

restaurants situated along seaside promenades, with outside tables.

Traditional paella is served throughout the region

Prices and Tipping

In beachside restaurants, prices are reasonable. A lunch will cost around €20–25. The *menú del día* may be even cheaper. The sky is the limit on prices charged by some of the top restaurants. Some regional dishes and seafood may be expensive. The price of the latter will depend on the weight of the ordered lobster or fish.

Mallorca and Ibiza tend to have the highest prices. The final bill includes service charges and tax and is, therefore, higher than the sum of the menu items. Normally, the tip does not exceed 10 per cent; it is usual to round up the bill.

Most restaurants welcome credit cards, though American Express is less common. Some bars take Visa, but small sums are normally paid in cash. Some small restaurants, especially those not geared up for tourists, may not accept credit cards at all – so it is best to check in advance.

Recommended Restaurants

The *nueva cocina* food phenomenon that has swept Catalonia is making headway in the Balearics. Mostly it is found in owner-run establishments, where the chef takes time-honoured recipes, the finest local ingredients and gives them a contemporary, personal twist, both in taste and presentation. At the other end of the spectrum, home-cooked meals prepared in family-run restaurants can provide an equally memorable meal.

Both these categories, and more, have been considered when choosing the restaurants featured in this guide. They span a wide choice of budget ranges and tastes, and cover something for everyone. For the "best of the best", we've marked recommended restaurants as DK Choice. These are the island's most outstanding establishments, offering singular experiences that are unrivalled by anything on the mainland.

Juan y Andrea in Formentera, set against a stunning beach backdrop

The Flavours of the Balearics

This quartet of beautiful islands, strategically positioned on ancient trading routes, has been fought over for thousands of years. Each occupying force – Arabs, Catalans, French and British among them – has left its mark, and the local cuisine reflects this. Mediterranean seafood, particularly spectacular lobster and crayfish, remains the most prominent local ingredient, but the islands are also known for their delicious pastries and desserts, like the feather-light *ensaimada* from Mallorca and the typical Ibizan *flaó*. Cured meats *(embutits)* and traditionally made cheeses are also local specialities.

Locally grown oranges

Mediterranean sea produce in a Mallorcan fish market

Mallorca and Menorca

Seafood predominates in the Balearic Islands. Menorca is renowned for *caldereta de llagosta* (spiny lobster stew), once a simple fishermen's dish but now a delicacy *(see p105)*. The classic Mallorcan dish is *pa amb oli*, a slice of toasted country bread rubbed with garlic and drizzled with local olive oil. Menorca's creamy garlic sauce *all i oli* is a delicious accompaniment to meat and seafood dishes, and the island also produces fine cheese, *formatge de Maó*.

Ibiza and Formentera

Seafood also reigns supreme on Ibiza and its quieter little sister, Formentera, especially in *calders* (stews) such as *borrida de rajada* (skate with potatoes, eggs and pastis) and *guisat de peix*. Pork is the staple meat. For a picnic, try *cocarrois*, pastries filled with meat, fish or vegetables, and *formatjades*, soft-cheese-filled pastries flavoured with cinnamon. Delicious local desserts include *gató* (almond cake served with ice cream) and Ibizan *flaó*, made with creamy cheese and eggs, and flavoured with mint.

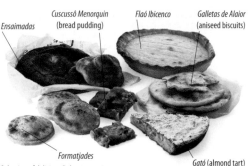

Ensaimadas — Cuscussó Menorquin (bread pudding) — Flaó Ibicenco — Galletas de Alaior (aniseed biscuits) — Formatjades — Gató (almond tart)

Selection of delicious Balearic pastries

Regional Dishes and Specialities

All i oli

Fish and shellfish (particularly the revered local lobster) are omnipresent in the Balearics, particularly along the coast. Try them simply grilled to fully appreciate their freshness (many seaside restaurants have their own fishing boats), but you will also find wonderful, slow-cooked stews which are bursting with flavour. The rugged inland regions provide mountain lamb and kid, along with pork, which is also used to make *embutits*, including spicy Mallorcan *sobrasada* which is delicious with *pa amb oli*. The tourist industry has not killed the longstanding farming tradition on the Balearics, which produce plentiful fruit and vegetables. Mallorca makes its own robust wines, particularly around the village of Binissalem, while Menorca, thanks to the long British occupation of the island, makes its own piquant gin.

Tumbet de peix A fish pie, made with layers of firm white fish, peppers, aubergine (eggplant) and sliced boiled egg.

Where to Eat and Drink

Mallorca

ALARÓ: Traffic €
Regional
Plaça de la Vila, 7, 07170 Alaró
Tel *971 879 117* **Closed** *Tue*
Located in an old manor with a
pleasant terrace by a garden
and pool. The *lechona* (suckling
pig) is a speciality.

**ALCÚDIA: Meson de los
Patos** €€
Seafood
*Cami de Ca'n Blau 42, Parque
Natural de S'Albufera, Bahía
d'Alcúdia, 07410*
Tel *971 890 265* **Closed** *Mon; 6 Jan–
mid-Feb*
This eatery is located in the
beautiful Parc Natural de
S'Albufera. The menu includes
a variety of outstanding fish
dishes and an excellent
selection of island wines.

**ALCÚDIA: Restaurante
Jardín** €€€
Regional
C/ Tritones s/n, 07410, Port d'Alcúdia
Tel *971 892 391* **Closed** *Nov–Mar*
Michelin-starred fine dining with
a choice of service indoors, or in
the pretty outdoor garden. Well-
planned and beautifully
designed menu.

BINISSALEM: Es P'dal €
Bistro
Passeig des Born 8, 07350
Tel *971 511 061*
A pub-style old bar serving
quality pizzas and tapas with a

The elegant interiors of Restaurante Jardín,
a Michelin-starred restaurant in Alcúdia

good selection of beers and
local wines. A good place to
have a drink or a coffee.
Occasional live music.

BINISSALEM: Can Arabí €€
Mediterranean
Cami Bellveure, km 1.200, 07350
Tel *971 512 211* **Closed** *Mon*
Enjoy appetizing Mallorcan
and Mediterranean cuisine at
this country-style restaurant.
The daily menu is prepared
using fresh, locally sourced,
organic ingredients.

BUNYOLA: I un poc mes €
International
Santa Bàrbara 3, 07110
Tel *971 148 378* **Closed** *Sun dinner
& Mon*
A small cantina serving fresh
local fare in creative dishes with
Asian influences.

DK Choice

CAIMARI: Ca Na Toneta €€
Regional
Horitzó 21, 07314
Tel *971 515 226* **Closed** *winter:
Mon–Thu*
In a stylishly renovated
country house, Maria and
Teresa Solivellas treat their
customers like old friends.
Located amid the untouched
landscape near the village of
Caimari, Ca Na Toneta works
closely with local producers and
farmers to provide authentic
homecooking, though the
dishes have a contemporary
touch. The six-course menu is
worth the indulgence.

CALA RAJADA: La Casita €
Regional
C/ es Farallo 6, 07590
Tel *971 563 731* **Closed** *Tue*
The chef at this delightful
restaurant serves meat and fish
prepared to his own exacting
recipes. The restaurant also has
a *bodega* with a range of
island wines.

**CALA RAJADA: Cavall
Bernat** €€€
Fusion
*C/ Maressers 2, Cala Sant Vicenç,
07469*
Tel *971 530 250* **Closed** *Nov–Apr:
Sun*
Offering a mix of classic Mallorcan
dishes and international recipes
(with a *cocina nueva* touch),
Cavall Bernat is a stylish, slightly
formal establishment.

<table>
<tr><td colspan="2">Price Guide</td></tr>
<tr><td colspan="2">For a three-course meal for one,
including half a bottle of house wine,
service and tax.</td></tr>
<tr><td>€</td><td>up to €30</td></tr>
<tr><td>€€</td><td>€30–€60</td></tr>
<tr><td>€€€</td><td>over €60</td></tr>
</table>

CALA RAJADA: Ses Rotges €€€
French
C/Rafael Blanes 21, 07590
Tel *971 563 108* **Closed** *Jan–mid-
Mar; Sun dinner;*
Mallorcan-influenced, classic
French dishes and great
home-made desserts. The
terrace overlooks a lovely
subtropical garden.

CALVIÀ: Ca na Cucó €€
Regional
Avenida Palma 14, 07184
Tel *971 670 083* **Closed** *Summer:
Sat lunch*
Classic Mallorcan cuisine in a
traditional stone house with a
terrace that overlooks the
Calvià seafront.

CALVIÀ: Lila Portals €€
Contemporary
Passatge Mor 1, Portals Nous, 07181
Tel *971 676 894*
Splendid terrace overlooking
the beach, this place serves
creative Mediterranean dishes
and surprising desserts. Tapas
dishes are served all day.

**CAMPANET: Es Mirador
Monnaber** €€
Contemporary
Possessió Monnaber Nou, 07310
Tel *971 877 176*
Attached to a regal country
house hotel, Es Mirador Monnaber
offers a choice of classic dishes
with a modern touch.

**COLÒNIA DE SANT JORDI:
Pep Serra** €€
Seafood
C/ Gabriel Roca 87, 07638
Tel *971 655 399* **Closed** *Mon–Fri;
Oct–Mar;*
Enjoy freshly caught fish and a
selection of other sea produce at
this charming seafront restaurant.
Don't miss the outstanding
langoustine paella.

**COLÒNIA DE SANT JORDI:
La Playa** €€€
Seafood
C/ Mayor 25, 07638
Tel *971 655 256* **Closed** *Mon lunch*
In a typical Mallorcan house on
the beach, this hotel and restau-
rant serves paella, lobster salad
and fresh fish straight off the boat.

For more information on types of restaurants *see page 153*

Charming indoor seating at the well-reviewed Santi Taura in Lloseta

DEIÀ: Café Miró   €€€
Regional
Cami de Son Canals s/n, 07179
Tel *971 639 011*   **Closed** *Sun*
Located in a splendid 17th-century country house, this bistro serves excellent local, island cuisine. Michael Douglas is known to be a regular.

DEIÀ: El Olivo   €€€
Mediterranean
Son Canals s/n, 07179
Tel *971 639 011*   **Closed** *Winter: Mon & Tue*
Set inside a former olive mill, with additional seating out on a lovely terrace, this famous restaurant offers delightful options. The *menú degustación* is a memorable feast. Dress formally.

ESCORCA: Es Guix   €€
Regional
Urbanización Es Guix, 07315
Tel *971 517 092*   **Closed** *Tue; Jan & Mar: Mon–Thu*
Outstanding traditional restaurant overlooking a rock pool in a lovely forested setting. Located near the Monestir de Lluc.

ESPORLES: Meson de la Villa   €€
Regional
C/ Nou de Sant Pere 5, 07190
Tel *971 610 901*   **Closed** *summer: Sun & lunch; winter: Wed & Sun–Tue dinner; July*
This townhouse restaurant prides itself in being the first truly Castilian grill in Mallorca. Food is prepared in a rustic wood-burning grill.

FELANITX: Sa Llotja   €€€
Mediterranean
C/Pescadors s/n Porto Colom, 07670
Tel *971 825 165*   **Closed** *Mon; Nov–Dec*
Appetizing Mediterranean cuisine based on fresh seasonal fare, particularly fish and vegetables.

Key to Price Guide *see page 155*

The restaurant occupies a beautiful 15th-century building overlooking the harbour.

INCA: Celler Ca'n Ripoll   €
Regional
C/ Jaume Armengol 4, 07300
Tel *971 500 024*   **Closed** *Sun dinner*
A winery from the 1760s, Celler Ca'n Ripoll is an atmospherically restored national heritage building. Try the island classics, such as the roast milk lamb, and for dessert, anything with fresh almonds.

INCA: S'Angel   €
Tapas
Plaza del Ángel 2, 07300
Tel *971 880 473*
A choice of innovative Mediterranean dishes, *pintxos* and an amazing selection of gin and tonics.

INCA: Cellar Can Amer   €€
Regional
C/ Pau 39, 07300
Tel *971 501 261*   **Closed** *May–Sep: Sat & Sun; Winter: Sun dinner*
Hidden away in Inca's market, this award-winning restaurant serves classic Mallorcan cuisine. The recipes have been developed over decades of research into the origins of Mallorcan food.

DK Choice

LLOSETA: Santi Taura   €€
Regional
C/Joan Carles I 48, 07360
Tel *656 738 214*   **Closed** *Mon lunch, Tue & Sun dinner; Aug: 2 weeks*
Local chef Santi Taura is a food anthropologist of sorts –he unearths old island recipes and reinterprets them. The restaurant offers a tasting menu, which changes weekly. With each course, the waiter (or often Santi himself) explains the cultural history of what's on your plate. Book in advance.

MANACOR: La Reserva Rotana   €€€
International
Cami de Bendris, km 3, 07500
Tel *971 845 685*   **Closed** *lunch; mid-Nov–mid-Feb*
On the patio of this handsome 17th-century hotel, chef Cristian Denz combines Mallorcan and international recipes to create wonderful gourmet delights, all presented with panache.

MONTUÏRI: Pizzeria Es Moli   €
Bistro
C/ es Molinar 51, 07230
Tel *971 646 508*   **Closed** *Wed*
A pleasant restaurant set in an old windmill with fantastic views. Delicious home-made pizzas, fresh pasta and Italian salads on offer.

PALMA: Bar Cuba Colonial   €
Mediterranean
C/ Sant Magí 1, 07013
Tel *971 452 237*
A lovely café with tables on the street. At night, it becomes a bar and salsa club with an à la carte menu on offer.

PALMA: Bon Lloc   €
Vegetarian
C/ San Feliu 7, 07012
Tel *971 718 617*   **Closed** *Sun & Mon–Wed dinner*
One of the rare vegan and vegetarian restaurants in Mallorca, Bon Lloc offers a choice of light meals, cooked using local ingredients.

PALMA: Ca'n Torrat   €
Regional
Camino Maravillas, 25. Exit 11, Autopista de Palma (3 km from the airport) S'Arenal, 07610
 Tel *971 262 055*   **Closed** *Wed*
Famed for its wood-fired barbecue and grill, Ca'n Torrat offers traditional local dishes such as suckling pig, roast lamb and fried fish.

Lovely outdoor seating under the trees at El Olivo, Deià

PALMA: Café L' Antiquari €
Tapas
C/ Arabi 5, 07003
Tel *871 572 313* **Closed** *Sun*
A relaxed place with an
interesting decor and a friendly,
almost hippy, vibe. Helpings
are sizable but not too large,
and the brunches are
absolutely delectable.

PALMA: Can Punta €
International
C/ Vicario Joaquin Fuster 105, 07006
Tel *971 274 334* **Closed** *Summer:*
Mon; Winter: dinner (except Fri &
Sat & Tue)
Pretty café and restaurant on the
waterfront at Portixol. The menu
includes Greek-inspired salads,
tapas, and coffee and snacks
throughout the day.

PALMA: Cappuccino €
Café
C/ de Sant Miquel 53, 07002
Tel *971 719 764* **Closed** *Sun*
In the heart of Palma, this stylish
café offers great morning coffee,
light lunches and wonderful
evening drinks.

PALMA: Club Nautico
Cala Gamba €
Seafood
Passeig Cala Gamba s/n, 07007
Tel *971 262 372* **Closed** *Mon*
With its nautical theme and large
windows that overlook the marina,
this restaurant is a must-visit. The
menu includes an interesting
choice of locally-caught fish.

PALMA: Fibonacci Pan €
Bistro
C/Vicario Joaquin Fuster 95, 07006
Tel *971 249 961*
Scandinavian bakery that offers
excellent sandwiches, cakes,
croissants and top-rate coffee.
Also serves light salads and
soups at lunchtime.

PALMA: Koh €
Asian
C/de Servet 15, 07013
Tel *971 287 039* **Closed** *Sun & lunch*
In Palma's Santa Catalina district,
Koh serves tasty and tangy dishes
– curries, noodles, barbecued
meats and Vietnamese rolls. Street
-food nights on Wednesdays.

PALMA: Molta Barra €
Tapas
Carrer del Pes de la Farina 12,
07001
Tel *658 419 162* **Closed** *Sun & Mon*
With delightful tapas and *pintxos*
at good prices, this popular
eatery is an integral part of the
night scene in the buzzing Sa
Gerreria area.

La Taberna de la Bóveda, Palma, offering
food from Castile and the Basque Country

PALMA: Quina Creu €
Bistro
C/ Corderia 24, 07001
Tel *971 711 772* **Closed** *Sun*
Views of an ancient street to
accompany good, unpretentious
bistro fare. Eclectic, retro decor
and a friendly ambience.

PALMA: La Taberna
de la Bóveda €
Tapas
Paseo Sagrera 3, 07012
Tel *971 720 026* **Closed** *Sun*
Popular tapas bar with pretty
period decor. Serves large
helpings of Basque Country and
Castilian favourites.

PALMA: Tast €
Tapas
Calle Unión 2, 07001
Tel *971 729 878* **Closed** *Sun*
Popular local place that serves
top-quality tapas and *pintxos*,
with bite-sized canapés made
with farmhouse cheese and
charcuterie (cooked cold meats).

PALMA: La Bodeguilla €€
Tapas
C/ Sant Jaume 3, 07012
Tel *971 718 2/4*
A superb tapas bar with a dining
room upstairs, this Palma
institution serves typical
Mallorcan cuisine.

PALMA: El Gallego €€
Seafood
C/ Carmen 16, 07003
Tel *971 710 313* **Closed** *dinner*
(except Thu–Sat)
Popular noisy local eatery that
serves Galician seafood specialities.
Try the steamed mussels,
octopus or cod with *salsa verde*.

PALMA: Forn de Sant Joan €€
Regional
C/ Sant Joan 4, 07012
Tel *971 728 422*
One of Palma's best restaurants,
housed in an old bakery spread
over four floors that was
converted into an eatery in
1992. Serves imaginative dishes
with a modern touch.

PALMA: Misa €€
Bistro
C/ Can Maçanet 1, 07003
Tel *971 595 301* **Closed** *Sun*
This brasserie offers carefully
prepared, French-inspired dishes,
cooked using top-quality
ingredients, in an informal and
relaxed setting. Book in advance.

PALMA: Nassau Beach
Club €€
Seafood
Passeig de Portixol 5, 07004
Tel *664 449 053*
Enjoy salads and ciabattas, or
sushi and fresh fish, lounging on
a deck chair on the white sandy
beach. The Sunday brunches
have live DJs.

PALMA: Las Olas Bistro €€
Fusion
C/ Can Fortuny 5, 07001
Tel *971 214 905* **Closed** *Sun,*
Mon & Tue dinner
A smart little eatery that serves
Mediterranean lunches by day
and Asian cuisine by night.

PALMA: Tasca de Blanquerna €€
Tapas
C/ Blanquerna 6, 07003
Tel *971 290 108* **Closed** *Sun & Mon*
dinner
Contemporary restaurant that
serves dishes with Asian and
Mediterranean influences created
by the renowned chef Marc Fosh.

The exquisite dining area at Misa in Palma,
renowned for its French-inspired cuisine

For more information on types of restaurants *see page 153*

The modernistic interiors of Simply Fosh in the hotel Convent de la Missió in Palma

PALMA: Toque €€
Belgian
C/ Federico García Lorca 6, 07014
Tel 971 287 068 **Closed** Sun & Mon
A Belgian family restaurant,
serving the most delicious
mussels, escargots in green
sauce, steak tartare and
premium desserts; all
accompanied by a good selection
of Belgian beers, French and
local wines. Book in advance.

PALMA: Wasabi Blue €€
Fusion
C/ Trafalgar 41, 07007
Tel 971 264 602 **Closed** Oct–Mar;
Tue & Sun dinner
Renowned fusion restaurant
by the seafront. It serves
remarkable sushi and uses local
fish to make a variety of makis,
rolls and sashimi.

DK Choice

PALMA: Simply Fosh €€€
Mediterranean
C/ de la Missió 7A, 07003
Tel 971 720 114 **Closed** Sun
British chef Marc Fosh has
garnered a reputation of
being one of the island's
finest chefs. Simply Fosh is a
stylish restaurant located in
the hip Convent de la Missió
hotel, where Fosh makes use
of local ingredients to create
the most extraordinary
Mediterranean delights. The
menu changes seasonally. It
offers a good wine list and a
truly memorable experience.

POLLENÇA: 3/65 Restaurant €€€
Regional
Crta Palma–Pollença PM 220, km
49.9, 07460
Tel 971 535 353 **Closed** daily
lunch & Tue (except Aug); Dec–Jan

Part of the chic boutique hotel
Son Brull, this elegant restaurant
serves gourmet cuisine created
from fresh local ingredients and
produce of the hotel's own
certified organic farm.

**PORT DE POLLENÇA:
The Codfather** €
Seafood
C/ de Levante 14, 07470
Tel 629 044 082 **Closed** daily
lunch; Nov–Mar
British-style fish and chips at
this bustling eatery with an
outdoor garden. Enjoy all the
usual favourites, including
mushy peas and gravy.

**PORT DE POLLENÇA: Hell's
Kitchen** €
International
C/ Verge del Carme 8, 07470
Tel 971 867 163 **Closed** Winter: Mon
& Tue
A friendly café run by expats that
offers home-made cuisine, from

Diners at the busy Hell's Kitchen in Port de
Pollença, offering international cuisine

curries to pasta, and even British
staples such as the traditional
Sunday roast.

**PORT DE POLLENÇA:
Laguna** €
International
Edificio Bonança, Calle El Faro 15,
07470
Tel 971 864 919 **Closed** Nov–Mar
Delicious cocktails and
appetizing meals by the pool,
in keeping with the laid-back,
tropical ambience.

**PORT DE POLLENÇA:
Neptuno** €
Seafood
C/ Migjorn 8, 07470
Tel 971 867 859
A bright, nautical-themed
eatery that serves tapas and
home-made meals. It also has
a special children's menu.
Reservations essential.

**PORT DE POLLENÇA:
Corb Mari** €€
Seafood
Passeig Anglada Camarassa 91,
07470
Tel 971 867 040 **Closed** Mon
(except Jun–Aug); Dec–mid-Mar
While it specializes in grilled
meat, Corb Mari also whips up
some of the best paellas in
Pollença. Don't forget to try
the barbecued prawns, squid
kebabs and monkfish.

**PORT DE POLLENÇA:
Iru** €€
Contemporary
Paseo Anglada Camarasa 23,
07470
Tel 971 867 002 **Closed** Tue
(except in summer); mid-Nov–Feb
Innovative fish and meat dishes,
served on a sunny terrace near
the Port of Pollença. Reasonably
priced, with light pastas and
salads at lunchtime.

PORT DE POLLENÇA:
La Llonja €€
Seafood
Moll Vell s/n, 07470
Tel *971 868 430* **Closed** *Nov–Mar: Tue*
An elegant place with a weekly menu that is based on what the fishermen bring in. Try the legendary lobster stew – it is absolutely divine.

PORT DE POLLENÇA:
Stay €€
International
Muelle Nuevo s/n, 07470
Tel *971 864 013*
A charming glass-fronted restaurant with great views that sits right on the port. It serves delicious fish, pasta and salads.

PORT DE SÓLLER:
Es Fanals €€€
Seafood
Calle Belgica s/n, 0/108
Tel *971 637 886*
Part of the luxurious Jumeriah resort, this lunch-only, alfresco restaurant serves stellar seafood against a spectacular Mediterranean backdrop.

PORTO COLOM:
Sa Sinia €€
Seafood
Calle Pescadores 28, 07670
Tel *971 824 323* **Closed** *Mon; Nov–Jan*
Among the finest restaurants in Mallorca, Sa Sinia is well-known for its unique seafood creations, home-made desserts and warm, friendly service.

DK Choice

SA COMA:
Es Molí d'en Bou €€€
Regional
Calle Liles s/n, 07560
Tel *971 569 663* **Closed** *Mon, Tue–Fri lunch & Sun*
Awarded a Michelin star in recognition of chef Tomeu Caldentey's subtle, creative interpretations of Mallorcan cuisine, Es Molí d'en Bou has been a success since it first opened in 2000. Enjoy the artistry of the tasting menu or dishes such as suckling pig with apples and *sobrasada* or *solomillo* with white asparagus and clams.

SÓLLER: El Guia €
Regional
C/ Castañer 2, 07100
Tel *971 630 227*
The dining room of an old-fashioned, family-run hotel in the heart of Sóller; offers friendly ambience and well-prepared classic dishes. A local favourite.

SÓLLER: Muleta de Ca S'Hereu €€
Regional
Camp de sa Mar s/n, Platja de'n Repic, 07100
Tel *971 186 018*
Rustic eatery at a charming rural hotel; serves modest salad lunches but generous home-cooked meals in the evenings.

SÓLLER: Sa Cova €€
International
Plaça Constitució 7, 07100
Tel *971 633 222* **Closed** *Sun dinner*
Enjoy rabbit in garlic sauce, crab with snails, or couscous with vegetables and meats. Vegetarian dishes are also available.

SÓLLER: Bens d'Avall €€€
Regional
Urb. Costa Deià. Ctra Sóller–Deià, 07100
Tel *971 632 381* **Closed** *Mon & Tue lunch; Winter: Mon–Thu*
A wonderful setting with stunning views of the coast and Deià. The food, which builds upon the best of local ingredients, is outstanding as well.

VALLDEMOSSA: C'an Costa €€
Regional
Carretera Deià, km 2.5, 07170
Tel *971 612 263* **Closed** *Nov–Mar; Mon–Fri dinner & Tue*
Charming rural restaurant with simple, rustic-style cooking. The suckling pig is a speciality.

Menorca

ALAIOR: Ca'n Jaumot €
Tapas
C/ Sant Joan Baptista 6, 07730
Tel *971 378 294* **Closed** *May–Aug: Sun*
A popular local rendezvous, offers a wide assortment of tapas, pizzas, salads and sandwiches, together with a good collection of wines.

ALAIOR: Es Forn de Torre Solí Nou €€
Regional
Urb Torre Solí Nou, 07730
Tel *971 372 898*
Excellent meat and poultry *a la brasa* (char-grilled). The best tables in this attractive restaurant are those on the breezy terrace.

CALA EN PORTER:
Sa Païssa €
Bistro
Av da Central 54, 07730
Tel *971 377 389*
Conveniently located in the centre of Cala en Porter in an eponymous hostel, Sa Païssa offers a fairly good selection of well-cooked dishes. Breakfast, lunch and dinner available.

CIUTADELLA: Bar Aurora €
Tapas
Plaza Alfons III 3, 07760
Tel *971 481 994*
Located in one of Ciutadella's most charming squares, Bar Aurora is a tapas institution and local favourite. Try the meatballs and grilled squid.

CIUTADELLA: Es Tastet €
Regional
C/ Carnisseria 9, 07760
Tel *971 384 797* **Closed** *Feb; summer: Sun lunch; winter: Sun dinner*
A wonderful, friendly place for breakfast, as well as creative tapas, pasta and fish through the day. The owner takes pride in cooking with fresh market produce.

CIUTADELLA: Cas Ferrer de Sa Font €€
Regional
C/ Portal de Sa Font 16, 07760
Tel *971 480 784* **Closed** *Nov–Mar; Jun–Aug: Sun lunch*
Spread out over three rooms of an imposing 17th-century mansion, this restaurant offers a small but worthy menu. The dishes are mostly island specials, cooked using organic produce from its own kitchen garden.

The stunning outdoors at Es Forn de Torre Solí Nou, Alaior

Table laid out at the Son Granot restaurant, part of a beautiful rural hotel in Es Castell

CIUTADELLA: Casa Manolo €€
Seafood
Marina 117–121, 07760
Tel *971 380 003*   **Closed** *Nov–Apr*
Well-known harbourfront
restaurant that serves good local
grilled fish with rice.

CIUTADELLA: Es Puntet €€
Regional
Jose Maria Cuadrado (Ses Voltes) 24,
07760
Tel *971 484 863*   **Closed** *Sun*
A pleasant restaurant that
serves innovative Menorcan
cuisine. Superb home-made
cakes and good breakfasts. Order
dessert at the start of the meal –
always made fresh, they take
time to prepare.

CIUTADELLA: Es Tast de na
Silvia €€
Mediterranean
Passeig de Portixol 21–22, 07760
Tel *971 387 895*   **Closed** *Wed; Nov–*
Mar
Top-notch Mediterranean cuisine
served in a romantic ambience.
One of the best among a series
of touristy restaurants in the area.

CIUTADELLA: Café Balear €€€
Seafood
Pla de Sant Joan 15, 07760
Tel *971 380 005*
One of the best fish eateries
on the island. Formerly a
fishermen's quayside inn, Café
Balear has its own boat that
goes out every morning to
catch the day's menu.

ES CASTELL: Club Nautic
es Castell €€
Seafood
C/ Miranda de Cales Fonts 2, 07720
Tel *971 362 542*   **Closed** *Mon,*
Wed & Sun dinner
A former fort on the harbour, this
nautical club offers a marine
menu. Stunning views.

ES CASTELL: Sant Joan de
Binissaida €€
Regional
Cami de Binissaida 108, 07720
Tel *971 355 598*   **Closed** *Nov–Apr*
Savour traditional Menorcan
dishes in the stone-walled dining
room, or in the lush gardens of
this beautiful rural hotel.

ES CASTELL: Son Granot €€
Regional
Carretera Sant Felip s/n, 07720
Tel *971 355 555*
Old family recipes for traditional
dishes, prepared with fresh
vegetables from the kitchen
garden of this charming country
hotel. The Georgian-style colonial
building dates back to 1712.

ES MERCADAL: Es Moli
d'es Racó €€
Regional
C/ Major 53, 07740
Tel *971 375 392*
No-frills country restaurant
that makes good use of an
old windmill. Has top-class
traditional food and a good
choice of island wines.

ES MIGJORN GRAN:
S'Engolidor €€
Regional
C/ Major 3, 07749
Tel *971 370 193*   **Closed** *Nov–Mar;*
Mon & daily lunch
To be found behind the simple
façade of a four-room hotel, this
restaurant is a treat. The menu
features a choice of delicious
Menorcan dishes – don't miss out
on the tender baby lamb and
aubergine stuffed with fish.

FERRERIES: Liorna €
International
C/ Econòm Florit (C/ de Dalt) 9,
07750
Tel *971 373 912*   **Closed** *summer:*
Mon; winter: Mon–Thu

Damia Coll's restaurant doesn't
just look like an art gallery, it is
one. Choose from a diverse
range of options: pizzas, sushi
and Thai specials.

FERRERIES: El Mirador €€
Regional
Platja Cala Galdana s/n, 07750
Tel *971 154 503*
This charming eatery, located
on a rocky headland, offers
gorgeous views and delicious
house specials, which usually
include paella and fresh
fish-of-the-day. It also has an
excellent wine list.

FERRERIES: Meson El Gallo €€
Regional
Ctra Cala Galdana, km 1.5, 07750
Tel *971 373 039*   **Closed** *Mon;*
summer: lunch (except Sat & Sun);
winter: dinner (except Fri & Sat);
Dec & Jan
A short walk out of Ferreries,
the signature dish of this
farmhouse restaurant is *gallo*
(rooster) paella. Also popular are
the lip-smacking steaks, best
relished with Mallorcan cheese.

FORNELLS: Ca Na Marga €€
Regional
Urbanización "Ses Salines", Parc
núm. 1, 07748
Tel *971 376 410*   **Closed** *Nov–Apr;*
lunch
Family-run restaurant in Ses
Salines, where fish, meat and
vegetables *a la brasa* (char-
grilled) are the mainstay.

FORNELLS: Sa Rumbada €€
Seafood
C/ Gumersindo Riera 27, 07748
Tel *971 376 777*   **Closed** *Nov–Apr*
This attractive seaside restaurant
in Fornells has a splendid
terrace and a laid-back ambience.
Don't miss the famed, delicious
lobster stew.

Key to Price Guide *see page 155*

MAÓ: Sa Gavina II €
Regional
Moll de Llevant 157, 07701
Tel *609 048 699*
Small restaurant serving traditional food and home-made bread. Ask for the *raciones* (portions) menu to try more than one dish.

MAÓ: Restaurante Way €
Japanese
Moll de Llevant 216, 07701, Port de Maó
Tel *971 362 272*
A matchless Japanese restaurant where the sushi, maki and tempura are made using local catch. They also serve Chinese.

MAÓ: Cap Roig €€
Seafood
Ctra Sa Mesquida 13, 07589, Sa Mesquida
Tel *971 188 383* **Closed** *mid–Oct–Easter*
Named after the star of its menu – scorpion fish – Cap Roig is highly recommended. Its *caldereta de llagosta* (lobster stew) is also excellent, as is the Norway crab or crayfish, when available. Enjoy your food with stunning sea views from the cliff-top location.

MAÓ: Casa Sexto €€
Seafood
C/ Vassallo 2, 07703
Tel *971 368 407* **Closed** *Sun dinner*
Galician cuisine using fresh regional ingredients, including a variety of seafood, shellfish and cheese.

DK Choice

MAÓ: La Minerva €€€
Regional
Moll de Llevant 87, 07701
Tel *971 351 995* **Closed** *Mon; Jan*
A classic hangout for the island's yacht club crowd, La Minerva is the place to be seen. If you are lucky enough to get a table on the floating terrace in the harbour, you will be served the longest menu in Menorca. A wide range of meat dishes are on offer, as well as fish, notably the seafood *zarzuela* (stew).There is also a good fixed-price menu.

SANT LLUIS: Pan y Vino €€
Regional
Cami de la Coixa 3, Torret, 07710
Tel *971 150 201***Closed** *Tue; Dec–mid Feb; Sun dinner; winter: Fri lunch*
French chef Patrick James prepares elaborate local dishes with a French touch in this charming restaurant that is based in an old farmhouse.

Ibiza

EIVISSA: Locals Only €
Mediterranean
Plaça del Parc 5, 07800
Tel *971 301 997* **Closed** *Mon*
Opened by Tito Piazza, ex-chef of the famous Cipriani in New York, this restaurant serves local cuisine. Cocktails and brunch also available.

EIVISSA: La Masia d'en Sort €
Contemporary
Ctra de Sant Miquel, km 1, 07800
Tel *971 310 228* **Closed** *Mon (except Aug); daily for lunch*
A handsome 200-year-old country house with lovingly prepared island classics, to be enjoyed under lemon trees.

EIVISSA: Ca n'Alfredo €€
Seafood
Paseo Vara de Rey 16, 07800
Tel *971 311 274* **Closed** *Mon & Sun dinner; Nov: 2 weeks*
The oldest restaurant in Eivissa, located in a mansion on the port. Its menu is largely based on fish and rice.

EIVISSA: La Brasa €€€
International
Carrer de Pere Sala 3, 07800
Tel *971 301 202* **Closed** *winter: Sun*
This incredible restaurant, with a pleasant garden, is part of a villa in the old town.

EIVISSA: Las Dos Lunas €€€
International
Ctra Ibiza–San Antonio, km 5.4, 07840
Tel *971 198 102* **Closed** *Nov–April*
One of the most exclusive restaurants in Ibiza, Las Dos Lunas has an Italian and Mediterranean menu. Get a chance to rub elbows with many visiting celebrities.

EIVISSA: El Faro €€€
Seafood
Plaça Sa Riba 1, 07800
Tel *971 313 233* **Closed** *Oct–Apr*
Large terrace and palm-shaded garden. One of the best places to eat fish in Ibiza.

EIVISSA: El Olivo €€€
French
Plaça de la Vila 9, 07800
Tel *971 300 680* **Closed** *mid-Oct–mid-Apr; lunch*
Popular restaurant with a trendy terrace in the fashionable Dalt Vila. The cuisine is Ibizan-French with a *cocina nueva* edge.

EIVISSA: Sa Punta €€€
Fusion
Es Puet de Talamanca, 07819, Bahía de Talamanca
Tel *971 193 424* **Closed** *Nov–Mar*

The place to be seen in Sa Punta. An excellent restaurant with dishes that combine island cuisine with ritzy flourishes of Italian, Thai and Japanese.

FIGUERETAS: Soleado €€
Seafood
Paseo Ses Pitiusas s/n, 07800
Tel *971 394 811* **Closed** *Nov–Apr*
Right on Figueretas's palm-lined seafront, this large terrace restaurant reflects its French owners' culinary heritage.

SANT ANTONI DE PORTMANY: Rincon de Pepe €
Tapas
Sant Mateu 6, 07820
Tel *9/1 340 697* **Closed** *Nov–Mar*
Original quayside tapas bar and restaurant that offers a good variety. The staff operates a point-at-what-you want system that works well.

SANT ANTONI DE PORTMANY: Es Rebost de Ca'n Prats €€
Regional
C/ Cervantes 4, 07820
Tel *971 346 252* **Closed** *Tue; Jan*
For an authentic Ibizan dining experience in the heart of Sant Antoni, this family-run restaurant is regarded as one of the best.

SANT ANTONI DE PORTMANY: Sa Capella €€€
Regional
Ctra Sant Antoni–Santa Agnès, km 1, 07820
Tel *971 340 057* **Closed** *Nov–Mar; daily for lunch*
This former 16th-century chapel has been restored and transformed into a lovely restaurant with a terrace. The ambience is cool and the decor Modernist.

Seating overlooking the Figueretas seafront at Soleado

For more information on types of restaurants *see page 153*

The dining area at Sant Josep de Talaia's Es Torrent, located on the beach

SANT CARLES DE PERALTA:
Anita's Bar €
Tapas
Plaça de l'Església, 07850
Tel *971 335 090*
This hippy bar played a big role in Ibiza's counterculture. With its vine-covered patio and a range of tapas and pizzas, it remains a local favourite.

SANT JOSEP DE SA TALAIA:
El Destino €
Tapas
Calle de Talaia 15, 07830
Tel *971 800 341*   **Closed** *Sun; Nov–Mar*
The diverse and enduring patronage furthers El Destino's reputation as the most famous tapas bar and restaurant in Ibiza. Tapas and full *raciones* come with a twist of Moroccan and hints of Asian flavours, crossed with traditional island cuisine. Book in advance.

SANT JOSEP DE SA TALAIA:
Sa Caleta €€€
Seafood
Playa de es Bol Nou, 07830
Tel *971 187 095*   **Closed** *winter: dinner*
A beach club with a garden and sunloungers, Sa Caleta is an idyllic spot for a drink. The menu includes delicious grilled fish and seafood.

SANT JOSEP DE TALAIA:
Es Torrent €€€
Seafood
Cala d'es Torrent, Ctra Porroig to Sant Josep, 07839
Tel *971 802 160*   **Closed** *Nov–Easter*
With tables right on the beach, this wonderful eatery serves

superb fish, seafood and rice dishes. It is very popular with the locals.

SANT JOSEP DE SA TALAIA:
Es Xarcu €€€
Seafood
Cala Es Xarcu, Porroig, 07839
Tel *971 187 867*   **Closed** *Nov–Easter*
Informal eatery on the beach of a small, tranquil bay; serves local fish, hand-cut *jamón* (ham) and tapas under grass parasols.

SANT LLORENÇ:
Cami de Balafia €€
International
Ctra Sant Joan de Labritja, km 15.4 (Ctra Sant Llorenç), 07812
Tel *971 325 019*   **Closed** *Mon*
A hacienda-type patio under the stars, this is a family-run restaurant that serves juicy steaks and grilled meat dishes.

DK Choice

SANT LLORENÇ: La Paloma
€€
Mediterranean
C/Can Pou 4, 07812
Tel *971 325 543*   **Closed** *Oct–Jun: Mon; Nov*
Pretty garden restaurant surrounded by fruit orchards. In winter, it moves indoors to the renovated *finca*. It offers a small range of delicious Italian-inspired home-made dishes, prepared with local, organic ingredients. The café and bakery, also on the premises, are great for breakfasts and lunches.

SANT RAFAEL: El Ayoun €€€
Moroccan
C/ Isidor Macabich 6, 07816
Tel *971 198 335*   **Closed** *lunch*

As authentic as a Moroccan restaurant gets in Ibiza; variations on couscous and tagine, with some spicy starters.

SANT RAFAEL: El Clodenis €€€
International
Plaça d'Església s/n, 07816
Tel *971 198 545*   **Closed** *Apr–Jun: Sun; winter: Sun–Wed*
A great, whitewashed island house with terrace serving Provençal cuisine and traditional island dishes. Simple and good, just like the atmosphere.

SANT RAFAEL: L'Elephant €€€
Fusion
Plaça de l'Església s/n, 07816
Tel *971 198 056*   **Closed** *Nov–Apr; lunch*
A French fusion menu, with a good choice of fish, though there are also meat and vegetarian options. The decor is stylish and minimalist, and there is a lovely rooftop terrace.

SANTA AGNÈS DE CORONA:
Can Cosmi €
Regional
Plaza Iglesia, 07850
Tel *971 805 020*   **Closed** *winter: Tue dinner; mid-Dec–mid-Jan*
Historic institution that serves some of the best tortillas in Ibiza. Admire the work of local artists displayed on the walls.

SANTA EULÀRIA DES RIU:
El Bigotes €€
Seafood
Cala Mastella, Sant Carles, 07850
Tel *650 797 633*   **Closed** *Nov–Mar; daily for dinner*
Perched overlooking a crystalline *cala* (cove), El Bigotes serves fresh-off-the-boat fish in a picturesque outdoor setting.

The garden restaurant at La Paloma in Sant Llorenç, surrounded by fruit orchards

Bartender serves wine to customers at Bar Costa, a typical village country-inn in Santa Gertrudis de Fruitera

SANTA EULÀRIA DES RIU: Es Caliu €€
Regional
C/Sant Joan, km 10.8, 07840
Tel *971 325 075* **Closed** *Jul–Aug: lunch; end-Dec–end-Jan*
A must-visit country-style eatery that is well established on Ibiza's culinary map. Specialities include grilled steaks, suckling pig and rabbit.

SANTA EULÀRIA DES RIU: Can Pep Salvado €€
Regional
Ctra Es Canar, km 2.5, 07840
Tel *971 338 171* **Closed** *Mon*
Traditional Ibizan dishes such as mixed fish with *all i oli* and Spanish staples draw patrons to this roadside restaurant.

SANTA EULÀRIA DES RIU: La Casita €€
Bistro
Urbanización Valverde–Cala Llonga 60, 07849
Tel *971 330 293* **Closed** *Feb; Tue; lunch (except Sat & Sun)*
A pleasant country restaurant with a beautiful garden to relax in. The Summer menu includes green fig soup, goat's cheese and pesto salad – all absolutely delicious.

SANTA GERTRUDIS DE FRUITERA: Bar Costa €
Tapas
Plaça de l'Església s/n, 07819
Tel *971 197 021* **Closed** *Tue*
Famous for its *bocadillos* (hearty sandwiches) and art-adorned walls, Bar Costa is in every way a typical *venta* (country inn).

Formentera

ES CALÓ: Es Caló €€
Regional
C/ Vicari Joan Mari 14, Es Caló de Sant Agustí, 07872
Tel *971 327 311* **Closed** *Nov–Mar*

With stunning views over the sea and the cliffs of La Mola, this elegant beach restaurant has an open-air wood and stone dining room. Serves delicious regional specialities, such as fresh seafood and rice. The desserts are absolutely fabulous.

ES CALÓ: Restaurante Pascual €€€
Seafood
Ctra de Mola 12, 07860, Pilar de la Mola
Tel *971 327 014*
A large terrace and lovely gardens lend this eatery a beautiful ambience. The menu offers varieties of fresh fish.

LA MOLA: Blue Bar €
Bistro
Platja Es Migjorn Gran, Ctra Sant Ferran de Ses Roques–La Mola, km 8, 07871
Tel *666 758 190* **Closed** *Nov–Mar*
One of the original 1960s hippy beach bars; serves modest salads, tasty pasta, fish and a host of vegetarian options.

LA MOLA: Es Mirador €€
Seafood
Carretera de la Mola, km 14.3, 07860
Tel *971 327 037* **Closed** *mid-Oct–Apr*
This charming restaurant can be found at the easternmost promontory of the island, with views of Ibiza in the distance. Apart from its spectacular setting, it offers tasty island fare such as paella and fresh fish.

LA SAVINA: Aigua €€
International
Puerto de la Savina s/n, 07870
Tel *971 323 322*
The menu at this beach club includes Italian-inspired dishes and sushi, with cocktails served at the Gin Bar late into the evening.

LA SAVINA: Bellavista €€
Seafood
Port de la Savina, 07870
Tel *971 323 324*
One of Ibiza's best restaurants away from the beach, Bellavista has a large terrace offering views of the port.

> ## DK Choice
>
> ### PLATJA ILLETES: Juan y Andrea €€€
> Seafood
> *Platja Illetes s/n, 07860*
> **Tel** *971 187 130* **Closed** *Oct–Apr*
> From fresh fish and shellfish to lobster (caught by the restaurant's fishing boat), Juan y Andrea serves excellent food. Local rice dishes are a speciality, as are the grilled prawns and the lobster *ajillo* (chopped garlic). The eatery overlooks Playa de Illetas, one of the wildest and most beautiful beaches in the Mediterranean.

A retro snooker table in the eclectic interiors of Blue Bar, La Mola

For more information on types of restaurants *see page 153*

SHOPPING IN THE BALEARIC ISLANDS

As elsewhere in Spain, the islands produce a wide variety of good leatherware, with Inca, in Mallorca, having a worldwide reputation for footwear. Items of clothing including hippy jewellery found on market stalls are most in evidence on Ibiza, which is also known for its fashion trend, "ad-lib". Locally produced ceramics also make good souvenirs and are available on all of the islands, as are other island crafts including embroidery and basketwork. Local produce should also not be ignored, and bringing home a string of garlic, some spicy sausages or a good bottle of Mallorcan wine is as good a way as any of remembering the holiday.

Ceramics shop in Maó, Menorca

Where to Buy

Souvenirs of the Balearic Islands can be bought almost anywhere and the number of small shops offering all sorts of knick-knacks and mementos is truly amazing. They can be found in the historic parts of towns, in tourist centres and near harbours and beaches. Almost every hotel has its own boutique. There are also numerous shops selling clothes and anything that may be useful on the beach, including mattresses, mats, hats, beach balls and sun-block creams.

The items offered by boutiques can also be found in larger shopping centres, where you can buy food and various factory products. Palma has the largest choice of shops while Maó, in Menorca, has quite a few outlets and can cater for most holidaymakers' tastes.

Factory shops are good places to buy souvenirs. They offer slightly lower prices and a much larger selection of goods. The specialist centres are also great places to hunt for souvenirs including pottery or synthetic pearls.

Opening Hours

The large shops in tourist centres are usually open from

Boutiques and restaurants along a seaside promenade

9am until 9pm. Some close for a siesta between 2pm and 5pm. Boutiques have similar opening hours. Shops along the beaches open virtually non-stop. These are the most reliable places to buy food and other basic articles. During high season most shops remain open seven days a week.

Provincial towns and villages do not have such regular opening hours and are more attuned to the pace of life of the local people than to holiday-makers. Shops in small villages may also close at weekends.

How to Pay

When shopping in small shops, food stores and markets, it is customary to pay in cash. Only some larger stores, such as hypermarkets or factory shops, or those selling jewellery, cosmetics, clothes and books, will accept payment by credit cards.

Markets

Markets are an integral feature of the Mallorcan scenery. They are held at weekly intervals, mostly in the provincial towns and villages of the island. They mainly serve the local population, although during high season they also offer many goods aimed at tourists. Besides everyday domestic items, most of them sell fruit, vegetables and sometimes locally produced sauces and preserves. Markets tend to start in the mornings and end early in the afternoon.

Hippy markets are held mainly on Formentera and Ibiza. Aimed squarely at visitors, they offer colourful clothes reminiscent of the fashions popular in the 1960s, as well as every type of ornament, including brooches, earrings, necklaces, belts and bracelets made of shells. These bustling markets are organized during the high season only and, unlike traditional Mallorcan markets, they are held every day.

Hippy bazaar in San Francesc on Formentera

Food

The Balearic Islands offer a number of unique food products that are specific to the region. The delicious *ensaimada* pastry, popular with tourists, is packed in distinctive octagonal boxes, making it easy to transport. Gourmets may be tempted by *sobrasada* – a spicy pork sausage produced in several varieties and used in many Balearic dishes. Strings of dried peppers, or olives prepared in a variety of ways, attract those who wish to bring back culinary souvenirs. All these products can be bought in markets and food stores. Shops that sell exclusively Balearic food are very attractive. The sheer number and variety of colourful

products on display will tempt anyone to step inside.

The most popular alcohols produced on the islands include gin from Maó and herb liqueurs. You can taste the local gin in the Maó distillery *(see p100)*. Liqueurs are produced in a great number of varieties on all the islands and can be sampled in the shops that sell them. Balearic wines are also well worth trying. The best wines come from the Binissalem region on Mallorca, where a grand wine festival is held every year in September. There are two main wine-producing regions in the Balearic Islands – Binissalem and Pla i Llevant, both on Mallorca. Wines that are especially worth sampling include those from the cellars of Jaume de Puntiró, Macià Batle, Vins Nadal, Ànima Negra, Pere Seda and Miquel Gelabert.

Dried peppers

Souvenirs

These days it can be difficult to buy genuine local handicrafts on the Balearic Islands. Sometimes you can find them in markets, but you may find they

have been largely replaced by factory-made articles that imitate handicrafts. These include ceramics decorated with traditional patterns, typical of the islands. The most characteristic pottery items – the *siurells* produced mainly on Mallorca – are colourful whistles in the shape of people or animals, painted in white, red and green. They can be bought in many places at the markets, in small shops and in large stores that sell Balearic pottery. Popular, but expensive, is the glassware produced by the three glassworks on Mallorca. At the Ca'n Gordiola glassworks near Algaida you can witness the production process *(see p91)*. Equally popular are articles made of olive wood, such as bowls and mortars produced by the Olive-Art factory near Manacor.

Also close to Manacor is Perlas Majorica, a shop selling high-quality simulated pearls that can be bought in smart boutiques all over Europe, as well *(see p85)*.

Among the most popular souvenirs are espadrilles (traditional footwear) from Ibiza. Souvenirs from Menorca include leather goods such as wallets, handbags, jackets and sandals. T-shirts and baseball caps with humorous slogans and pictures are also popular.

Shop selling local delicacies in Palma

What to Buy in the Balearic Islands

The choice of souvenirs in the Balearic Islands is vast, but it can be difficult to find genuine local handicrafts among them. However, it is still possible to buy items from each of the islands that is characteristic of the place. In Mallorca, these include simulated pearls, glassware, dolls and wines from the Binissalem region; in Menorca – leather goods, textiles and local gin; in Ibiza – hippy souvenirs or club clothes.

Doll in regional costume

Ceramics

Ceramic items are among the most popular souvenirs. The variety of forms and designs is staggering. Many of those on offer have not actually been produced on the islands and it is best to buy from one of the local manufacturers.

Plate decorated with cobalt

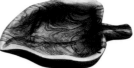

Colourful plate

Condiment container

Glass

The high-quality glassware produced on the Balearic Islands was once as popular as that made in Venice. To this day, the most popular articles of glassware are modelled on traditional designs.

Leaf-shaped bowl

Pestle and mortar

"Gordioli" goblet

Wooden Articles

Articles made of olive wood are very popular with visitors to the islands. They have a distinctive colour and are very durable. The choice is, however, limited to a few designs.

Leather wallet

Traditional sandals

"Lafiore" pots

Leather Goods

Menorca is famous for its leather goods. The factory shops sell virtually everything that can be made of leather, including wallets, coats and jackets. Many articles are made to order for large international companies.

Warm leather gloves

Woman's handbag

Hippy Jewellery
A large number of hippy products sold in Ibiza and Formentera have been produced by a flourishing cottage industry, though less authentic products are beginning to dominate. Even so, it is still worth visiting these markets, if only for their atmosphere.

Box from India

Earrings

Black pearl necklace

Belt with shells

Ring

Simulated Pearls
Simulated pearls are Mallorca's signature item. Though expensive, every item comes with a certificate of authenticity. You can buy ready-made jewellery as well as single pearls that you can use to make your own necklace or bracelet.

Necklace of simulated pearls

Wickerwork
Wickerwork is very popular with visitors to the Balearics and wickerwork items are among the most genuine Balearic products. The baskets of various shapes and sizes are particularly attractive.

Beach basket

Straw hat

Clothes
Clothes, including T-shirts with a variety of slogans and original designs, such as the ones sold on Menorca with the "Ecológica de Menorca" sign, are also popular. Club clothes likewise make interesting souvenirs.

Cap with "Mallorca" inscription

Printed T-shirts

Alcohol
A large selection of alcoholic drinks is on offer. Each island produces its own herb liqueur *(hierbas)*. All adult visitors to Menorca might try the local gin. Connoisseurs will not miss the chance to try Mallorcan wines, particularly the best of them – the red wine from Binissalem, but also white and rosé varieties from the same vineyards.

Herb liqueur

Almond liqueur

Local red wine

Handicrafts in the Balearic Islands

Ceramics are extremely popular in the Balearic Islands, just as in the rest of Spain. One of the most characteristic items of Mallorcan handicrafts is the *siurell* – a statuette-whistle that is made of painted clay. Sa Cabaneta, one of the Mallorcan parishes, is known as "clay country" due to the large number of pottery workshops that can be found there. Weaving and embroidery are also very popular and leather goods are plentiful, especially in Menorca. Mallorca has become famous for its production of simulated pearls.

Ceramic lamps on display in a market

Ceramics

The art of making pottery on the Balearic Islands goes back thousands of years. It was greatly influenced by the art of the Moors, who ruled the archipelago for several centuries.

The item you are most likely to see is the *siurell*, a statuette-whistle made of clay and painted white, with green and red decorations. It usually depicts a man sitting on a donkey or playing a guitar; but it can also be styled as a bull, a dog, a peacock, a rooster or even the devil. The origin of the *siurell* is uncertain; already known in Moorish times, it was most likely inherited from the Phoenicians. The Spanish artist Joan Miró was particularly taken with these little toy whistles and drew inspiration from them. The *siurell* was once a highly important item; a man would hand it to the lady of his choice – if she blew on it, it

meant "yes", but if she put it aside, it meant that the suitor had been rejected. The Romeria de Sant Marçal *(see p31)*, a lively fair held at the end of June in Sa Cabaneta, is dedicated to these clay whistles.

Original ceramic products with distinctive yellow and green glazing are produced in Felanitx in Mallorca. At the busy Sunday market in this small town, you can also purchase blue-and-white bowls and jugs, decorated with delicate floral or arabesque motifs.

In Pòrtol, near the small town of Santa Maria del Camí, there are a few remaining potters who produce traditional bulging pots made of red clay *(ollas)* and shallow bowls *(greixoneras)*.

In Ibiza, in the small village of Sant Rafael situated on the

route from Eivissa to Sant Antoni de Portmany, there are many pottery workshops producing beautiful bowls, vases and jugs based on ancient Carthaginian designs. Ceramic copies of the terracotta figurines dating from the Punic era (3rd century BC) displayed in archaeological museums in Eivissa – particularly busts of women – are popular as souvenirs from Ibiza.

Glassware

The earliest glass vessels found on the Balearic Islands date as far back as Roman times. In the 16th century, glassware from Mallorca competed successfully with popular Venetian products. Even today, the bestselling products tend to be copies of ancient designs.

There are three factories of artistic and household glass in Mallorca; the best known of these is the Can Gordiola glass museum near Algaida, on the road from Palma to Manacor. The oldest glassworks on the island, it has been run by the same family since 1719. Here, it is possible for visitors to watch the glassblowers at work. Using long, thin pipes, they can produce a variety of objects, from lovely small trinkets to large vases.

Traditional condiment pot

Clay pot production in a pottery workshop

Simulated Pearls

The production method for simulated pearls was patented in 1925 by Eduard Heusch, a German engineer. The recipe for producing a thin bead-coating layer is kept secret to this day, for obvious reasons, though it is said to contain fish scales mixed with resin.

Two factories in Manacor and Montuïri produce these simulated pearls, which are of good quality and, to the untrained eye, virtually impossible to distinguish from the real thing.

The beads are immersed repeatedly in a liquid compound, which imitates the natural process of pearl production. Afterwards, each pearl is polished by hand and weighed. The production process can be seen during a visit to the Perlas Orquidea factory. Be aware that the factory shop sells them at much lower prices than those charged by shops elsewhere.

Inside the Gordiola glass factory in Mallorca

Straw hat, popular in the islands

Wood and Wicker Products

Artifacts made of olive wood are very popular in the Balearic Islands and can be distinguished by their rich colour and unusual grain. Olivart, a factory in Palma, produces a number of basic household goods, such as bowls and mortars, as well as ornamental items and many other souvenirs.

The dwarf palm, or palmito, grows on many of the islands' mountain slopes. Its leaves are used, particularly in Artà, to weave chair seats, baskets, bags and the soles of the *espadrille* or *alpargatas*. In addition to this, local craftsmen produce a wide variety of bags and baskets woven from strong grass or jute, and hats that are popular with the locals and tourists alike.

Other Local Products

The Balearic Islands, and Menorca in particular, are famous for their production of excellent footwear. In Menorca the centre of the leather industry is Ferreries. Here, you can buy relatively inexpensive shoes, bags and leather clothes. It is worth taking a closer look at some of the sandal designs, which are unique to this island, locally known as *abarcas menorquinas*. In Mallorca the cheapest place to buy leather products is Inca.

Weaving and embroidery have a long local history. The traditional *robes de llengues* – print-decorated heavy linen fabrics – are often used to decorate Mallorcan homes, even today. They can be used for curtains and bedspreads as well as wall linings and furniture upholstery. Clothes that imitate hippy fashions from the 1960s are still very much in vogue, and designs produced in this style

An olive wood household bowl

continue to create a stir at the annual fashion shows. The fashion show Moda Ad Lib is held every June, in Eivissa, Ibiza. Clothes that are shown here can later be bought in Eivissa's fashionable boutiques – at high prices.

Traditional gold and silver jewellery has been produced by local craftsmen on the Balearic Islands for centuries. Although less fashionable now, it is still used as an addition to folk costumes. Similar to the enduringly popular fashion in clothing, the designs of gold jewellery are inspired largely by hippy culture. Silver and metal items can be bought at "hippy markets", particularly in Ibiza and Formentera.

A cobbler at work

ENTERTAINMENT IN THE BALEARIC ISLANDS

Ibiza is listed in the *Guinness Book of Records* as the world's most entertaining place. This is no doubt due to the number of nightclubs, bars and pubs packed into this small island. The other islands of the archipelago have plenty of entertainment on offer, however, and there are many clubs, concerts and shows to choose from. The range of

entertainment on available to visitors is much wider than this, however. At the height of the holiday season, the larger resorts open up casinos, concert halls, cinemas and theatres and also organize folklore, theatre and cinema festivals. On top of this, and perfect for the kids, are the many aquaparks and other amusement parks to enjoy.

Shelves of the many liqueurs on offer in a shop

Information

It is a good idea to find out what is on offer before you leave, as local tourist information offices may not always have details of forthcoming cultural events, particularly if they are held in another town. The Internet has a wealth of information on concerts, amusement parks and festivals and may sometimes include first-hand accounts of particular attractions.

Current details may often be found in the local press. Keep your eyes peeled, too, as many events are advertised on posters. Other valuable sources on what is happening are hotel reception areas.

Booking Tickets

Tickets to some of the major nightclubs in Ibiza, such as Amnesia and Privilege, can be booked before you go on holiday, over the Internet or by telephone. It is also advisable to book early for any guided tours.

In this case, you must know the organizer's telephone number or go to the local office. The same applies to concerts and music festivals. Hotel receptions will often be happy to do the booking for you. The earlier you book, the better your chances of getting a ticket. In many cases, tickets are only sold a short time in advance. Admission to many open-air events is often free.

Nightlife

Nightlife flourishes on the islands. Ibiza is particularly famous for it, but Mallorca also has many nightclubs (*discotecas*). The clubs usually open their doors between midnight and 1am and many remain open all night. Admission to the most famous and fashionable places in Ibiza and Mallorca is relatively expensive. Lesser-known venues tempt guests in with various gimmicks or free drinks. Earlier in the evening

Entry ticket to Jardines d'Alfàbia

you can visit bars and pubs. For those people who do not fancy the nightclubs, there are also casinos and many venues that put on artistic programmes.

Music and Theatre

Despite appearances, the cultural life on the Balearic Islands is not limited to pubs, clubs and religious festivals. Classical music, opera and theatre are all very popular with the locals, particularly on Mallorca and Menorca. Theatres and opera houses can be found in many places. Their repertoire includes mainly modern Spanish drama and there are frequent performances by visiting theatre and opera companies from mainland Spain, as well as from other European countries,including Germany, Italy and the UK.

The leading theatres are the **Teatre Principal** in Palma and **Fundació Teatre Principal de**

Tourist information office in Sant Antoni de Portmany, Ibiza

Partygoers enjoying themselves at Amnesia, Ibiza

Maó in Menorca. During the summer season, when the theatres close, theatre festivals come to take their place. These are mostly international events. Many of these include theatre workshops, which offer plenty of opportunities for audience participation.

Lovers of classical music will also find something on the islands. World-class musicians and orchestras frequently appear in the concert halls, such as the **Auditórium de Palma de Mallorca**. In addition, many music festivals and concerts are organized during the holiday season. In Menorca, there are three major festivals during the summer season – in Maó, Ciutadella and Fornells. Festivals taking place between June and September are held in concert halls, theatres and churches. Among the important musical events in Mallorca are the classical music festivals held in Palma (Jan–Apr) and the Chopin Festival in Valldemossa (Aug). Other popular events include international festivals of music in Deià (May–Sep) and Pollença (Jul–Aug) during the summer.

Popular Music

Lovers of jazz and rock have no cause to complain in the Balearic Islands, particularly during the summer season. Occasionally, top rock groups or pop stars make an appearance. You should enquire about dates and venues in the local tourist information office or look up events in the local press. There are also numerous local regular events, such as a Rock'n'Rostoll Festival in Maria de la Salut, in Mallorca, while cities such as Palma have many live music venues.

Some events have become a permanent fixture in the islands' cultural calendar. Anyone who loves jazz may know about Sant Climent in Menorca. On Tuesdays from May to October, "jam sessions" are held here. Two extremely popular events in Mallorca are the International Jazz Festival held every year during May and June in Cala d'Or, and the Mallorca Jazz Festival during August in Sa Pobla. In Palma, the Jazz Voyeur Festival runs from September to December.

Fiestas

When visiting the islands, it is worth including one of the fiestas in your itinerary. These are held not only as celebrations of patron saints, but may also commemorate historic events (mainly Medieval events) or celebrate important harvests (such as the grape harvest festival in Binissalem and the melon festival in Vilafranca de Bonany). These colourful, bustling celebrations, accompanied by music, dancing and feasting, can continue for several days, during which time the town's business life grinds to a halt as the local population joins in the fun.

Street processions with people dressed in regional costumes or their Sunday best are often spiced up by the *dimonis* – devils that personify evil, which are defeated in the end. This happens during the fiestas in Montuïri and Santa Margalida. An important element of many fiestas are the horse races and shows. The most interesting of these are held during the Sant Joan fiesta in Ciutadella (in June). The majority of fiestas, as well as other cultural and entertainment events, are held during the summer months, at the peak of the holiday season. Important events taking place outside the tourist season include the Procession of the Three Magi (Jan), the carnival (Feb) and the celebrations associated with Holy Week.

Sign for a horse show

Participants in a colourful fiesta

Amusement Parks

No visit to the Balearic Islands would be complete without a trip to a waterpark or theme park, especially if you have children. **Marineland** in Mallorca provides the opportunity to see the performing dolphins and sea lions and look at the colourful fish in the aquarium, while the thrills and spills of the waterparks can be great fun, especially when it is hot.

During the high season there are also many funfairs with carousels and circus troupes with acrobats and magicians. Magnificent horse shows are staged in Menorca.

Another form of entertainment in the islands is afforded by a visit to one of the numerous caves, especially in Mallorca. Some of these have their own light and music shows.

Museums

The islands' museums are sometimes overlooked, since they are not set up as tourist attractions. Some of the collections are quite modest, presenting the history of the town or region and its associated folklore. However, there are museums on the islands that are definitely worth visiting. These include the **Museu de Mallorca** in Palma *(see pp56–7)*, which displays works of art from prehistoric times up to the present day, illustrating the cultural development of the island. The **Museu de Menorca in Maó** is of a similar character, but its collection is more limited in its scope *(see p100)*.

Another worthwhile museum is the **Centre de la Natura de Menorca**, found in Ferreries *(see p110)*. It has a modern display showing all that is typical of the island's natural environment, culture and traditions. It is a nice idea to pop in here before you start exploring the island.

Children will probably be more interested in visiting the **Waxwork Museum** in

Glass-bottomed boat ride

Binissalem, in Mallorca. Here, they will be able to see wax likenesses of a number of famous people who are in one way or another associated with the island.

Excursions

Those looking for an active holiday will have no trouble finding plenty of outlets able to provide details of walking or cycling trails, and even organize excursions. For anyone looking for a less strenuous excursion, there are plenty of coach tours. It is, of course, possible to hire a car and drive to some of the most interesting places around the islands. You can also ask at tourist offices about guided tours. You might, however, bear in mind that some groups may contain a number of nationalities and you should be prepared to listen to a commentary in a variety of languages. Of all the tours and excursions on offer, possibly the most pleasant are **boat cruises**. These include glass-bottomed boat rides, and even submarine trips. The most pleasurable of these are sailing trips to remote little bays. This way it is possible to circumnavigate the whole of Ibiza or Menorca.

Logo of Menorca's natural history museum

Children

The Spanish are famously fond of children, and kids are welcomed in restaurants, especially at lunchtimes.

In terms of attractions, Mallorca has the lion's share, with waterparks, dolphin shows, caves and promenades for cycling. Fun shows, including mock pirate battles and jousting tournaments, are organized for the enjoyment of younger visitors. Out of season, there are visits by circuses and fairs to the islands and some of the larger clubs run youth afternoons at the weekends. **Palma Aquarium**, just outside the city centre, makes for a great day out.

Although the other islands have fewer attractions, there is still plenty to keep children entertained. Menorca has pony rides and riding shows, for example, while Ibiza's beaches and all the associated seaside attractions, such as snorkelling, beach games and banana rides, will keep most children happily occupied for the duration of your holiday.

Slides in a waterpark in Ibiza

DIRECTORY

Nightlife

BCM
Avda S'Olivera, Magaluf.
Tel 625 597 256.
W bcm-planetdance.
com
British-run entertainment
complex – the biggest
club on the island.

Menta
Avda Tucan, Alcúdia.
Tel 971 893 257.
Two dance floors, seven
bars and an indoor pool

Paladium Paguera
Avda 50, Paguera.
Tel 971 686 557.
A smaller club that gets
packed on the weekends.

Tito's
Paseo Marítimo, Palma.
Tel 971 730 017.
W titosmallorca.com
Upmarket club with a
cocktail bar and a great
view of the bay from the
club's glass elevator.
*See pp124–5 for details of
clubs on Ibiza.*

Theatres

Café Teatre Sans
C/C'an Sanç 5,
Palma, Mallorca.
Tel 971 727 166.

**Fundació Teatre
Principal de Maó**
C/Costa Deià 40, Maó,
Menorca.
Tel 971 355 603.
W teatremao.com
See p98 for further details.

Orfeó Maonès
C/ Verge de Gràcia 155,
Maó, Menorca.
Tel 971 363 942.

Teatre del Mar
Llucmajor 90, "Es Molinar",
Palma, Mallorca.
Tel 971 248 400.
W teatredelmar.com

**Teatre Municipal de
Manacor**
Avda del Parc s/n,
Manacor, Mallorca.
Tel 971 554 549.

Teatre Principal
Riera 2, Palma, Mallorca.
Tel 971 219 696.

Teatre de Vilafranca
Sant Martí 26, Vilafranca
de Bonany, Mallorca.
Tel 971 832 072

Trui Teatre
Camí Son Rapinya, 29,
Palma, Mallorca.
Tel 971 783 279.
W truiteatre.es

Music

Auditorl d'Alcúdia
Plaça de la Porta de
Mallorca 3, Alcúdia,
Mallorca. **Tel** 971 897 185.

**Auditórium de Palma
de Mallorca**
Paseo Marítimo 18,
Palma, Mallorca.
Tel 971 734 735.
W auditoriumpalma.
com

**Auditórium Sa
Màniga**
C/ Son Galta 4, Cala Millor,
Mallorca. **Tel** 971 587 373.

**Centro Cultural
Andratx**
C/ Estanyera 2,
Andratx, Mallorca.
Tel 971 137 770.
Concerts during the
summer.

Shows

Casino Mallorca
Porto Pi Centro, Mallorca.
Tel 971 130 000.
W casinodemallorca.
com

**Club Escola
Menorquína**
Ctra Ferreries–Cala
Galdana, Menorca.
Tel 971 373 497.

Es Foguero
Highway Palma–Santanyi,
Exit No 10, Mallorca.
Tel 617 700 516.
W esfoguero.com
Flamenco, ballet & cabaret.

**Pirates Adventure
Show**
Magaluf, Mallorca.
Tel 971 130 659.
W piratesadventure.
com

Son Amar
Ctra de Sóller, km 10 ,
Palmanyola, Mallorca.
Tel 971 617533 *(free).*
W sonamar.com

Son Martorellet
Ctra Ferreries–Cala
Galdana, km 1.7 km,
Menorca.
Tel 639 156 851.
W sonmartorellet.com

Amusement
Parks

Aguamar
Platja d'en Bossa, Ibiza.
Tel 971 396 790.
Open May–Oct.

Aqua Center
Urb Los Delfines,
Calanblanes, Menorca.
Tel 971 388 705.
W aquacenter-
menorca.com

Aqualand El Arenal
Autopista Palma–S'Arenal,
exit 13, Mallorca.
Tel 971 440 000.
W aqualand.es/elarenal
One of the world's largest
water-parks, which
includes a mini-zoo.

Aquarium Cap Blanc
Ctra Cala Grassió, Sant
Antoni de Portmany,
Ibiza. **Tel** 663 945 475.
W aquariumcapblanc.
com

Aventura Park
Ángel Guimerà 11, Palma,
Mallorca. **Tel** 871 949 452.

Club Hipico Son Gual
Ctra Puigpunyent-
Establiments, km 6.2,
Mallorca.
Tel 971 798 578.
W hipicasongual.com

Golf Fantasía
C/Tenis 3, Palmanova–
Calvià, Mallorca.
Tel 971 135 040.
W golffantasia.com
Crazy golf with a choice
of three circuits.

Marineland
C/ Garcilaso de la Vega 9,
Costa d'en Blanes, Calvià,
Mallorca. **Tel** 971 675 125.
W marineland.es
See p63 for further details.

Natura Parc
Santa Eugènia, Mallorca.
Tel 971 144 078.
W naturaparc.net

Palma Aquarium
Manuela de los Herreos i
Sorá 21, Mallorca.
Tel 902 702 902.
W palmaaquarium.com

Safari-Zoo
Ctra Porto Cristo–Son
Serva, km 5.
Tel 971 810 909.
W safari-zoo.com

Western Park
Ctra de Cala Figuera,
Magaluf, Mallorca.
Tel 971 131 203.
W westernpark.com
Long-established
waterpark on the edge of
town.

Excursions

**Riding Academy
Mallorca**
Son Magraner. Cami d'
Ullastre, 39, Palma.
Tel 610 419 223.
Special courses for children.

Barcos Azules
Passeig Es Través 3, Port
de Sóller, Mallorca.
Tel 971 630 170.
W barcosazules.com
Island boat trips.

Mar Cabrera
Colònia de Sant Jordi,
Mallorca. **Tel** 971 656 403.
W marcabrera.com

OUTDOOR ACTIVITIES

The warm climate and diversity of the landscape on the Balearics make them an excellent place for all types of sport. The most popular of these are, of course, water sports and you will find windsurfing, sailing and diving are all well catered for. Those looking for an activity holiday of this kind will have the chance to practise their favourite sports under professional supervision. Cycling, horse riding and golf are also popular in the islands and many travel bureaux and agents offer equipment hire, from yacht charter to bicycle rental. Some hotels also have their own facilities and can often hire out equipment.

Surfer riding the waves in Cala Major, in Mallorca

Windsurfing

The conditions for windsurfing are not as impressive here as they are in the Canary Islands because the local winds are not strong enough for advanced surfers. As a consequence, the Balearic Islands are not popular with professionals, but this makes them a very good place for beginners to pick up some of the basic techniques.

Although the number of schools is rather limited, all of the islands have at least one school that teaches basic windsurfing and offers equipment hire. Surfing enthusiasts will also be able to find suitable spots in the Balearic Islands; however, do not expect the "ultimate wave".

Sailing

Sailing is the most popular water sport in the Balearic Islands. Major international regattas include the King's Cup and the Princesa Sofia Trophy held in Mallorca. These are high-profile events and attract many of the world's leading sailors; King Juan Carlos is a frequent competitor. The Trofeo Almirante Conde de Barcelona, held in August, features regattas with classic sailing boats. Almost every coastal town has its own marina and these are visited by yachts from all over Europe. Many vessels remain here for the winter.

Of course, you do not have to own a yacht in order to cruise the Balearic Islands. Many firms offer sea-going vessels for charter. Smaller inshore catamarans can be rented by the hour on local beaches. You can also find many clubs or schools that are able to teach you the rudiments of sailing.

The popularity of sailing is so great that during the high season the marinas tend to be very busy, even though the mooring charges are extremely high. Some boats moor in sheltered bays, accessible only by sea.

Fishing

Despite the fact that the local waters teem with fish, fishing is not a popular sport here. A few agents organize trips, however. Further information is available from the Asociación Balear de Pesca (see p177) or from the Club Nautics.

Beach Activities

During the high season, beaches employ lifeguards so it is safer to bathe and swim. Most beaches are sandy and situated in small bays. Sailing yachts and fishing boats sometimes anchor at the mouth of the bay and these are only a hazard if you swim out too close to them. The beaches can be busy and are sometimes short of space for beach sports. Nevertheless, a few of them have areas designated for volleyball, and even on busy beaches you can still find space to kick a ball around or play frisbee.

Diving and Snorkelling

The clear, clean coastal seawaters, combined with the diversity of underwater flora

Catamarans on Es Pujols beach in Formentera

Beach volleyball, popular throughout the islands

and fauna, create ideal conditions for diving, and the sport is as popular as sailing throughout the islands. Every seaside resort has at least one diving centre *(centro de buceo)* where you can hire equipment, go for a test dive with an instructor or enrol on a course. A one-week stay would be sufficient to complete the beginners' course in scuba diving. The organizers ensure proper supervision by a qualified instructor and provide all the necessary equipment.

People hoping to dive in deeper waters must hold a proper diving certificate, such as PADI, CUC, CMAS/ FEDAS or SSI. Holders of these certificates can join expeditions, some of which explore underwater caves. One of the best places to dive is the water around Cabrera, about 18 km (11 miles) off the coast of Mallorca. In 1991, Cabrera and its surrounding waters were awarded the status of a national park – the first park of its kind in Spain. Diving here requires the permission of the park ranger.

A much cheaper but equally exciting way of getting a glimpse of underwater life is to go snorkelling. A snorkeller can observe the wonders of the deep while floating on the surface of the water almost anywhere. Perhaps the most interesting places are the small bays rarely visited by tourists, where nature has hardly been touched by the hand of humans. A word of warning: snorkelling can be dangerous if you are distracted and collide with nearby rocks.

Motorboat with parachute waiting for the adventurous to paraglide

Other Water Sports

Other water sports that are popular with visitors include taking out a high-speed water-bike or **paragliding**. Paragliding behind motorboats (similar to hang-gliding) offers a wonderful way to see the islands. You can

also take water-skiing lessons or (an easier option) bump along on a rubber raft, towed by a speeding boat.

Alternatively, visitors might like to join a sea trip by kayak. The most interesting routes go to the islands such as Conillera, near Ibiza, or Dragonera, off Mallorca. Equally exciting are trips to the waters of Formentor (Mallorca) and Cavalleria (Menorca).

Hiking

Hiking around the islands is becoming popular. The best area for hiking is probably the mountainous regions of Mallorca. The trails leading through the Serra de Tramuntana are difficult; however, they offer a wonderful experience and breathtaking scenery. Trekking across the mountains along rough paths requires suitable footwear and clothing and this activity should not be undertaken alone, as there are potential hazards such as sudden changes in the weather and unexpected ravines.

Menorca also offers many hiking trails. Most of these lead through the local nature reserves, of which the island has 18. The regions of S'Albufera, Cap de Favaritx and Cap de Cavalleria are truly magnificent areas for hiking. Many agents organize themed excursions, such as birdwatching trips. If setting off without a guide, you should make sure you have a good map, as many tourist trails are not signposted.

Snorkelling in shallow waters in Menorca

Cyclists in a boulevard in Palma, Mallorca

Two-Wheeled Sport

Cycling is very popular here, and renting a bicycle from one of the numerous hire firms is inexpensive. Cycling is an excellent way to explore the towns or get to a nearby beach. On the island of Formentera it is the most popular form of transport, along with the scooter.

More ambitious cyclists may want to undertake longer trips, and all types of terrain can be encountered on the islands, from long, flat stretches of coast through to steep mountain roads. The islands also offer many interesting trails for mountain bikes, although the routes leading through the wild mountain terrains on Mallorca, or the coastal crags of Menorca, are best undertaken with a guide. Agents who organize these tours generally offer guides and equipment.

Horse Riding

Horse riding is another popular island sport and there are several riding centres on the islands that provide facilities for beginners as well as for advanced riders. The riding areas and trails are

deliberately set amid beautiful scenery, but you should not expect romantic gallops along the beach. All horse riding is done under the supervision of an instructor. There are many riding centres in Menorca and this is where they breed the famous Menorcan black horses that play such a prominent part in many fiestas. As well as riding lessons and outings, many centres also stage displays of horse breaking. For those who fancy a flutter, regular horse races are held on Mallorca and Ibiza.

Caving

Caving and associated pursuits, such as canyoning and rock climbing, are still in their infancy in the Balearics but growing in popularity.

Only a handful of Mallorca's caves, including the Drac and Hams *(see p84)*, are open to all; most are reserved for experienced potholers. Adventurers can therefore explore the caves of the Tramuntana mountains and, on Menorca, try sea-cave diving as well. Organized caving expeditions offer anything from a half-day guided starter's cave trip, to day- and even week-long caving holidays, with all equipment provided.

The steep rocks along the coast of Mallorca and the inland regions are good places for rock climbing, too, providing various degrees of difficulty. Companies such as **Rocksport Mallorca** offer walking, canyoning and rock

climbing at beginner and advanced levels. **Diving Center Ciutadella** offers sea-cave diving training at various sites around the Menorca. Cave exploration can be dangerous and is only recommended for people who have been trained and have the proper equipment. Before embarking on any adventure sport, check your insurance cover.

Climber on a rock face near Valldemossa, Mallorca

Other Sports

The warm climate and varied terrain mean that most sports can be enjoyed somewhere in the islands. Surprisingly, for such a dry region, there are even places that are good for canoeing, a very popular sport in Spain but one that requires a high level of fitness. When planning these expeditions you should seek advice from the organizers, who will not only inform you about the best routes but will also ensure suitable supervision.

The good aerodynamic conditions on Mallorca make the island suitable for hang-gliding and paragliding *(see p175)*. These sports are not popular in the other islands of the archipelago. The best lifting currents are found in the inland regions. This is where beginners' courses are held and where you can also meet experienced hang-gliders. The islands' weather conditions are also favourable for **ballooning**. A number of companies and some of the more exclusive hotels on the island can organize hot-air balloon flights.

Sea-cave diving – growing in popularity

DIRECTORY

Ballooning

Mallorca Ballons
Tel 971 596 969.
w mallorcaballoons.com

Caving

Diving Center Ciutadella
Ciutadella, Menorca.
Tel 651 644 319.
w diveinnmenorca.com

Rocksport Mallorca
Tel 629 948 404.
w rocksportmallorca.com

Diving

Aqua Diving Center
Port Sant Antoni de Portmany, Ibiza.
Tel 617 280 055.
w aquadivingcenter.com

Big Blue
C/ Marti Ros García 6, Palmanova, Mallorca.
Tel 971 681 686.
w bigbluediving.net

Blue Water Scuba
Cala'n Bosch, Menorca.
Tel 971 387 183.
w bluewaterscuba.co.uk

Octopus
Canonge Oliver 13, Port de Sóller, Mallorca.
Tel 971 633 133.
w octopus-mallorca.com

Skualo
C/ Lepanto, Cala Ratjada, Mallorca.
Tel 971 564 303.
w skualo.com

Sub Menorca
Cala'n Bosch.
Tel 659 194 734.
w submenorca.info

Vellmari Formentera Diving
Marina de Formentera 14, Puerto de la Savina, Formentera.
Tel 971 322 105.
w vellmari.com

Fishing

Asociación Balear de Pesca
C/ Joan Miró, 325, Calanova, Palma, Mallorca.
Tel 971 702 088.

Federación Española de Pesca y Casting
Navas de Tolosa 3, Madrid.
Tel 915 328 352.
w fepyc.es

Hiking

Dia Complert
Passeig Marítim 41, Fornells, Menorca.
Tel 609 670 996.
w diacomplert.com

Ecoibiza
Juan Carlos 1, Ediflcio Transat, Eivissa, Ibiza.
Tel 971 302 347.
w ecoibiza.com

Mallorca Activa
Son Pereto 9, Palma, Mallorca.
Tel 971 783 160.
w mallorcaactiva.com

Horse Riding

Ca'n Paulino
Ctra Vieja de Algaida s/n, Llucmajor, Mallorca.
Tel 664 384 924.
w canpaulino.com

Club Hípico Es Puig
Ctra San Miquel, km 5.5, Cami de Cas Ramons, Santa Gertrudis de Fruitera, Ibiza.
Tel 600 059 343.
w cuadrasespuig.com

Hípica Son Gual
Ctra Puigpunyent to Establiments, km 6.2, Palma, Mallorca.
Tel 608 532 096.
w hipicasongual.com

Menorca a Cavall
Ctra Es Mercadal-Ferreries, km 24, 3 Santa Rita, Es Marcadel, Menorca.
Tel 971 374 637.
w menorcaacavall.com

Riding Academy Mallorca

See p173.

Sailing

Centro Wet Four Fun
Platja d'Es Pujols, Formentera.
Tel 609 766 084.
w wet4fun.com

Club Náutico el Arenal
C/ Roses s/n, S'Arenal, Mallorca.
Tel 971 440 142.
w cnarenal.com

Club Náutico Ciutadella
Cami de Baix s/n, Ciutadella, Menorca.
Tel 971 383 918.
w cnciutadella.com

Club Náutico Porto Cristo
C/ Vela 29, Porto Cristo, Mallorca.
Tel 971 821 253.
w cnportocristo.com

Club Náutico Sant Antoni
Paseo Marítimo s/n, Sant Antoni de Portmany, Ibiza.
Tel 971 340 645.
w esnautic.com

Escuela Balear de Náutica
C/ Aragón 28 bajos, Palma, Mallorca.
Tel 971 909 060.
w escueladenautica.com

Real Club Náutico de Palma
Muelle de Sant Pere s/n, Palma, Mallorca.
Tel 971 726 848.
w realclubnauticopalma.com

Windsurfing

Cesar's Watersports
Playa S'Arganassa, Santa Eulalia del Rio, Ibiza.
Tel 971 330 919 or 670 629 961 *(mobile)*.
w watersportscesars.com

Club Náutico Sa Ràpita
Explanada del puerto s/n, Sa Ràpita, Mallorca.
Tel 971 640 001 or 971 641 535 (courses).
w cnrapita.com

Windsurf Fornells
Bahia Fornells, Menorca.
Tel 664 335 801.
w windfornells.com

Golf in the Balearics

Golf is a relative newcomer in the Balearics, but it is catching up fast, with a growing number of modern and environmentally sensitive golf courses on Mallorca, Menorca and Ibiza. Blessed with a mild climate and boasting excellent facilities, these courses attract golfers all year round. The Federación Balear de Golf oversees a total of 26 courses on the three larger islands, as well as an ever-expanding range of competitions and trophies, training and practice facilities, and junior championships. Formentera has a ferry link that makes a round of golf on Ibiza a viable possibility.

Teeing off on one of the many courses in the Balearic Islands

General Information

The Balearic Islands' golf culture is just over 40 years old, which means that courses have been designed to meet the demands of the modern golfer. They are also mindful of the fact that golfers are here for a holiday. Consequently, in addition to training and activities (some organize tournaments, for example), all courses offer extensive leisure amenities – clubhouses, restaurants, bars and shops.

Spain's proactive attitude towards the disabled has also seen the Balearics' disabled sports council **FEBED** (Federació Balear d'Esports per a Persones amb Discapacitat) active in promoting access, facillities, training and tournaments for disabled golfers at the **Real Golf de Bendinat** course in Mallorca.

There are golf tournaments every week of the golf year, although the most important date is the Baleares Doubles, held at Mallorca's **Golf Santa Ponsa II** course in June.

Green fees range from €50 to €150 a day, depending on the course and the season. Many clubs and holiday agencies offer discounts on fees and equipment hire. All of the golf courses included in the directory listings are recommended by the **Federación Balear de Golf**.

Mallorca

The first ever golf course in Spain opened on Gran Canaria in the Canary Islands only in 1891, some 200 years after St Andrews in Scotland. The first golf course in the Balearics was the **Golf Son Vida**, opened in 1964 a few kilometres outside Palma, in an idyllic valley setting with views of the sea and the Serra de Tramuntana mountains.

Most Balearic golf courses offer extensive and modern facilities, in addition to adv-anced grounds-maintenance technology. Already considered one of the key golf destinations in Europe, Mallorca is drawing leading course design architects such as Robert Trent Jones Jr, Bradford Benz, Falco Nardi and José Gancedo.

In 1967, Son Vida was followed by the **Golf Son Servera** course, designed by John Harris, near Artá. It was another 10 years before the next golf course opened; the first of the (now three) **Golf Santa Ponsa** courses, designed by Falco Nardi, is still the largest on the island. It was followed in 1978 by another John Harris course, **Golf de Poniente**, still regarded as one of the toughest on Mallorca. Laid out among pine and olive groves, the par-72 Poniente has 18 holes and a number of "character-building" bunkers planted along its *recorrido* (course).

The 1980s and 1990s saw another 23 courses open in quick succession in the Balearic Islands. Perhaps the ultimate so far is the exclusive **Golf Son Muntaner**, opened in 2000 and winner of two awards for sensitive ecological course management. **Golf Son Termens** has also been praised for its sympathetic approach to pre-existing landscape in its planning.

Most courses cater to all levels of player ability, although a few are designed to put even the most experienced enthusiast through their paces. **Golf de Pollença**, for example, integrated among ancient olive groves on a gentle hill overlooking the Bahia de Pollença, admits that "none of the holes is easy", and deems most to be suitable for mid- to

Beautiful views across Bahia de Alcúdia from Golf Alcanada

high-experience players and professionals. The Robert Trent Jones Jr-designed **Golf Alcanada**, opened in 2003, is blessed with sea views of the splendid Bahia de Alcúdia from every hole, although players are advised to beware the 58 bunkers Jones has included in the design of this idyllic but testing course. **Golf de Andratx** has declared each of its holes a *reto*, or challenge, while the course at **Golf de Canyamel** is still considered the toughest on the island.

Landscape and climate make Mallorca an ideal setting for golf. It is impossible to say which golf course boasts the most impressive architecture, although Son Muntaner is the most exquisitely manicured. **Golf de Capdepera** is set in a lush valley surrounded by scenic mountains, while the Poniente is set among mature pine and olive woodlands. The most

striking course is **Pula Golf**, whose grounds, located in an old country estate, are shared with some of the most important *talayot* structures on the island.

Menorca

Menorca and Ibiza are still a considerable way behind Mallorca; however, it is only a matter of time until they catch up. Menorca's main course, **Golf Son Parc**, is an unusual course with a 69 par and an ingenious course by Dave Thomas that requires strategic thinking to negotiate rocky bunkers, several lakes, reedbeds and, not least, a resident colony of peacocks.

Ibiza

The only golf course on the island of Ibiza, **Golf de Ibiza** is something of an oddity. The old Roca Lisa nine-hole course has now been absorbed into the larger, neighbouring Golf de Ibiza, with a new 18-hole course, giving it a 27-hole total. The shorter course is said to be the easier terrain; however, all 27 holes are still described as difficult.

The challenging course of Golf de Ibiza

DIRECTORY

General Information

Febed
Avda Uruguay s/n, 07010 Palma de Mallorca.
Tel 971 701 481.
W febed.es

Federación Balear de Golf
Camí Son Vida 38, 07013 Palma de Mallorca.
Tel 971 722 753.
Fax 971 711 731.
W fbgolf.com

Mallorca

Golf in Mallorca
W golfinmallorca.com

Golf Alcanada
Carretera del Faro s/n, 07400 Puerto de Alcúdia.
Tel 971 549 560.
Fax 971 897 578.
W golf-alcanada.com

Golf de Andratx
Carrer Cromlec 1, 07160 Camp de Mar.
Tel 971 236 280.
Fax 971 236 331.
W golfdeandratx.com

Golf de Canyamel
Avda des Cap Vermell s/n, 07589 Capdepera.
Tel 971 841 313.
Fax 971 841 314.
W canyamelgolf.com

Golf de Capdepera
Carretera Artá–Capdepera, km 3.5, 07570 Artá. Tel 971 818 500.
Fax 971 818 193.
W golfcapdepera.com

Golf de Pollença
Carretera Palma–Pollença, km 49.3, 07460 Pollença.
Tel 971 533 216.
Fax 971 533 265.
W pollensagolf.com

Golf de Poniente
Carretera Cala Figuera s/n, 07182 Magaluf.
Tel 971 130 148.
Fax 971 130 176.
W ponientegolf.com

Golf Santa Ponsa I, II & III
Av. Golf s/n, 07180 Santa Ponsa.
Tel 971 697 589.
W golf-santaponsa. com

Golf Son Muntaner
Ctra Son Vida, 07013 Palma.
Tel 971 783 030.
Fax 971 783 031.
W sonmuntanergolf. com

Golf Son Servera
Urbanización Costa de los Pinos, 0/550 Son Servera.
Tel 971 840 096.
Fax 971 840 160.
W golfsonservera.com

Golf Son Termens
Carretera S'Esglaieta, km 10, 07110 Bunyola.
Tel 971 617 862.
Fax 971 617 895.
W golfsontermens.com

Golf Son Vida
Urbanización Son Vida, 07013 Palma.
Tel 971 791 210.
Fax 971 791 127.
W sonvidagolf.com

Pula Golf
Carretera Son Servera–Capdepera, km 3, 07550 Son Servera.
Tel 971 817 034.
Fax 971 817 035.
W pulagolf.com

Real Golf de Bendinat
C/ Campoamor s/n, Urb Bendinat, 07181 Calviá.
Tel 971 405 200.
Fax 971 700 786.
W realgolfbendinat. com

Vall d' Or Golf
Ctra. cala d'Or Portocolom, km 7.7, 07669 S'Horta (Felanitx).
Tel 971 837 001.
W valldorgolf.com

Menorca

Golf Son Parc
Urbanización Son Parc s/n, 07740 Es Mercadal, Menorca.
Tel 971 188 875.
W golfsonparc menorca.com

Ibiza

Golf de Ibiza
Carretera Jesús a Cala Llonga s/n, 07840 Santa Eulària des Riu.
Tel 971 196 052.
Fax 971 196 051.
W golfibiza.com

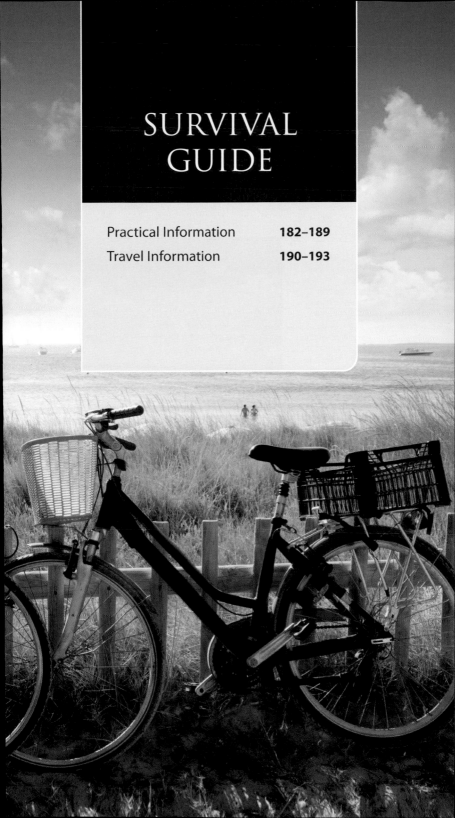

SURVIVAL
GUIDE

PRACTICAL INFORMATION

The Balearic Islands are one of Europe's most popular holiday destinations. The islands have invested heavily in tourism and are geared up to receive multitudes of visitors. Hotel and catering facilities are extensive and there are plenty of attractions for the whole family to enjoy. In general, the islands are safe for visitors, although, as with any other busy resort destination, holidaymakers are vulnerable to crimes such as bag-snatching. Such crimes can be avoided if you take sensible precautions. A well-developed information service, especially on the Internet, makes researching and planning a trip here a relatively straightforward business. During the peak period tour operators tend to snap up the available accommodation, but outside the summer season it is fairly easy to book a room in advance.

When to Visit

Each season has something to offer. Nevertheless, the tourist season is at its busiest from July until September. It peaks in August, which coincides with the hottest weather on the islands. The hotels, bars and restaurants fill up, beaches are full of sun-lovers and the clubs are crowded. At the height of the season you are more likely to hear German or English being spoken than Spanish or Catalan.

West End in Sant Antoni de Portmany, Ibiza

Anyone who dislikes crowds should plan their visit for the period before the high season or when things begin to quieten down. In May, June, late September and early October, the weather is still warm enough for sunbathing. Springtime is between February and April. This is the best time for hiking, as the flowers are in bloom, although there can be heavy rain and storms at this time of year. The islands are quietest during the autumn months and December.

Visas

Regulations covering admission to the Balearic Islands are the same as for the rest of Spain. Nationals of all the European Union member states do not require a visa to enter the Balearic Islands. People from other non-EU countries, including Australia, Canada, Israel, Japan, New Zealand and the USA, are likewise not required to obtain a visa before entry for tourist visits of up to 90 days. If in doubt, you should contact the Spanish Embassy or seek advice from a travel agent. Anyone who does require a visa must apply in person at the consulate in their own country.

Customs Regulations

Customs regulations state in detail the limits on goods imported to and exported from the Balearic Islands. Such information may be obtained from Spanish Embassies and travel agents. Specific customs queries may be referred to the *Departamento de Aduanas e Impuestos Especiales* (Customs and Excise Department) in Madrid. Remember that only adults are entitled to export alcohol and cigarettes in the quantities allowed by the regulations.

Nationals of non-EU countries may apply for VAT refunds on goods purchased in any of the islands' shops bearing the sign "Tax Free Shopping". The refund is worked out on the basis of the *formulari* (Global Refund Cheque), stamped by the Customs Officer at the point of departure before checking the luggage. The refund can be claimed at the airport, at any Cash Refund desk, or on returning home, by post or via bank transfer.

Strolling through Ciutadella, Menorca

◀ Bicycles parked by the Illetes Beach, one of the busiest beaches in Formentera

Language

The official joint language of the Balearic Islands is Spanish (Castilian). For many locals, however, the everyday language is Catalan. This bilingual culture can be felt when using local maps, where the names of places may be given in one or the other language. Catalan, in its turn, is divided into variants specific to each of the islands. In Mallorca it is known as *Mallorquín*, in Menorca as *Menorquín* and in Ibiza as *Eivissenc*.

During Franco's regime Catalan was banned and you risked a prison sentence if you were caught speaking it. Nevertheless, the local population has never abandoned its use and learning a few courtesy phrases in Catalan is a good way to win over the locals.

In tourist areas English and German are readily understood. Information signs and restaurant menus are generally multilingual. Greater problems with communication may be experienced away from the busiest areas. But even in the provinces, increasing numbers of people can speak at least one major European language as well as Spanish.

Tourist Information

You will find Tourist Information offices (*Informació turística*) in all of the larger towns and resorts. These offer free maps and information packs; they also have details of current cultural events, entertainment and available accommodation. However, the information they provide may be somewhat general in nature and it is usually limited to the town where the tourist office is located or to its immediate vicinity. If you want to go on an organized hike or cruise, it is best to enquire with the agent who organizes them (*see p173*). A valuable source of information is the Internet.

Horse-cab ride in Palma, Mallorca

Individual islands, towns, tourist offices, hotels, car hire firms and museums all have their own websites (*see p185*). They usually include photographs with text written in several languages. It is therefore much simpler to do your research before leaving home rather than once you are already there. While using websites you should check when they were last updated because some may quote last year's prices. The best websites are those which are run by the provincial government of the Balearic Islands and the Tourism Promotion Department "Ibatur" (*Institut Balear del Turisme*).

Signposts on Menorca

Youths/Students

The Balearics are an ideal destination for young holidaymakers. The fine weather, great beaches and clubs attract thousands of young people from all over Europe. Some also come in search of seasonal employment, combining work with pleasure. Holders of the International Student Identity Card (ISIC) and the Euro under-26 card are entitled to many benefits when visiting the Balearic Islands. They can get discounts on ferry travel, entrance charges to museums and galleries, and tickets to some of the other tourist attractions. Some travel agents offer cheap flights to cardholders.

Children

As with much of Spain, children are welcome in most places except the big clubs, which, of course, have age restrictions for obvious reasons. Most hotels can provide cots; some have all-day care, babysitting and special entertainment for youngsters. It is nevertheless worth checking in advance what facilities are available at any given hotel.

Restaurants in hotels and in towns are also good at providing for the needs of children. They have highchairs and have special menus for children. When hiring a car, you should have no problem getting a child seat.

Children visiting one of Menorca's historic sights

Market in Inca, Mallorca, with local produce

Facilities for the Disabled

The Balearic Islands are not particularly hospitable towards disabled people. Most hotels and restaurants are not adapted to serve guests who use wheelchairs, although new restaurants and hotels have to offer access by law. Many public places such as museums, galleries and shops are also inaccessible. When planning a visit, it is useful to use the services of an organization that deals with the issues of disabled people. **Handisport Mallorca** is a good first stop for advice. Or you can approach **COCEMFE** (the Spanish Association for the Disabled). Another helpful agency is **ILUNION Viajes**.

Public transport also presents problems for people in wheelchairs and moving from town to town can be difficult. Disabled visitors to Mallorca are able to use the services of a specialized company, such as EMT Special Bus Service.

Parking sign for the disabled

Excursions

Travel agents who sell holidays to the Balearic Islands usually also offer a choice of excursions for an additional fee. These are mostly day-long sightseeing trips, cruises, safaris, or visits to casinos, theatres or clubs. However, the prices you pay for these may be higher than those quoted by local tourist agents,

and it is worth browsing through leaflets displayed at the hotel reception desk, or calling in at one or two local tourist offices to check what is on offer.

Island Time

All the islands are 1 hour ahead of Greenwich Mean Time (GMT), 6 hours ahead of Eastern Standard Time and 9 hours ahead of Pacific Standard Time. The changeover to summertime, as with mainland Spain, takes place on the last Sunday in March. The clocks are put back on the last Sunday in October.

In terms of vocabulary, the word used to describe the early hours after midnight is *la matinada*. *El mati* means morning (up to 1pm); late afternoon and evening are translated as *la tarda*, while night is referred to as *la nit*.

Opening Hours

Museums and historic monuments are generally open from Tuesday to Sunday, from 10am to 2pm and again from 4pm to 6pm. As with most offices, they close for public holidays and fiestas. Tourist information offices have similar opening hours.

Some sectors of business are reassessing their traditional opening hours. Big department stores, for example, and hypermarkets tend to forgo the siesta and are generally open until 9pm or 10pm, though most still close on Sundays.

Theme parks and gardens are open seven days a week and they do not close for siesta. Most clubs open their doors late at night and stay open until morning. Many offices associated with tourism work shorter hours during the winter; some close altogether.

Electrical Supply

The mains voltage on the islands is generally 220V AC. A three-tier standard travel convertor will enable you to use foreign equipment. Mains sockets require the European-style two-pin, round-pronged plugs.

Religion

Like the rest of Spain the Balearic Islands are Roman Catholic and religion plays an important part in community life. All religious festivals are lavishly celebrated and at these times the offices in town remain closed. Church opening hours vary. Some, like the cathedral church in Eivissa,

Tourists resting in Dalt Vila, in Eivissa

have set sightseeing hours. Others, including Palma cathedral, expect a donation or charge an admission fee. Many churches are open only for services, that is early mornings or evenings (6–9pm).

When planning to visit a particular religious building, you should check its opening hours in advance. Hotel reception desks and tourist information centres can sometimes provide details.

Church statue

Toilets

Public toilets are few and far between, even in large towns. Bars and restaurants will usually allow non-guests to use their toilet facilities, but it is polite to ask permission first. When looking for a toilet you should ask for *servicios* or *aseos*. Doors leading to the men's toilets are marked *señores* or *caballeros*; to the ladies', *señoras* or *damas*. If there are no written signs, the doors will be marked with a picture of a male or female silhouette. (Sometimes you might see an amusing cartoon of a pipe-smoking man or a long-haired women with a fan.)

Special toilets designed for the disabled are a rarity on the islands, even in hotels, to say nothing of restaurants. In the future things should improve, however, as all newly built hotels and restaurants must by law be fully accessible to travellers with disabilities.

Customers relaxing at a café Palma

DIRECTORY

Embassies in Mainland Spain

Australia
Paseo de la Castellana 259D, 28046 Madrid.
Tel 913 536 600.
Fax 913 536 692.

United Kingdom
Paseo de la Castellana 259D, 28046 Madrid.
Tel 917 146 300.
Fax 917 146 301.

Consulates

France
Mallorca: C/Caro 1, 1st floor G, 07002, Palma.
Tel 971 730 301.
Fax 971 780 099.

Ibiza: Avda. Bme. Vte Ramón 10, 07800, Ibiza.
Tel 971 312 031.
Fax 971 314 008.

The Netherlands
Mallorca: C/San Miquel 36, 6th floor, 07002 Palma.
Tel 971 716 493.
Fax 971 726 642.

Germany
Mallorca: C/Porto Pi 8, 3rd floor D, 07015 Palma.
Tel 971 707 737.
Fax 971 707 740.

Menorca: C/Des Negres 32, 07703 Maó.
Tel 971 361 668.
Fax 971 369 012.

Ibiza: C/D'Antoni Jaume 2, 2–9th floor, 07800 Eivissa.
Tel 971 315 763.
Fax 971 315 763.

United Kingdom
C/Convent dels Caputxins 4, Edif Orisba B, 4th floor D, 07002 Palma de Mallorca.
Tel 902 109 356.
Fax 971 717 520.

Ibiza: Avda/ Isidoro Macabich 45, 1st floor, 07800 Eivissa.
Tel 902 109 356.
Fax 971 301 972.

Organizations for the Disabled

COCEMFE
Luis Cabrera 63, Madrid.
Tel 917 443 600.
W **cocemfe.es**
Handisport Mallorca
Tel 971 132 268.
W **handisportmallorca. org**

ILUNION Viajes
C/Forners 7, 07006 Palma de Mallorca.
Tel 971 774 684.
W **viajes.ilunion.com**
For blind travellers.

Tourist Information

Mallorca
Plaça de la Reina 2, Palma.
Tel 971 173 990.
Av. Argentina 1, Palma.
Tel 902 102 365.

Menorca
Muelle de Llevant 5, Maó.
Tel 902 929 015.
Plaça des Born, Ciutadella.
Tel 971 484 155.

Ibiza
Passeig Vara de Rey 1, Eivissa.
Tel 971 301 900.
Fax 971 301 740.

Passeig de ses Fonts. Sant Antoni de Portmany.
Tel 971 343 363.

Formentera
Port de la Savina.
Tel 971 322 057.

Tourist Information Websites

W **illesbalears.es**
W **spain.info**
W **balearweb.com**
W **caib.es**
W **visitbalears.com**

Mallorca
W **visitmallorca.com**
W **infomallorca.net**
W **a2zmallorca.com**

W **mallorcarutes.com**
W **mallorcanatural.es**

Menorca
W **menorca.net**
W **menorca.es**
W **visitmenorca.com**

Ibiza
W **ibiza.travel**
W **ibiza-online.com**
W **ibiza-spotlight.com**
W **descubreibiza.com**

Formentera
W **formentera.es**
W **guiaformentera.com**
W **formenteraonline.net**
W **visitformentera.com**

Personal Security and Health

The crime level on the Balearic Islands is lower than in other regions of Europe. Thefts do occur in the most crowded places and even in hotels, but they can be minimized by taking sensible precautions. Credit cards and money are best hidden away. Never leave anything visible in your car when you park it. It is also advisable to avoid carrying excessive amounts of cash. When in need, you can always ask a policeman for help. Basic medical help and advice is usually provided by a pharmacist. Holders of valid medical insurance can receive treatment in public hospitals and clinics.

Lifeguard on duty at Sant Elm beach, Mallorca

Personal Property

Before travelling abroad it is wise to make sure you have adequate holiday insurance in order to protect yourself financially from the loss or theft of your property. Even so, it is also advisable to take common-sense precautions against loss or theft in the first place. Travellers' cheques are a far safer option than cash. If you have two credit cards, do not carry them together and make sure you keep a separate note of credit card cancellation numbers. Particular care should be exercised in crowded places such as airports and bus stations. Patrolling policemen often remind visitors about the need to be careful. There are also cases of tourists falling victim to theft when drunk. Never leave a bag or handbag unattended and do not put a mobile phone, purse or wallet on a tabletop in a café. The moment you discover a loss or theft, report it to the local police. The police will give you a *denuncia* (written statement), which you will need to make an insurance claim. If you have your passport lost or stolen, report it to your consulate.

Beach notice board in Cala Millor

Spanish Police

The island police are friendly towards tourists. They are always ready to give advice and help. However, in case of any infringement of the law, they can be very firm and it is best not to try to argue with them.

As in the rest of Spain there are three types of police on the islands. The *Policía Nacional* (state police), the *Policía Municipal*, also known as the *Policía Local* (local police), and the *Guardia Civil* (National Guard). The force encountered most frequently by tourists is the *Policía Municipal*. Their officers are mostly encountered in small towns, and patrol the streets of crowded tourist resorts; they have a separate branch for traffic. The *Policía Nacional* wear dark-blue uniforms. They deal with more serious incidents and matters concerning foreign visitors; they also guard various important buildings in large cities. The *Guardia Civil*, dressed in green uniforms, patrol rural areas. You can see them while travelling the roads and wild areas of the Balearic Islands.

State police car or *Policía Nacional*, frequently seen around the islands

Beaches

During the high season most beaches have lifeguards. Many beaches have swimming areas marked by buoys, although this does not mean that swimming outside these areas is prohibited. Many beaches have Red Cross stations. Notice boards at the entrance to the beach give information on facilities such as showers or wheelchair access *(see left)*. Many smaller beaches do not have lifeguards. Nevertheless, swimming is usually safe, as beaches are generally situated in small coves with calm waters.

The majority of the Balearic Islands' beaches are sandy. However, those along the northern shores of the islands are often rocky. You should exercise special care when swimming off rocky beaches. It is also recommended that you use footwear when entering the water and that you watch out for underwater rocks when snorkelling.

The sun should be taken seriously while on the beach. Between noon and 6pm it is best not to stay exposed for too long. It can take only minutes to get sunburned and children are especially vulnerable. Be sure to apply a high-factor sunblock cream and also make use of an umbrella. Deckchairs and umbrellas can often be hired for a fee. Drink plenty of water to avoid dehydration.

Medical Care

The UK Foreign Office advises all travellers to buy medical insurance. However, visitors from EU countries are entitled to free national health treatment if they travel with a European Health Insurance Card (EHIC), which can be obtained in the UK from the Department of Health or from a post office before you travel. Note that Spanish health care does not cover all expenses, such as the cost of dental treatment. Having private health insurance can also avoid time-wasting bureaucracy. Visitors from outside the EU should always carry valid medical insurance.

In case of illness, you should report to a hospital or clinic. At night, patients are seen by the *Urgencias* (Emergency). You can also telephone the Cruz Roja (Red Cross) for help.

Decorative pharmacy sign

Pharmacies

Pharmacies have the same opening hours as other shops. They carry a green or red cross with the word *farmàcia*, or sometimes *apotecaria*. Details about those open at night and on public holidays can be found in the windows of all pharmacies. Most pharmacists in large towns

Firefighting aeroplane on Ibiza

Ambulance on Formentera

speak at least one foreign language. This is important, since when dealing with minor medical problems pharmacists are entitled to give advice and even dispense necessary medicines. In this instance, consulting a pharmacist may be enough. Balearic pharmacies sell several medicines over the counter that in other countries are available only on prescription. Away from the big towns, a *farmàcia* may be found in any small town or village. Here, opening hours may be shorter and they are not often open over the weekends. In smaller towns and villages the pharmacist may be less used to dealing with tourists and communication may be a problem as a result.

Fire Hazards

The Balearic Islands have a dry Mediterranean climate, with mild winters and hot summers. The summer heat often causes droughts since rain falls sporadically between October and February. This creates conditions where fire can spread extremely quickly. Parched woodlands, combined with the general layout of the land, makes firefighting very difficult. Often fire fighting necessitates aeroplanes and

helicopters dropping vast amounts of water. It is vital, therefore, when travelling on the islands or using picnic facilities, to remember to take great care to prevent a fire from starting. Before leaving, carefully check the remains of any bonfire and be sure to pick up glass, particularly bottles, that may also cause fire. It goes without saying that you should be especially careful when extinguishing cigarettes in country areas.

The island firefighters are called *Bomberos*, and as elsewhere in the world, they have a simple emergency telephone number *(see below)*.

DIRECTORY

Emergency Numbers

Police, Guardia Civil, Red Cross, Ambulance & Fire Brigade
Tel 112.

Pharmacies

Mallorca
Farmacia La Rambla C B Rambla Ducs de Palma 14, Palma de Mallorca.
Tel 971 711 511.

Menorca
Farmacia Segui Puntas, Avda Vives Llull 16, Maó.
Tel 971 360 993.

Ibiza
Farmacia Ferrer, c/ Formentera, 8, Figueretas, Eivissa.
Tel 971 302 737.

Formentera
Juan Torres Quetglas. c/ Santa Maria, Sant Francesc.
Tel 971 322 419.

Communication and Banks

The quality of telephone services in the Balearic Islands is high. Thanks to the transfer to digital technology in 1998, the line quality is generally good. The banking services on the islands are equally efficient and many foreign banks, mainly German, have branches here. The Spanish postal system functions quite so well but it may take a week or more for a letter posted in the Balearic Islands to reach its destination. When communicating with Spanish companies, it is best to use fax or email.

Bright and easy-to-spot post box belonging to the Spanish *correos*

Telephones

Most of the telephones in the Balearic Islands are owned and maintained by the Spanish company Movistar, although in some of the busier resorts you may see telephones belonging to other companies. This competition means that even in a small place you should have no problem finding a public telephone – if not in a street kiosk, then in a bar or restaurant.

Card-operated telephones vary, as there are two types of phonecards. One has a black magnetic strip with an encoded value. The other has a PIN number that must be entered before the connection can be made. If you plan on spending a long time in Spain, it is worth buying a cheap mobile phone with a rechargeable card – mobiles can be purchased for as little as €25. Alternatively, buy a pay-as-you-go SIM card for your phone.

When dialling a number you should remember that in Spain you must always dial the full nine-digit number, even if you are in the same area. The code for the Balearic Islands is 971. A call from Mallorca to Menorca will cost the same as one from Palma to Andratx. When telephoning the Balearic Islands from the UK, Ireland and New Zealand, you must first dial 0034 (the country code for Spain) and then the subscriber's number starting with the area code (971). When calling a mobile phone number you should dial the country code, followed by the subscriber's number. To phone the UK from the Balearic Islands dial 0044, then area code (minus the 0), then number; to phone Ireland dial 00353, then area code (minus the 0), then number; to phone the US or Canada dial 001, then area code, then number.

There are four tariffs for international calls. These apply respectively to EU countries, other European countries and northwest Africa, North and South America, and the rest of the world. A call from a public telephone costs 35 per cent more than one made from a private phone, but is still cheaper than from a hotel.

Telephone kiosk

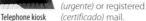

Logo of Movistar

Postal Service

The Spanish postal system is now quite efficient, and postcards and letters sent from the islands take a couple of days to reach the addressee. If a message is urgent, it is much better to send it by fax or email. It is also possible to send express *(urgente)* or registered *(certificado)* mail.

Post offices are open between 8:30am and 2:30pm Mondays to Fridays (main offices are open to 8:30pm), and between 9:30am and 1pm Saturdays. If you only want stamps, these are also sold at kiosks bearing the sign *timbre* or at tobacconists; or, ask at your hotel reception. Postal charges depend on where the item is being sent to and fall into bands that include the EU, the rest of Europe, the USA and the rest of the world. Post offices also accept telegrams, registered mail and parcels. Letters and cards can be mailed in a yellow post box.

Many hotels, as well as some shops, offer services of companies other than the Spanish post. They are, however, no more efficient. If you use one of these and buy an appropriate stamp, remember to post your letter in the correct box.

Currency

The Euro (€) is the common currency of the European Union. It went into general circulation on 1 January 2002, initially for 12 participating countries. Spain was one of those 12 countries, and the Spanish peseta was phased out in January 2002. Euro notes, in denominations of €5 to €500, are identical throughout the Eurozone countries, while the coins have one side identical (the value side), and one side with an image unique to each country.

Banks and Cash Dispensers

Most banks are open from 8am until 2pm. Some have longer opening hours or work in the afternoons on a rota system. After the switch to the euro, most bureaux de change closed. Now the easiest way to change currency is in a bank, at the counter marked *cambio*.

To do this you will need to show your passport or other ID. Most banks charge a small commission for this.

Alternatively, you can withdraw money from one of the many cash dispensers that work 24 hours. They accept all major credit cards and do charge a commission, but the exchange rate is usually better than at banks.

One of the many cash dispensers available on the islands

Credit Cards and Traveller's Cheques

The most popular credit cards are **Visa** and **MasterCard**. However, most cash dispensers, as well as shops, hotels and restaurants, will also accept **American Express** or

Diners. When you pay with a card, cashiers will usually pass your card through a reading machine. Sometimes you may be asked to punch in your PIN number. Some smaller places, such as market stalls and independent shops may not accept credit cards.

Traveller's cheques are by far the safest way of carrying money. When you lose a cheque you don't automatically lose the money and it can be quickly replaced. These may be cashed in banks and bureaux de change. The most popular traveller's cheques are American Express, Visa and Thomas Cook, but overall their use is declining. Banks charge a commission for cashing a cheque.

Radio and Television

Numerous pubs and cafés have a television and it is easy to watch major sporting events live, including many English and German league soccer matches. Hotels have a larger selection of TV channels. Besides Spanish national TV, such as TVE1 and TVE2, there are a number of local channels including Catalan TV3 and Canal 33. These broadcast mainly Spanish news and light entertainment shows..

You can tune into the BBC's World Service 24 hours a day online or through audio channels offered by local TV providers in some hotels.

Newspapers

Several local newspapers are published on each of the islands. These cover mainly local issues and they can also be valuable

Popular dailies published in the Balearic Islands

sources of information for visitors who want to find out about forthcoming cultural and sporting events. They also publish useful addresses and telephone numbers. Some of the local newspapers have foreign-language supplements.

In many towns, kiosks and hotels sell Spanish national papers as well as British and German newspapers. The majority of the popular EU publications arrive on the Balearic Islands with a minimum delay.

DIRECTORY

Post Offices

Mallorca
Constitucio 6,
Palma.
Tel 971 228 610.

Menorca
C/ Bon Aire 15, Maó.
Tel 971 356 629.
Pl Borne 9, Ciutadella.
Tel 971 380 081.

Ibiza
Avda Isidor Macabich 67,
Eivissa.
Tel 971 399 769.

Lost or Stolen Credit Cards

American Express
Tel 900 994 426.

Diners Club
Tel 902 401 112.

MasterCard
Tel 900 971 231.

Visa
Tel 900 991 216.

Kiosks selling papers in Passeig d'es Born in Palma, Mallorca

TRAVEL INFORMATION

Most visitors arrive on the Balearic Islands by air. This is not only the fastest, but often also the cheapest, way of getting here. The airports are on Mallorca, Menorca and Ibiza. Served by international airlines, these are mostly charter flights, though there are also regular scheduled flights from the UK. Alternatively, you can fly to mainland Spain and change planes. During peak season, Palma's airport is one of the busiest in Europe. Sea links are equally convenient, but you must first get to the Spanish coast. The routes from Barcelona, Dénia and Valencia to the Balearic Islands are served by large ferries that may carry cars, and also by fast catamarans.

Palma airport's departure hall, Mallorca

Air Travel

Regular links between large Spanish cities and the Balearic Islands are provided by the Spanish carriers **Iberia**, **Vueling** and **Aireuropa**. There are also regular flights between the Balearic Islands (mainly Mallorca) and countries that provide the greatest numbers of visitors, such as Germany and Britain, as well as Austria, Switzerland, France and the Netherlands.

The Balearic Islands are featured by a wide range of European tour operators – ask your travel agent for advice. Package holidays operate year-round and feature both scheduled and charter flights. Palma, Ibiza and Menorca are also served by low-cost airlines **easyJet**, **Ryanair** and **bmibaby** with flights from London Gatwick, Stansted, Luton, Bristol, East Midlands, Manchester, Liverpool, Newcastle and Glasgow. Flights from the UK take

under 3 hours. These relatively short flight times mean that the islands are popular for annual holidays as well as "mini-breaks". Flights from the US require changing planes in London, Barcelona or Madrid.

Flights Between the Islands

The only carrier providing flights between the islands is **Iberia**. The flight from Mallorca to Menorca takes only 30 minutes. For that reason this is a convenient way of travelling. Before island-hopping, it is a good idea to find out what type of aircraft you are going to fly in. Some are quite small and you may not be able to take large hand luggage. Travelling in a small, packed and stuffy light aircraft can be a little unpleasant for anybody who suffers from claustrophobia or other health problems. Even in the best of weather, the flight may be bumpy and a small aircraft makes this more noticeable. However, flying between the islands will not only save you time but will also give you the chance to see magnificent views of the archipelago.

Multilingual information sign at Palma's airport

Airports

Son Sant Joan airport on Mallorca is situated on the outskirts of Palma, around 11 km (7 miles) from the centre of the island's capital. The nearby motorway provides a fast road link to Palma. The airport has many shops, car hire agents and tourist information centres.

Over the last few years, the airport has been constantly extended for the needs of tourists. Despite its size, it is difficult to get lost here. There is only one terminal, where check-ins are made on the second floor, and boarding is on the fourth floor. Individual zones are well signposted, but be prepared for long walks when making your way from one sector of the airport to another. Menorca's airport is near the island's capital – Maó. This is the smallest of the Balearic airports. Ibiza's airport is a dozen or so kilometres from Eivissa and is far busier. The traffic increases particularly during weekends, when club-goers from all over Europe arrive for the Saturday–Sunday revel. The aircraft touching down here are often

Colourful aircraft at Ibiza's airport

Ferries in Maó's harbour, Menorca

painted in the most fantastic designs. When taking off or landing in Eivissa, you get a bird's-eye view of the town and of Dalt Vila. Frequent bus services operate from all the main airports and can take you straight to the city centres.

Ferries

Anyone who plans to take their own car or motorcycle to the islands must use a ferry. These run frequent and regular services between large towns on the Spanish mainland and the harbours of Mallorca, Menorca and Ibiza. Journey times are quite reasonable; it takes 7 hours by ferry from Barcelona to Palma for example.

The large ferries operated by **Trasmediterranea** sail from Barcelona and Valencia to Palma and Maó. They also provide transport to Ibiza. The latter may be reached from Barcelona (10 hours) or Valencia (about 4 hours). **Balearia**, a smaller ferry company, also has services to the islands. If you're in a hurry, you can also use Trasmediterranea's high-speed ferry service, which carries up to 900 passengers and 265 cars and can take you from Valencia to Ibiza in 3 hours. Inter-island services are equally diverse. You can choose a fast Trasmediterranea catamaran or a slower ferry run by a company like **Iscomar**. Both of them have bars for passengers.

Using ferries to hop from island to island will always be cheaper than flying and it can

be a very pleasant option. Arriving by sea and catching your first glimpse of Maó's ancient harbour is an unforgettable experience. Some islands can only be reached by sea. These include Cabrera, Formentera and Dragonera. A journey by ferry from Ibiza to Formentera takes about 1 hour; by catamaran it takes about 30 minutes. Ticket prices for ferries providing links between the islands are reasonable, but going by a catamaran will cost you more. Price differences between the competing companies are greater for longer routes, but prices depend mostly on the time of year. The lowest prices can be obtained after high season, from October until December, and again from the end of January until the end of March. In the period from Easter until the beginning of July – known as the "half-season" – the ferry prices tend

BALEARIA
Logo of Balearia ferry lines

to go up again. Children up to the age of 12 are entitled to a 50 per cent reduction, and infants travel free.

DIRECTORY

Airports

w aena.es
Tel 902 404 704.

Mallorca – Son Sant Joan
Tel 971 789 655.

Menorca
Tel 971 157 000.

Ibiza
Tel 971 809 000.

Airlines

Aireuropa
w aireuropa.com

bmibaby
w bmibaby.com

easyJet
w easyjet.com

Iberia
w iberia.com

Ryanair
w ryanair.com

Vueling
w vueling.com

Ferry Lines

Baleària
w balearia.com

Iscomar
w iscomar.com

Trasmediterranea
w trasmediterranea.es

Pleasure boat – an enjoyable way to travel to smaller ports

Getting Around the Islands

The Balearic Islands have only two railway lines, both of which are in Mallorca. The first is an historic line from Palma to Sóller; the other links Palma with Manacor, via Inca. To explore the more remote parts of the island, as well as the remaining islands of the archipelago, you will need a car, a scooter or a bicycle. On Formentera, a scooter and bicycle are the best means of transport. When travelling round the islands, you should pay particular attention to the numerous motorbike riders. Weekend motorbike rallies and races are held in Mallorca, although they are strongly opposed by the *Guardia Civil*.

Scenic, winding road leading to Sa Calobra, Mallorca

Roads

Roads and signage on the Balearic Islands are generally good, although there is a shortage of hard shoulders. As a consequence, stopping along the road in order to admire the scenery can be difficult and dangerous and is not recommended. The only free motorway runs along the coast of Badia de Palma, encircling Mallorca's capital. Its second segment links Palma with Inca. To use the segment between Alfàbia and Sóller that passes through the tunnel under Serra de Tramuntana, you have to pay a toll. During the morning and afternoon rush hour in the areas around Palma and other industrial towns like Inca or Manacor, you may experience traffic jams.

Take great care when you are trying to reach some beaches or sights off the beaten track. The roads leading to them can be narrow, steep and winding. Problems can arise when two cars try to pass each other. Some beaches and sights inland can only be reached along unmade, bumpy roads and to travel to these requires a four-wheel drive vehicle.

Maps

When hiring a car you will normally be given an outline road map of the island. It will show the main roads on which it is safe to drive. Unfortunately the maps are not always up to date and it is advisable to buy one of the maps sold in bookshops, souvenir shops or petrol stations. The folding B&B maps are particularly good. Please note that town and street signs now appear in Catalan rather than Spanish (Castilian), so make sure you get a map marked in Catalan.

Car and Scooter Hire

Companies will be falling over themselves to rent you a car almost as soon as you have landed, as all major car hire companies, **Avis, Hertz** and **Europcar** have their desks at the airports. It is, however, worth taking your time to search for a small local firm that may offer you a better price.

The price of car hire depends on the time of year, the size of the car and the length of hire. Advance booking can also affect the price. It is worth not only comparing the prices quoted by the various companies but checking exactly what the quote includes.

When hiring a car, you will have to show your passport and valid driver's licence. You should also carefully check the conditions regarding insurance and any restrictions about driving on rough tracks or taking the car from one island to another. Be sure to inspect the condition of the car, as you will have to return it in the same condition or pay a fine. The terms and conditions of hire can vary greatly from company to company. Check carefully before signing any contract.

Scooters are a very popular form of transport, particularly on Formentera and Ibiza. Hire rates for these are much lower and they can transport you to

Car and bike rental service in Ibiza

Petrol station run by the Cepsa chain

DIRECTORY

Hiring a Car

Avis
w avisworld.com

Europcar
w europcar.es

Hertz
w hertz.com

Spain Car Rental
w rentspain.com

Bus Stations

Autobuses
Sant Antoni de Portmany, Ibiza.
Tel 971 340 510.
w ibizabus.com

Empresa Municipal de Transportes Urbanos de Palma
Ansolm Clavé 5, Palma, Mallorca
Tel 971 214 444. w emtpalma.es

Transportes Menorca
Tel 971 360 475.
w tmsa.es

Train Stations

Palma-Inca
Tel 971 177 777.

Tren de Sóller
Tel 902 364 711.

places that cars cannot reach. Many people learn to ride a scooter during their holidays.

Rules of the Road

Driving on the Balearic Islands is no different to driving in any other European country. You should remember the speed limits, which are 120 km/h (74 mph) on motorways, 90 km/h (56 mph) on major roads and 40 km/h (25 mph) in towns. The fines for breaking the speed limits are high, just as they are for drunken driving. The highest permitted blood alcohol level is 0.025 per cent.

Sign for a parking meter

Buying Petrol

Petrol station pumps are generally operated by the staff. Only a few are automatic and open 24 hours. Menorca, Ibiza and Formentera have very few petrol stations. The same applies to the Serra de Tramuntana region of Mallorca. When touring these areas you should remember that a car uses more fuel on mountainous terrain than on a flat road. It is therefore worth filling the tank before setting off.

Town Driving

If at all possible, you should avoid driving in large town centres and popular resorts. Many streets in historic towns are narrow, with one-way traffic. Cars parked alongside pavements make driving conditions even more difficult. Popular resorts are always

crowded and it can be hard to find a parking space.

Most car parks charge fees, and there are fines for non-payment. Paid car parking spaces along pavements are marked with a blue line. Generally, the parking fees apply from 9am to 1pm and from 5pm to 8pm on weekdays, and from 9am to 1pm on Saturdays. In many towns, such as Eivissa, parking in these spaces is limited to a set time. A yellow line painted along the pavement means that parking is prohibited. In Palma and Maó, use one of the underground car parks. Here, there is no time limit on parking, but you may have to wait in a long queue.

Buses

Bus links between major towns as well as between large and small towns are very good. Links between small towns and villages are less efficient. Of the large towns, only Palma has its own municipal bus network. Bear in mind that during weekends bus services are less frequent. When planning a further

Bicycle and "quadcycle" on a promenade

journey, particularly on Mallorca, check your options for the return journey.

Ibiza has a special night bus service during high season, taking guests to the most popular clubs and ferrying them between Sant Antoni de Portmany and Eivissa.

Taxis

For travelling around town, it is best to hire a taxi. Most taxis in Palma have a black-and-cream colour scheme. The driver is obliged to turn on the meter at the start of the journey, and the sum displayed is the one you pay. For disabled people, taxi transport is by far the most convenient, as you can order a specially adapted vehicle. Taxis to the airport charge an additional airport and luggage fee. For taxis on Mallorca, call 971 755 440; on Menorca, call 971 367 111; and on Ibiza, call 971 398 483.

General Index

Acknowledgments

Dorling Kindersley would like to thank the following people whose contributions and assistance have made the preparation of this book possible.

Consultant Chris Rice

Factcheckers Paula Canal, Bernat Fiol, John Gill

Proofreaders Stewart Wild, Nikky Twyman

Indexer Helen Peters

Additional Contributors Tony Kelly, Jeffrey Kennedy, Andrew Valente

Additional Photography Ian Aitken, Simon Bracken, Joe Cornish, Neil Lucas, Ian O'Leary, Coline Sinclair

Revisions and Relaunch Team Tora Agarwala, Claire Baranowski, Sonal Bhatt, Paula Canal, Jo Cowen, Emma Brady, Gadi Farfour, Anna Freiberger, Lydia Halliday, John Gill, Sumita Khatwani, Phil Lee, Sonal Modha, Alison McGill, Caroline Mead, Marianne Petrou, Mani Ramaswamy, Alice Reese, Farah Sheikh, Azeem Siddiqui, Lucinda Smith, Susie Smith, Sylvia Tombesi-Walton, Priyansha Tuli, Hugo Wilkinson, Conrad Van Dyk, Ajay Verma, Richa Verma

Senior Editor Jacky Jackson

Managing Editor Helen Townsend

Publishing Manager Kate Poole

Special Assistance
Wiedza i Życie would like to thank the following people for their help in creating this guide.

Martin & Toni Cornell, Zbigniew Dybowski, Joanna Egert-Romanowska, Christiane Hagen, Martin Hagmüller, Javier Lopez Silvosa, Barbara Sudnik.

The publisher would also like to thank the people and institutions who allowed photographs of their property to be reproduced, as well as granting permission to use photographs from their archives:

AENA, Gabinete de Comunicación-Aeropuertos de Baleares; Aeropuerto de Palma de Mallorca (Elisabet Royo Romero); AFP in Warszawie (Piotr Ufnal); Aguamar in Platja d'en Bossa; Amic Hotels in Palma (Andreu Llabrés); Amnesia in Sant Rafael (Stéphane Schweitzer, Aymeric Huot-Marchand); Banys Àrabs in Palmie (Doña Pilar); National Library in Warsaw (Iwona Grzybowska); Centre Perles in Palma (Lluc Antonio Bibiloni, Carolina Gato); Corbis – Agencja Free in Warsaw (Gabriela Ściborska); Coves de Campanet (Maria Antònia Siquier); Eden in Sant Antoni de Portmany (Gemma); El Divino in Eivissa; Els Calders (Javier Marqués); Es Paradis in Sant Antoni de Portmany; Fundació Pilar i Joan Miró in Cala Major (Núria Sureda, Joan Insa); Grupo Aspro-Ocio (Omar García Melcon); Ibatur (Esteve Rigo Ribas); La Granja (Manuel Moragues Marqués); La Residencia in Deià (Arantza Zamora); La Reserva Puig de Galatzó (Heike Killisch); Modas Leather in Ferreries (Suzanne Sparkes-Keeble); Museu d'Art Espanyol Contemporani in Palma (Antonio Barcelo); Museu de Lluc in Monasteri de Luc (Elvira González); Museu de Mallorca in Palma (Guillem Rosselló Bordoy); Museu de Menorca in Maó (Anna Fernandez); Naviera Universal Española, S.L. in Barcelona (Núria Alvarez); paulunderhill.com (Paul Underhill); Safari-zoo Mallorca (Miquel Brunet Alós)

Picture Credits

a–above; b–below/bottom; c–centre; f–far; l–left; r–right; t–top.

Works of art have been reproduced with the permission of the following copyright holders: *Personage and Bird* and *Mosaic* in Parc de la Mar, Palma Joan Miró © Succession Miró/ADAG, Paris and DACS, London 2011: 62c/52bl; *La Fustaria* Guillermo Perez Villalta © DACS, London 2011 60tl.

The publisher is grateful to the following individuals, companies and picture libraries for permission to reproduce their photographs:

4Corners Images: Sime/Schmid Reinhard 13bl, 10cla; **Aena:** 190cla; **AFP** 187bl; **Alamy Images:** Paul Bourdice 154cla; City Image 166cb; Greg Balfour Evans 116; Xavier Fores-Joana Roncero 128–9; imagebroker/White Star/Monica Gumm 179cr; naqele stock.com 11cr; WENN UK 23tl; Wolfgang Pölzer 176bl; Superstock 71cl; The Geoff Williamson Image Collection 178tr; **Amnesia:**124t, 171tl.

Celda de Frederic Chopin y George Sand: Cartuja de Valldemossa 71bc; **Club de Golf Alcanada:** 178bl; **Corbis:** 38c, 39br, 124ca, 125b; Franz-Marc Frei 33cra; Roger Halls 115tr; Bob Krist 23br; Vittoriano Rastelli 137b; Hans Georg Roth 95b; James A Sugar 25bl, 33cl, 41crb; Cueva des Hams 83tl; Werner Forman 8-9.

El Divino: 124b; **Dreamstime.com:** Alessandro0770 15tc; Emanuel Corso 192br; Foxirisha 15br; Jpmora 106-7; Lunamarina 2-3, 180-1; Victor Pelaez Torres 14cl; Xoriguer 136. **Es Forn de Tore Soli Nou:** 159tc.

Fotolia: nito 18; **Fundació Pilar i Joan Miró:** 62b; **Getty Images:** Gonzalo Azumendi 46; Michele Falzone 94; Doug Pearson 144–5.

La Granja: 69bc, **Grupo Aspro-Ocio:** 45bl, 63tl, 63bl, 63br, 91tr, 92clb, 93bl, **Hell's Kitchen:** 150bc; **Hemispheres Images:** Michel Gotin 12bl; **Ibatur:** 30br, 31c, 32cla, 171br; **Ibiza Gran Hotel:** 151bl.

Piotr Kiedrowski: 153bc, 167cb; **Restaurante Jardin:** 155bl; **Juan y Andrea:** Iris Esteve 153br; **Julius and Hanna Komarniccy:** 24c, 30cl, 167la; **Wesley Kutner:** 21bl, 23tl, 152c. **Andrzej Lisowski:** 21tr, 25br, 27br, 32b, 100ca, 124cb, 125c, 133br, 175tl, 182bl, 183br, 184br, 190br.

Carlos Minguel: 28clb, 28bl, 29c, 29cb, 29bl, 29br; **Misa, Palma:** 157br; **Pawel Murzyn:** 16c, 16b, 19b, 24bl, 24br, 27crb, 29tl, 33bl, 44cla, 93tl, 123b, 132c, 170cl, 174cla, 182cra; **Museu de Mallorca:** 56c, 56bc, 56tr, *Paris i Helena* Ca. 1665 Mattia Preti 56cla, 57bl, 57c, 57crb, *Cabeza de Mercurio* Jaume and Rafael Blanquer Ca 1630– 1650 57ca.

La Paloma: 162br; **Robert Pasieczny:** 26clb, 38br, 41bl, 45tl, 49br, 68tr, 68cla, 70tl, 72br, 74c, 172tr; **Paulunderhill.com:** 124tr; **La Reserva Puig de Galatzó:** 65tc, 65tc, 65c; **La Residencia:** 148br, 156br; **Santi Taura:** 156tl; **Biel Salas Servera:** 27c, 27ca, 27cb, 28tr, 28br, 29tc, 88clb, 89tl; **Simply Fosh:** 153cl, 158t; **Soleado:** 161br; **Son Granot:** 147c, 150tc; *Restaurant Stay:* 152cl; **Superstock:** Album/ Oronoz/Album 39cr; **Telefonica:** 188c.

Andrzej Zygmuntowicz and Ireneusz Winnicki: 5c, 105br, 152bc, 153tc.

Front Endpaper: **Alamy Images:** Greg Balfour Evans Lcla; **Dreamstime.com:** Xoriguer Lbr; **Getty Images:** Gonzalo Azumendi Rbl; Michele Falzone Rcr.

Jacket: Front - **4 corners:** Olimpio Fantuz/SIME Main; Dreamstime. com: Dominik Michálek bl.

All other images © Dorling Kindersley
For further information see: www.dkimages.com

Special Editions of DK Travel Guides
DK Travel Guides can be purchased in bulk quantities at discounted prices for use in promotions or as premiums. We are also able to offer special editions and personalized jackets, corporate imprints, and excerpts from all of our books, tailored specifically to meet your own needs.

To find out more, please contact:
in the US **specialsales@dk.com**
in the UK **travelguides@uk.dk.com**
in Canada **specialmarkets@dk.com**
in Australia **penguincorporatesales@ penguinrandomhouse.com.au**

Phrase Book

In Emergency

Help!	**Auxili!**	*ow-gzee-lee*
Stop!	**Pareu!**	**pah**-*reh-oo*
Call a doctor!	**Telefoneu un metge!**	*teh-leh-fon-***eh**-*oo oon meh-djuh*
Call an ambulance!	**Telefoneu una ambulància!**	*teh-leh-fon-***eh**-*oo oo-nah ahm-boo-***lahn**-*see-ah*
Call the police!	**Telefoneu la policia!**	*teh-leh-fon-***eh**-*oo lah poh-lee-***see**-*ah*
Call the fire brigade!	**Telefoneu els bombers!**	*teh-leh-fon-***eh**-*oo uhlz boom-***behs**
Where is the nearest telephone?	**On és el teléfon més proper?**	*on-ehs uhl tuh-leh-fon mehs proo-***peh**
Where is the nearest hospital?	**On és l'hospital més proper?**	*on-ehs looss-pee-tahl mehs proo-***peh**

Communication Essentials

Yes	**Sí**	*see*
No	**No**	*noh*
Please	**Si us plau**	*sees plah-***oo**
Thank you	**Gràcies**	**grah**-*see-uhs*
Excuse me	**Perdoni**	*puhr-***thoh**-*nee*
Hello	**Hola**	*oh-lah*
Goodbye	**Adéu**	*ah-they-***oo**
Good night	**Bona nit**	*bo-***nah** *neet*
Morning	**El matí**	*uhl muh-***tee**
Afternoon	**La tarda**	*lah* **tahr**-*thuh*
Evening	**El vespre**	*uhl* **vehs**-*pruh*
Yesterday	**Ahir**	*ah-***ee**
Today	**Avui**	*uh-voo-***ee**
Tomorrow	**Demà**	*duh-***mah**
Here	**Aquí**	*uh-***kee**
There	**Allà**	*uh-***lyah**
What?	**Què?**	*keh*
When?	**Quan?**	*kwahn*
Why?	**Per què?**	*puhr keh*
Where?	**On?**	*ohn*

Useful Phrases

How are you?	**Com està?**	*kom uhs-***tah**
Very well, thank you.	**Molt bé, gràcies.**	*mol beh* **grah**-*see-uhs*
Pleased to meet you.	**Molt de gust.**	*mol duh* **goost**
See you soon.	**Fins aviat.**	*feenz uhv-***yat**
That's fine.	**Està bé.**	*uhs-***tah** *beh*
Where is/are …?	**On és/són…?**	*ohn ehs/sohn*
How far is it to…?	**Quants metres/ kilòmetres hi ha d'aquí a …?**	*kwahnz meh-truhs/kee-***loh**-*muh-truhs yah dah-***kee** *uh*
Which way to …?	**Per on es va a …?**	*puhr on uhs* **bah** *ah*
Do you speak English?	**Parla anglès?**	**par**-*luh an-***glehs**
I don't understand.	**No l'entenc.**	*noh luhn-***teng**
Could you speak more slowly, please?	**Pot parlar més a poc a poc, si us plau?**	*pot par-***lah** *mehs pok uh pok sees plah-***oo**
I'm sorry.	**Ho sento.**	*oo* **sehn**-*too*

Useful Words

big	**gran**	*gran*
small	**petit**	*puh-***teet**
hot	**calent**	*kah-***len**
cold	**fred**	*fred*
good	**bo**	*boh*
bad	**dolent**	*doo-len*

enough	**bastant**	*bahs-***tan**
well	**bé**	*beh*
open	**obert**	*oo-***behr**
closed	**tancat**	*tan-kat*
left	**esquerra**	*uhs-***kehr**-*ruh*
right	**dreta**	**dreh**-*tuh*
straight on	**recte**	**rehk**-*tuh*
near	**a prop**	*uh* **prop**
far	**lluny**	*lyoonyuh*
up/over	**a dalt**	*uh* **dahl**
down/under	**a baix**	*uh* **bah**-*eeshh*
early	**aviat**	*uhv-***yat**
late	**tard**	*tahrt*
entrance	**entrada**	*uhn-***trah**-*thuh*
exit	**sortida**	*soor-***tee**-*thuh*
toilet	**lavabos/ serveis**	*luh-***vah**-*boos/ sehr-***beh**-*ees*
more	**més**	*mess*
less	**menys**	*menyees*

Shopping

How much does this cost?	**Quant costa això?**	*kwahn kost ehs-shoh*
I would like …	**M'agradaria …**	*muh-grad-uh-***ree**-*ah*
Do you have…?	**Tenen…?**	*tehn-un*
I'm just looking, thank you	**Només estic mirant, gràcies.**	*noo-mess ehs-***teek** *mee-***rahn** **grah**-*see-uhs*
Do you take credit cards?	**Accepten targes de crèdit?**	*ak-***sehp**-*tuhn* **tahr**-*zhuhs duh* **kreh**-*deet*
What time do you open?	**A quina hora obren?**	*ah* **keen**-*uh oh-ruh* **oh**-*bruhn*
What time do you close?	**A quina hora tanquen?**	*ah* **keen**-*uh oh-ruh* **tan**-*kuhn*
This one.	**Aquest.**	*ah-***ket**
That one.	**Aquell**	*ah-***kehl**
expensive	**car**	*kahr*
cheap	**bé de preu/ barat**	*beh thuh preh-***oo**/ *bah-rat*
size (clothes)	**talla/mida**	*tah-***lyah**/**mee**-*thuh*
size (shoes)	**número**	*noo-***mehr**-*oo*
white	**blanc**	*blang*
black	**negre**	*neh-gruh*
red	**vermell**	*vuhr-***mel**
yellow	**groc**	*grok*
green	**verd**	*behrt*
blue	**blau**	*blah-***oo**
antique store	**antiquari/botiga d'antiguitats**	*an-tee-***kwah**-*ree/ boo-***tee**-*guh/dan-***tee**-*ghee-tats*
bakery	**el forn**	*uhl forn*
bank	**el banc**	*uhl bang*
book store	**la llibreria**	*lah lyee-bruh-***ree**-*ah*
butcher's	**la carnisseria**	*lah kahr-nee-suh-***ree**-*uh*
pastry shop	**la pastisseria**	*lah pahs-tee-suh-***ree**-*uh*
chemist's	**la farmàcia**	*lah fuhr-***mah**-*see-ah*
fishmonger's	**la peixateria**	*lah peh-shuh-tuh-***ree**-*uh*
greengrocer's	**la fruiteria**	*lah froo-ee-tuh-***ree**-*uh*
grocer's	**la botiga de queviures**	*lah boo-***tee**-*guh duh keh-vee-***oo**-*ruhs*
hairdresser's	**la perruqueria**	*lah peh-roo-kuh-***ree**-*uh*
market	**el mercat**	*uhl muhr-***kat**
newsagent's	**el quiosc de premsa**	*uhl kee-***ohsk** *duh* **prem**-*suh*

post office	l'oficina de correus	loo-fee-**see**-nuh duh koo-**reh**-oos
shoe store	la sabateria	lah sah-bah-tuh-**ree**-uh
supermarket	el supermercat	uhl soo-puhr-muhr-**kat**
tobacconist's	l'estanc	luhs-**tang**
travel agency	l'agència de viatges	la-**jen**-see-uh duh vee-**ad**-juhs

Sightseeing

art gallery	la galeria d'art	lah gah-luh **ree**-yuh **dart**
cathedral	la catedral	lah kuh-tuh-**thrahl**
church	l'església/ la basílica	luhz-gleh-**zee**-uh/ lah buh-zee-lee-kuh
garden	el jardí	uhl zhahr-**dee**
library	la biblioteca	lah bee blee oo-**teh**-kuh
museum	el museu	uhl moo-**séh**-oo
tourist information office	l'oficina de turisme	loo-fee-**see**-nuh thuh too-**reez**-muh
town hall	l'ajuntament	luh-djoon-tuh-**men**
closed for holiday	tancat per vacances	tan-**kat** puh bah-**kan**-suhs
bus station	l'estació d'autobusos	luhs-tah-see-**oh** dow-toh-**boo**-zoos
railway station	l'estació de tren	luhs-tah-see-**oh** thuh **tren**

Staying in a Hotel

Do you have a vacant room?	¿Tenen una habitació lliure?	teh-**nuhn** oo-nuh ah-bee-tuh-see-**oh** **lyuh**-ruh
double room with double bed	habitació doble amb llit de matrimoni	ah-bee-tuh-see-**oh** **doh**-bluh am **lyeet** duh mah-tree-**moh**-nee
twin room	habitació amb dos llits/ amb llits individuals	ah-bee-tuh-see-**oh** am **dohs lyeets**/ am **lyeets** in-thee-vee-thoo-**ahls**
single room	habitació individual	ah-bee-tuh-see-**oh** een-dee-vee-thoo-**ahl**
room with a bath	habitació amb bany	ah-bee-tuh-see-**oh** am **bah**nyuh
shower	dutxa	**doo**-chuh
porter	el grum	uhl **groom**
key	la clau	lah **klah**-oo
I have a reservation.	Tinc una habitació reservada.	ting oo-nuh ah-bee-tuh-see-**oh** reh-sehr-**vah**-thah

Eating Out

Have you got a table for...?	Tenen taula per...?	teh-**nuhn** tow-luh puhr
I would like to reserve a table.	Voldria reservar una taula.	vool-**dree**-uh reh-sehr-**vahr** oo-nuh tow-luh
The bill please.	El compte, si us plau.	uhl **kohm**-tuh sees plah-oo
I am a vegetarian.	Sóc vegetarià/ vegetariana.	sok buh-zhuh-tuh-ree-**ah** buh-zhuh-tuh-ree-**ah**-nah
waitress	cambrera	kam-**breh**-ruh
waiter	cambrer	kam-**breh**
menu	la carta	lah **kahr**-tuh
fixed-price menu	menú del dia	muh-**noo** thuhl **dee**-uh
wine list	la carta de vins	lah **kahr**-tuh thuh veens
glass of water	un got d'aigua	oon **got** dah-ee-gwah

glass of wine	una copa de vi	oo-nuh **ko**-pah thuh **vee**
bottle	una ampolla	oo-nuh am-**pol**-yuh
knife	un ganivet	oon gun-ee-**veht**
fork	una forquilla	oo-nuh foor-**keel**-yuh
spoon	una cullera	oo-nuh kool-**yeh**-ruh
breakfast	l'esmorzar	les-moor-**sah**
lunch	el dinar	uhl dee-**nah**
dinner	el sopar	uhl soo-**pah**
main course	el primer plat	uhl pree-**meh** plat
starters	els entrants	uhlz ehn-**tranz**
dish of the day	el plat del dia	uhl plat duhl **dee**-uh
coffee	el cafè	uhl kah-**feh**
rare	poc fet	pok **fet**
medium	al punt	ahl **poon**
well done	molt fet	mol **fet**

Menu Decoder

l'aigua mineral	**lah**-ee-gwuh mee-nuh-**rahl**	mineral water
sense gas/ amb gas	sen-zuh gas/ am gas	still/sparkling
al forn	ahl **forn**	baked
l'all	lahlyuh	garlic
l'arròs	lahr-**roz**	rice
les botifarres	luhs **boo**-tee-fah-rahs	sausages
la carn	lah **karn**	meat
la ceba	lah seh-buh	onion
la cervesa	lah-sehr-**ve**-sah	beer
l'embotit	lum-boo **teet**	cold meat
el filet	uhl fee-**let**	sirloin
el formatge	uhl for-**mah**-djuh	cheese
fregit	freh-**zheet**	fried
la fruita	lah froo-**ee**-tah	fruit
els fruits secs	uhlz froo-**eets** seks	nuts
les gambes	lahs **gam**-bus	prawns
el gelat	uhl djuh-**lat**	ice cream
la llagosta	lah lyah-**gos**-tah	lobster
la llet	lah **lyet**	milk
la llimona	lah lyee-**moh**-nah	lemon
la llimonada	lah lyee-moh-**nah**-thuh	lemonade
la mantega	lah mahn-**teh**-gah	butter
el marisc	uhl muh-**reesk**	seafood
la menestra	lah muh-**nehs**-truh	vegetable stew
l'oli	loll-ee	oil
les olives	lahs oo-**lee**-vuhs	olives
l'ou	**loh**-oo	egg
el pa	uhl **pah**	bread
el pastís	uhl pahs-**tees**	pie/cake
les patates	lahs pah-**tah**-tuhs	potatoes
el pebre	uhl peh-**bruh**	pepper
el peix	uhl **pehsh**	fish
el pernil salat serrà	uhl puhr-**neel** suh-lat sehr-**rah**	cured ham
el plàtan	uhl **plah**-tun	banana
el pollastre	uhl poo-**lyah**-struh	chicken
la poma	lah poh-**mah**	apple
el porc	uhl **pohr**	pork
les postres	lahs **pohs**-truhs	dessert
rostit	rohs-**teet**	roast
la sal	lah **sahl**	salt
la salsa	lah **sahl**-suh	sauce
les salsitxes	lahs sahl-**see**-	sausages
sec	chuhs **sehk**	dry
la sopa	lah **soh**-puh	soup
el sucre	uhl-**soo**-kruh	sugar
la taronja	lah tuh-**rohn**-djuh	orange
el te	uhl **teh**	tea
les torrades	lahs too-**rah**-thuhs	toast

la vedella	*lah veh-***theh***-lyuh*	*beef*
el vi blanc	*uhl* **bee blang**	*white wine*
el vi negre	*uhl* **bee neh**-*gruh*	*red wine*
el vi rosat	*uhl bee roo-***zaht**	*rosé wine*
el vinagre	*uhl bee-***nah**-*gruh*	*vinegar*
el xai/el be	*uhl* **shah***ee/ uhl* **beh**	*lamb*
el xerès	*uhl shuh-***rehs**	*sherry*
la xocolata	*lah shoo-koo-* **lah**-*tuh*	*chocolate*
el xoriç	*uhl shoo-***rees**	*red sausage*

Numbers

0	**zero**	**seh**-*roo*
1	**un** (*masc*)	**oon**
	una (*fem*)	**oon**-*uh*
2	**dos** (*masc*)	**dohs**
	dues (*fem*)	**doo**-*uhs*
3	**tres**	**trehs**
4	**quatre**	**kwa**-*truh*
5	**cinc**	**seeng**
6	**sis**	**sees**
7	**set**	**set**
8	**vuit**	**voo**-*eet*
9	**nou**	**noh**-*oo*
10	**deu**	**deh**-*oo*
11	**onze**	**on**-*zuh*
12	**doce**	**doh**-*dzuh*
13	**tretze**	**treh**-*dzuh*
14	**catorze**	*kah-***tohr***-dzuh*
15	**quinze**	**keen**-*zuh*
16	**setze**	**set**-*zuh*
17	**disset**	*dee-***set**
18	**divuit**	*dee-voo-***eet**
19	**dinou**	*dee-***noh**-*oo*
20	**vint**	**been**
21	**vint-i-un**	*been-tee-***oon**
22	**vint-i-dos**	*been-tee-***dohs**

30	**trenta**	**tren**-*tah*
31	**trenta-un**	**tren**-*tah* **oon**
40	**quaranta**	*kwuh-***ran***-tuh*
50	**cinquanta**	*seen-***kwahn**-*tah*
60	**seixanta**	*seh-ee-***shan**-*tah*
70	**setanta**	*seh-***tan**-*tah*
80	**vuitanta**	*voo-ee-***tan**-*tah*
90	**noranta**	*noh-***ran**-*tah*
100	**cent**	**sen**
101	**cent un**	**sent oon**
102	**cent dos**	**sen dohs**
200	**dos-cents** (*masc*)	**dohs**-**sens**
	dues-centes (*fem*)	**doo**-*uhs* **sen**-*tuhs*
300	**tres-cents**	**trehs**-**senz**
400	**quatre-cents**	*kwah*-*truh*-**senz**
500	**cinc-cents**	**seeng**-**senz**
600	**sis-cents**	**sees**-**senz**
700	**set-cents**	**set**-**senz**
800	**vuit-cents**	*voo*-*eet*-**senz**
900	**nou-cents**	*noh*-*oo*-**cenz**
1,000	**mil**	**meel**
1,001	**mil un**	**meel oon**

Time

one minute	**un minut**	**oon** *mee-***noot**
one hour	**una hora**	**oo**-*nuh* **oh**-*ruh*
half an hour	**mitja hora**	**mee**-*juh* **oh**-*ruh*
Monday	**dilluns**	*dee-***lyoonz**
Tuesday	**dimarts**	*dee-***marts**
Wednesday	**dimecres**	*dee-***meh**-*kruhs*
Thursday	**dijous**	*dee-***zhoh**-*oos*
Friday	**divendres**	*dee-***ven**-*druhs*
Saturday	**dissabte**	*dee-***sab**-*tuh*
Sunday	**diumenge**	*dee-oo-***men**-*juh*